Interpersonal
Communication
in Organizations

Interpersonal Communication in Organizations

A Perceptual Approach

Richard C. Huseman
James M. Lahiff
John D. Hatfield

THE UNIVERSITY
OF GEORGIA

Holbrook Press, Inc.
Boston

Printed in the United States of America

Library of Congress Cataloging in Publication Data

Huseman, Richard C
   Interpersonal communication in organizations

   Includes bibliographical references and index.
   1. Communication. 2. Interpersonal relations.
I. Lahiff, James, joint author. II. Hatfield,
John, date, joint author. III. Title.
P90.H87   001.5   75-26626
ISBN 0-205-04897-8

Contents

Preface

In his interesting collection of interviews entitled *Working*, Studs Turkel includes one with a telephone operator. She resents the organizational rules that constrain her from giving the customer any more than token assistance. She is limited to a set number of phrases and is unable to talk with those persons who have problems and who obviously need to talk to someone. "I'm a communications person who can't communicate," she laments.

This is the enigma that is certainly not limited to telephone personnel, for it describes a situation that everyone experiences. Humans are communicators by nature. Their sense of well-being is determined largely by the quality of their interactions with others. Many—like the telephone operator—*do* chafe under organizational policies that inhibit communication. For others, the constraints are internal, fostered by uncertainty and an unfamiliarity with the ingredients of effective interpersonal communication.

Interpersonal Communication in Organizations is based on the premise that effective communication takes place when others respond appropriately and all derive mutual satisfaction. The book is written from a perceptual perspective; that is, with a constant awareness of the interwoven nature of the relationship between the processes of communication and perception. Just as it is our perceptions of others that determine what and how we communicate with them, so too, it is their image of us that determines the success of the interaction as well as the potential for mutual growth.

Part One deals with the theoretical fundamentals that provide the individual with a foundation upon which to further develop as an interpersonal communicator. In the first chapter, the reader is introduced to the communication process and to those factors that most affect it. The process is illustrated in several communication models. In Chapter 2 there is a brief survey of the early theories of perception and a consideration of possible causes of the great diversity in human perception. The third chapter treats the motivation process and introduces those theories that have a special relevance for the interpersonal communicator.

Chapters 4, 5, and 6 familiarize the reader with the prerequisites to effective communication. A discussion of language as a shaping force of one's reality and the meaning of nonverbal cues is included in chapters 4 and 5. The sixth chapter examines communication and conflict in various settings. The importance of this topic is evident in the growing recognition of conflict as a major cause of organizational problems.

Part Two opens with a consideration of listening and how to improve one's listening habits. Chapters 8 through 11 deal with two formats of interpersonal communication in which every individual, regardless of occupation, participates regularly—interviewing and small group communication.

Chapters 12 and 13 deal with public speaking and writing. These topics are appropriate because no matter what type of organization one is employed in or belongs to—business, government, education—that person will be expected to be a competent communicator in those two formats. Also, very often one's effectiveness in interpersonal interaction hinges on one's abilities to write or speak in public. This book will be many students' only involvement with a course in communication. Such broad coverage is in their best interest and will enable the students to function well in a variety of situations.

R.C.H.

J.M.L.

J.D.H.

part
one

Theoretical Considerations

1

Communication Process

The planet earth is frequently described as a spaceship hurtling along an irrevocable path. Traveling this charted course, the individual is depicted as existing at the whim of forces against which he is defenseless and routinely buffeted.

MAN AND HIS INSTITUTIONS

The institutions in modern-day society have reached gargantuan proportions and, to the individual, resemble labyrinths that are unimpressionable and unyielding. Everywhere man looks, he is confined by a faceless and impersonal system. The government taxes the individual and uses the funds for purposes alien to the individual's wishes. It provides inadequate services that must be supplemented by the individual.

A person is hired by a giant corporation for as long as he is needed and then disengaged or, in the current jargon, "dehired." Business organizations that extend across national boundaries uproot employees at will, depositing them in locales where the worker's only tie is to his job, thereby strengthening his dependence upon it.

From grade through graduate school, students are shaped or misshaped in a system that seems to mass produce graduates who universally share one overriding characteristic—a mental sameness to all other graduates. The educational and occupational fate of the individual hinges on the satisfaction of requirements, regulations, and policies created by administrators, now long forgotten, for reasons also long forgotten.

Although Thoreau was referring to a less complicated time when he said, "The mass of men lead lives of quiet desperation," he might well have been describing the sense of futility man experiences when drawn into confrontation with the institutions that regulate his life. Thoreau's belief that, "What is called resignation is confirmed desperation," foretold man's alienation from the system as he recognized that what had originally been created to serve him was now controlling him.

The love-hate relationship existing between man and society's institutions has been the theme for countless movies, books, and plays. Although many of these stories are fictional, there is no shortage in fact of such incidents. In real-life situations, however, there is one redeeming feature that allows the individual to maintain his equilibrium no matter how ominous the crisis may appear. That is the ability to interact and exchange information with others.

LEVELS OF COMMUNICATION

There are many different ways to categorize communication. In textbooks in public speaking, it is sometimes done on the basis of the purpose of the speech. Journalism sources may do it according to its media. In his treatise on nonverbal communication, Knapp divides his subject into the six nonverbal variables that most influence human communication.[1] This book's emphasis is on interpersonal communication and might be visualized at the midpoint on a communication continuum with intrapersonal to the left and public to the right.

Intrapersonal Communication

Intrapersonal communication occurs within the individual. A person who thinks through a problem is communicating at this level, as is the person who talks to himself. The encoding phase of the communication process, discussed later in this chapter, occurs at this level; however, in true intrapersonal communication, the message remains there. According to Brooks, this is the "base of operations" for the other levels, for it is here that the communication behaviors are formed—behavior that will be observable on the other levels.[2]

Public Communication

Public communication is the transmission of a message to a large group of persons. While it may occur in a face-to-face setting, the size of the audience precludes any significant verbal feedback. There may be considerable non-verbal feedback, but its diversity renders the immediate and accurate interpretation of it unlikely. The traditional public speech is a familiar example of this type of communication.

This level of communication is not limited to the public speech, however, for it also includes those means of mass communication that are products of modern technology. These mass media include television, books, radio, and the like. Public communication is uninvolving. It is further characterized by its impersonality and the rapidity with which it can reach a large and heterogeneous population.

Interpersonal Communication

Interaction with others is one aspect of interpersonal communication. Persons meet and talk face to face. They exchange ideas as well as emotions and opinions. The person who operates a punch press eight hours a day often lives from one work break to the next, for those are the only times when he is able to use his mind.

While all jobs do not treat the mind as optional equipment, insights into how it feels when one must "reason" with an inanimate object are readily available. The man whose credit card has been incorrectly billed by a computer and who seeks redress knows the feeling. So does the man who is arrested for violating an ordinance that should no longer even be on the books but that is enforced by an unsympathetic judge who "goes by the book."

Another characteristic of interpersonal communication is that all parties involved are active participants. There is a give and take of information with the participants playing a variety of roles.

There is no arbitrary size limit at which an interaction ceases to be interpersonal in nature, although there must be at least two participants. What *is* necessary is that the participants be close enough together so that they can conversationally interact and the personal mannerisms and nuances of one will be apparent to the others.

What, then, is interpersonal communication? It is interaction of a conversational nature involving an exchange of verbal and nonverbal information between two or more participants in a face-to-face setting.

Perhaps too much of a point is made of the redemptive qualities of interpersonal communication. There is no intent to deceive the reader into believing that it is invariably satisfying. Such exchanges as the following, reported by Michael Gartner of *The Wall Street Journal*, certainly leave one dissatisfied and frustrated:

DINER   What's today's "special"?

WAITRESS   —Roast beef—it comes with corn and lima beans.

DINER   Please don't bring the lima beans. I'm on a diet.

WAITRESS   O.K. But I'll have to charge you 'a la carte.' There's no substitutions on the special.

DINER   I don't want a substitute.

WAITRESS   —Makes no difference.

DINER   How much more would the special without lima beans cost?

WAITRESS   —One dollar more.

DINER   Then give me the special with the beans and bring an extra dish. (*The waitress then brings his food. He puts lima beans on the extra plate and beckons waitress back.*)

DINER   Take this plate (with the beans) away please.

WAITRESS   Well, that's different.

One gets the impression that no matter how long the diner had discussed the matter with the waitress the outcome would have been unchanged. Thus interpersonal communication is not by definition satisfying; however, it is involving and it has the potential to satisfy.

GOALS OF INTERPERSONAL COMMUNICATION

When a person rises to give a public speech that person has—or should have—a goal in mind. There are few experiences as frustrating as being a member of an audience to a speaker who persists in bewildering his listeners as to his exact purpose. Interpersonal communication is directed toward the following goals: mutual pleasure, catharsis, overt response, and covert response. The fact that they are discussed separately should not suggest a mutual exclusiveness, for most interpersonal unions are directed at some combination of these goals.

Mutual Pleasure

Thomas Wolfe is one of the most often quoted authors on the subject of the sense of isolation experienced by all. In *Look Homeward Angel* he described the state of his central character:

> He understood that men were forever strangers to one another, that no one ever comes really to know anyone, that imprisoned in the dark womb of our mother, we come to life without having seen her face, that we are given to her arms a stranger, and that, caught in that insoluble prison of being, we escape it never, no matter what arms may clasp us, what mouth may kiss us, what heart may warm us.[3]

It is the reduction of loneliness and the provision of pleasure to all participants that is a common goal of interpersonal communication. Much of the speech used for this purpose is aimed solely at maintaining bonds between individuals. Malinowski termed this *phatic* communication.[4] It includes small talk, greetings, and rap sessions in general.

The cleaning lady in a hospital, as described by an occupational therapist, has the natural instinct to recognize and satisfy this need in others.

> The nurses, the doctors, the medical students, are set up on a rigid status kind of system. If you buy into this kind of system, you buy the idea that "I'm not quite as good as the guy above me." The resident doesn't strike back at the attending man when he has a bad day. He strikes out at the nurse. The nurse strikes out at the hospital aide or the cleaning lady.
>
> Many patients tell me the best person for them has been the cleaning lady. Yet the doctors and nurses, everybody is saying that the cleaning lady just does a rotten job—"That dirt's been on the floor three days!" The cleaning lady deals with the patient on a human level. She's scrubbing the floor in the room and the patient says, "My son didn't come to visit me today." The cleaning lady smiles and says, "I know how you feel. I know how I'd feel if my son didn't come to visit me if I was sick." The cleaning lady doesn't see the patient as a renal failure or an illesotomy. She just sees a poor lady who's sick.[5]

The uninvolved observer who perceives such interaction as purposeless is very wrong. It has a most important purpose—to engender human warmth.

Catharsis

Felix Lopez defines catharsis as "the process by which one person obtains a release from unpleasant emotional tensions by talking about the source of these tensions and expressing his feelings."[6] In much communication that has this goal, the role of the receiver is of secondary importance since, while his presence is necessary, his input is minimal. He may function as a "sounding board" off which the sender "bounces" his verbalized feelings.

One of the nicest compliments that can be paid a person is that he or she is a good listener. When seeking catharsis, that is the type of person one needs. A person cannot help but respond emotionally to the way he is treated each day. In many situations, a person is neither free nor able to express feelings at the moment he would like to.

When the quality control supervisor tells the lathe operator that his work is substandard and that he'd better improve, their status difference will probably keep the operator from arguing very vehemently. Although he will not tell the supervisor what he'd like to, it is unlikely that he will forget the incident. He will probably soon tell it to another or others, wife, co-worker, or bartender, perhaps, and in this retelling, he will most likely go beyond describing the actual incident. He will amplify it somewhat by saying what he would like to have said to the supervisor and, having said it, he'll feel a little better.

Overt Response

Much of one's interpersonal communication is directed at eliciting an observable response from the receiver. While the response being sought may be either immediate or delayed, the sender is aware of it from the inception of the interaction; his goal in this role is a desired response.

The probation officer recognizes that there may be quite a difference between the level at which the client functions and the level at which he wishes him to function. Although the officer is pleased to hear his client discuss his aspirations and plans for the future, he will be more interested in how the client performs. The purpose of his direction and encouragement is to have the client respond as desired.

The clothing salesman may seek a covert response, such as tacit approval of his stock, as a preliminary step. What he is ultimately working for, however, is to make a sale.

At times, a person's communication strategy may dictate that a series of overt responses be attained in a predetermined sequence prior to the ultimate response. The political candidate may conduct a door-to-door campaign in which he will meet the voters and seek to secure the signatures necessary for his inclusion on the ballot. Later, he will seek financial support from them and later still, he will seek an endorsement from the editor of the newspaper. Each of these steps is preliminary, however, to the ultimate desired response—his election by the electorate.

Covert Response

Unlike the overt response, which is observable and verifiable, the covert is not. Covert responses include subtle changes such as the modification of attitudes or beliefs. When an advisor counsels a student, he may try to instill in him a more positive outlook toward the science courses he must take. He may never realize whether or not he succeeded. While the cocktail lounge that features an "attitude adjustment hour" is seeking an overt response—the buying of drinks—there may be various covert responses on the part of the customer. He may become more relaxed, pleasant, and receptive to a good meal. Conversely, he may become so internally disturbed that he eventually picks a fight with the man seated next to him.

In day-to-day interpersonal communication, it is not possible to separate the goals as neatly as this chapter does. They are intertwined, one with the other, for human interaction usually has multiple purposes. Regardless of one's primary goal, however, its attainment is dependent upon achieving an understanding with another.

COMMUNICATION MODELS

Understanding and the subsequent desired responses will not come about unless all the elements in the process of communication are considered. The ability to do this requires a constant recognition and awareness of them.

Communication may be conceptualized and better understood with the aid of definitions and models. Numerous examples of both are available. Some provide more insight than others. Any determination of the benefits of a particular model or definitions is substantially related to the needs and perspective of the person viewing the definition of a model or definition.

Thomas Nilsen has provided an excellent compilation and categorization of definitions of communication.[7] He observes that two categories of definitions exist. The first category includes definitions in which the sender deliberately seeks to evoke a response in the receiver. The second category includes definitions of communication that do not require that intention to evoke a response be present. Sereno and Mortensen have suggested a definition that captures the dyadic nature of communication explored in this chapter. They suggest that communication be defined as "a process by which senders and receivers of messages interact in given social contexts."[8]

This definition identifies communication as the interaction between people. This relational perspective focuses on the interaction of senders and receivers of messages rather than the intrapersonal process in which stimuli are translated into meaning by receivers. This approach has been the focus of most models that have been developed as explanations of the process of communication. The following sections are devoted to a brief summary of communication models. Models are presented, for the most part, chronologically, and in increasing order of complexity. Each one, from Lasswell's early oversimplified model to Barnlund's transactional models, provides insights that other models have failed to consider. Taken together, these models identify the basic elements of the communication process experienced by two or more individuals.

Advantages and Limitations of Models

Before these models are explained, a few statements about the advantages and limitations of models may help the student's understanding of them. Alphonse Chopanis provides an important critique of models and model building. His work is used as a basis for the following discussion of communication models—of which there is a profusion. Chapanis proposes the following definition of models:

> Models are representations, or likenesses, of certain aspects of complex events, structures, or systems, made by using symbols or objects which in some way resemble the thing being modeled.[9]

Two basic types of models exist. The replica model recreates on a smaller scale the object that it models. A standard desk globe of the world is an example of this type. Symbolic models, a second type, are abstractions that analogize a real event or process in words or other symbols. Communication models are of this latter type. Most combine words and diagrams to symbolize the process. Models vary widely in the exactness with which they represent their intended process.

Models focus on the essential factors of a process. No model can represent all of the parts of a process that it seeks to describe. If it did so, it would no longer be a model; instead it would be the process itself. The model builder must pick and choose among elements in a process as he designs his symbolic representation. Ideally, the elements chosen should represent the essential features of a process. The best model captures the essence of a process. Most models fall short of this goal; this is evident in several communication models outlined in pages ahead.

Essential elements within a model should be displayed as they interact in reality. The variables of a model should be outlined so that an observer has some understanding of how one element affects another. The models which follow do not attempt an elaborate explanation of the interaction of the variables. For the most part, variables are identified without explicit definition of the effects of one on another.

A model that identifies the essential elements of a process and explores the relationships or interaction of those variables, will clarify a complex event that otherwise defies easy understanding. To the extent that a model identifies elements or demonstrates their interaction, complexity is reduced. Lasswell's model reduces the process of communication to its very basic level. A reductionist approach allows the student of communication to handle the process with ease.

Models help us learn complex skills. Better interpersonal communication is certainly a goal of the increasingly large amount of research and theory that has come out of the field. A model that reduces the complexity of the communication process should assist a student in learning to communicate better. A good model will identify areas or elements that can be manipulated by the student in improving communication. Unfortunately, a model that reduces the complexity of an event may not necessarily increase the ease with which a skill can be learned, for identification of more than the essential elements of a process is necessary for a model to be instructive. Barnlund's model explains the relationship among various types of cues that affect communication. The interaction of those cues and the verbal or nonverbal behavior that results is more instructive than Berlo's identification of variables affecting essential elements of the communication process. For a model to serve well as a teaching device, it must explain relationships among the essential elements of a skill.

The models which follow are presented in ascending order of complexity. Each is particularly valuable in its identification of new relationships between elements and the process of communication.

An additional contribution of models is their ability to amuse us. They are enjoyable to build, and they are interesting to examine. This is hardly an intrinsic characteristic of the models, but is an extrinsic characteristic of models that may be of most value. Dean Barnlund makes the following observation about models. "Ultimately, the adequacy of any model depends upon the degree to which it stimulates research and to which it can organize diverse findings into an intelligible pattern."[10] A primary extrinsic contribution of models, then, is their ability to generate research.

Despite the contributions of any model, including those which follow, they are plagued by certain limitations. They may oversimplify or overgeneralize. This problem results in a model that, while simplifying a complex event, may be of little practical value. Second, a model is not reality. No matter how closely it analogizes a process, it is not the process. This limitation is so important that it should always be used as a filter in examining a model. Third, most models are not empirically validated. While many are based on inferences drawn from research and intuitively cogent theories, they do lack empirical validation.

Lasswell

Harold Lasswell's interest in the role of mass media in society led him to pose five questions that help to isolate the essentials of the communication process.[11] Lasswell felt that these five questions indicated the major variables in an act of communication:

> Who
> Says What
> In Which Channel
> To Whom
> With What Effect?

These simple questions isolate several key elements in the process. The source (Who) is the originator of the message. He initiates the process of communication. The source is the person who, through verbal and nonverbal symbols, intentionally or unintentionally structures the cognitive field of the *receiver* (To Whom), a second element identified by Lasswell. The receiver is the person who perceives stimuli transmitted by the source. These stimuli are the verbal and nonverbal symbols that the source sends as a message (Says What) to the receiver. Lasswell's model identifies the message as an element in the process, but fails to include nonverbal messages. Lasswell's emphasis on the verbal aspects of a message overlooks an extremely important body of stimuli available to a sender. (Nonverbal communication is examined in detail in Chapter 5.) The fourth element identified by Lasswell's model is the channel of communication. Channels are the means of conveyance of the stimuli that the sender produces.

The final element in Lasswell's model is the *effect* of the message. This element isolates an important aspect of communication. The effect is identified independently from the source, message, or receiver. It is instructive to recognize that the intentions of the source may not coincide with the effect of the message. This may be due to a number of variables that are explored in more recent models of communication. The effect of a message is within the province of a receiver's interpretation of the stimuli, the source, and other variables. The interaction of these elements leads to the attachment of meaning to stimuli and this interpretation is called perception. It is examined in Chapter 2.

Shannon and Weaver

At nearly the same time that Lasswell described an act of communication in five steps, Shannon and Weaver, two mathematicians, were developing a model to explain a communication system and its problems [see Figure 1.1].

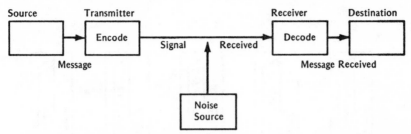

FIGURE 1.1 Shannon and Weaver, model of communication.

This model possesses the essential elements necessary for generalization to the human communication process. Consequently, it has been used extensively in explaining communication as a process of interaction between two humans.

The model explains communication in the following way.[12] An information source (the *Who* in Lasswell's model) originates a message that is encoded into verbal and nonverbal stimuli (transmitter). This message is then transmitted in its encoded form to a receiver who decodes the message and provides it with some meaning at its destination. The Shannon and Weaver model adds a new element to the communication process—a noise source. The message originated and encoded by the sender may not be equivalent to the message of the receiver. The noise in the process accounts for the differences between messages.

In the Shannon and Weaver model, the message refers to the meaning that each individual in the communication dyad attaches to the verbal and nonverbal symbols emitted by the sender. The model identifies an essential proposition of semantics—meaning is in people. A recognition of this situation requires some element to account for it. The Shannon and Weaver model offers a "black box" explanation. A noise source exists between the meaning of the sender and the receiver. It is now recognized that this noise may be physical or psychological. Physical noise may include physiological impairments of hearing, vision, or speech, or environmental disturbances such as others' talking or contextual distractions. Psychological noise is usually attributed to the process of perception. Whatever the cause of the noise, Shannon and Weaver's model identifies an important property of the communication process. The meaning attributed to a message by the sender may not be the meaning attributed to that same message by the receiver.

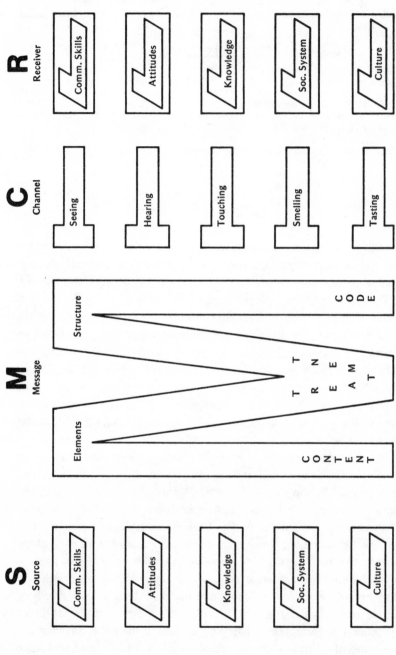

Reprinted from *The Process of Communication: An Introduction to Theory and Practice* by David K. Berlo. Copyright © 1960 by Holt, Rinehart and Winston, Inc. Reprinted by permission of Holt, Rinehart and Winston, Inc.

FIGURE 1.2 Berlo, model of communication.

Berlo

Berlo's model identifies four essential elements of the communication process: Source, message, channel, and receiver[13] [see Figure 1.2]. Its chief contribution is to succinctly identify factors that affect these four elements.

Additional factors could, of course, be added to any of the four elements Berlo identifies. To those factors that affect the source and receiver could be added perception. Specific delineation of verbal and nonverbal stimuli could be included in the message. Channels, which include only the five senses, might be expanded with a perspective that covers such things as telephone, television, radio, etc. Certainly the message that one receives on the telephone is considered and interpreted differently from that which one hears on the radio.

Berlo's model, then, while adding to our understanding by specifying factors that affect the elements of the communication process, suffers from its inability to include all of the factors such as the few additions included here. This model also fails to capture the dynamism that gives the feeling of communication.

Dance

Although linear models like those of Shannon and Weaver or Berlo have greatly advanced our understanding of the process of communication, both models have failed to include feedback in the process. Communication does not begin and end as neatly as the previous models have described. Communication is more circular or continuous, and it is this quality of communication that led Dance to postulate his helical model of communication[14] [see Figure 1.3].

Dance's model includes feedback in a dynamic model of communication that also emphasizes the effect of past experience on communication. A helix by means of its geometrical shape demonstrates that communication, while moving forward and adding new experiences, is also dependent on its past. The helix turns back on itself yet moves onward as well. The communication process, then, is affected by learning. It can correct itself through the intervention of feedback, an essential element of communication, explained in the following paragraph.

The inclusion of feedback in a model of communication is a significant advancement in our understanding. The concept of feedback originated in cybernetics where it operated as a self-regulating agent in a closed system.

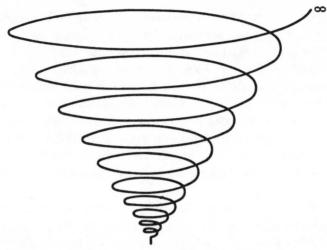

From "Toward a Theory of Human Communication" by Frank E. X. Dance, in *Human Communication Theory*, edited by Frank E. X. Dance. Copyright ©1967 by Holt, Rinehart and Winston, Publishers. Reprinted by permission of Holt, Rinehart and Winston, Publishers.

FIGURE 1.3 A helical spiral as representation of human communication.

Feedback allows a system to correct itself. An excellent example of a system that operates on this principle is a heating unit in a home. The thermostat automatically regulates the amount of heat in the room on the basis of the feedback it receives through its built-in thermometer. In a similar manner, feedback serves to correct the perceptions of a communicator. One can ascertain whether his behavior is interpreted properly by another. Appropriate corrections in the sender's verbal and nonverbal cues can then be made.

Barnlund

Barlund contributes to the development of communication models in several ways. First, he explicitly outlines the assumptions upon which his model is based. Those assumptions include the following: 1) Communication describes the evolution of meaning; 2) Communication is dynamic; 3) Communication is continuous; 4) Communication is circular; 5) Communication is unrepeatable; 6) Communication is irreversible; 7) Communication is complex. [15] Second, his model distinguishes between intrapersonal and interpersonal communication. Third, inclusion of nonverbal behavior as well as verbal behavior is evident in the model. Fourth, he impacts communication in a behavioral framework. Finally, he identifies some of the variables that explain the element of noise identified by Shannon and Weaver. In explaining his transactional model, Barnlund first develops a model of intrapersonal communication [see Figure 1.4].

P. represents the person who decodes (D) and encodes (E) verbal and nonverbal cues. Three general types of cues to which the individual may attribute meaning are available. Public cues (C pu) exist in one's environment in two forms. Natural cues include physical objects and their attributes that are independent of man's intervention. They include the temperature, humidity, color and properties of minerals, vegetable life, animal life, etc. Artificial cues include those modifications and manipulations of one's environment. Processing and arranging of wood, plastic, and glass are examples.

A second type of cue is essentially private. The private cues (C pr) may include the words or pictures in a magazine the person is reading. Private cues also include music from earphones or some clothing that is too tight. Before anyone else enters the environment, the intrapersonal model of communication includes nonverbal behavioral cues (C beh_{nv}). These cues include the nonverbal behavioral acts of a person in straightening a tie or turning the page of a book.

The number of cues that might affect a person's behavior is virtually infinite. This phenomenon is exhibited by the jagged lines at either end of the series of private, public, and behavioral cues in Figure 1.5. A person confronted by an environment filled with these cues responds only to a few of

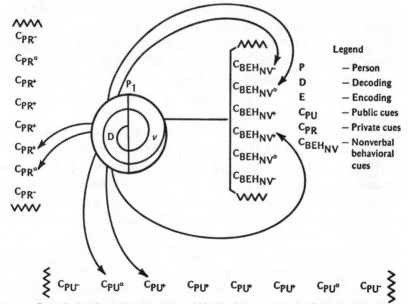

Legend

P	— Person
D	— Decoding
E	— Encoding
C_{PU}	— Public cues
C_{PR}	— Private cues
$C_{BEH_{NV}}$	— Nonverbal behavioral cues

Dean C. Barnlund, "A Transactional Model of Communication," reprinted from *Language Behavior: A Book of Readings*, edited by Johnnye Akin, Alvin Goldberg, Gail Myers, and Joseph Stewart, p. 59. Copyright © 1970 by Mouton & Co. N. V. Publishers. Reprinted by permission of Mouton & Co. N. V. Publishers.

FIGURE 1.4 Barnlund, interpersonal communication.

them. And those cues to which he responds may either assist or hinder his pursuits. Consequently, tentative valences are assigned to indicate the positive, negative, or neutral (+, −, 0) effect of cues.

Barnlund succinctly provides possible interaction between a hypothesized "Mr. A" who sits in the reception room of a clinic and assorted cues in the following illustration.

> At the moment he is faintly aware of an antiseptic odor in the room, which reinforces his confidence in the doctor's ability to diagnose his illness (C pu +). As he glances through a magazine (C pr 0) he is conscious of how comfortable his chair feels after a long day on his feet (C pr +). Looking up he glances at the Miro reproduction on the wall, but is unable to decipher it (C pu 0). He decides to call the nurse. As he rises he clumsily drops his magazine (C beh$_{nv}$−) and stops to pick it up, crosses the room (C beh$_{nv}$0), and rings the call bell firmly and with dignity (C beh$_{nv}$+).[15]

This illustration presents Barnlund's model of intrapersonal communication as it accounts for the cognitive processes in the hypothetical, "Mr. A."

Barnlund's model is completed with the addition of a second person. This complication of the communication process is brought about by the introduction of the interpersonal element with its affect on existent cues and its addition of other cues [see Figure 1.5].

The second person (P_2) in the model could be the introduction of a physician in the illustration reported above. This physician, Dr. B, is presented the same set of public cues (C pu) but his attention may be drawn to ones which Mr. A may not have noticed. Due to the variant backgrounds of the two men, cues observed by both may be interpreted differently. Consequently the same public cue (C pu) may possess one valence for P_1 and another for P_2.

An individual involved in interpersonal communication must not only interpret his private cues (C pr), the public cues (C pu) to which his attention is drawn, his own nonverbal cues (C beh nv) and his verbal cues (C beh$_v$), but he must also attend to the verbal (C beh$_v$) and nonverbal cues (C beh$_{nv}$) of the person with whom he communicates. In this process, a communicator will regulate his own cues and attempt to gauge the effect of his cues on the other person.

As awareness of each other reaches a sufficient level, the behavioral cues may be referred to as a message (M). At this point, even before verbal cues are issued, interpersonal communication has occurred. The addition of verbal cues is understood as the supplying of additional meaning to the instance of dyadic communication. Barnlund explains how persons determine meaning in this model.

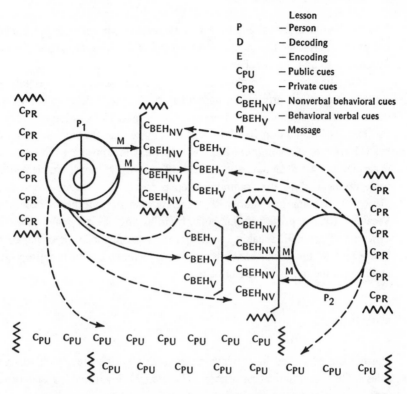

Dean C. Barnlund, "A Transactional Model of Communication," reprinted from *Language Behavior: A Book of Readings*, edited by Johnnye Akin, Alvin Goldberg, Gail Myers, and Joseph Stewart, p. 55. Copyright © 1970 by Mouton & Co. N. V. Publishers. Reprinted by permission of Mouton & Co. N. V. Publishers.

FIGURE 1.5 Barnlund, interpersonal communication.

> Meaning is cumulative (or ambiguity reductive) and grows as each new cue, of whatever type, is detected and assigned some sort of valence. Verbal cues are distinctive only in the sense that they constitute a special form of behavior, are finite in number, and are presented in a linear sequence.[16]

Unfortunately, Barnlund's model appears to equate the reception of the assorted cues with meaning. Some additional operation on those cues is necessary before they become meaningful. This is apparent when one examines the model closely. Both Mr. A and Dr. B may observe the Miro reproduction on the wall; yet Mr. A does not attach any meaning to it. Presumably, Dr. B, in whose office the picture is hung, attaches some meaning to the picture. Barnlund does note that the experiences of the interactors determine what kind of meaning is attached to this common public cue (C_{pu}); however, the model does not explicitly identify any processes which operate on the cues to convert them into meaning. Although the model offers additional insights into the process of communication, it fails to identify a crucial and necessary element which, for example, converts the public cues (C pu) available to everyone into the kind of meaningful units which lead to additional behavior in the dynamic process.

Despite this shortcoming, Barnlund provides several new insights into the communication process. Of particular importance in developing an understanding of the communication process is this model's inclusion of the social context. As indicated in Barnlund's model, more than the verbal and nonverbal behavior of the communicators is important in conveying messages. The occasion, the time of day, the social and physical context, are elements of some importance in the communication process. All of us are aware of the difficulty in communication with someone who has another appointment. Speaking with a professor immediately following a class may result in a different effect than speaking with that same professor in his or her office. The effect of the social context on dyadic communication is appropriately included in the model just described.

SUMMARY

The models presented in previous pages have identified several crucial variables in the communication process. The *sender* with his or her experiences and interpretations emits verbal and nonverbal stimuli. A *receiver*, who attends to the *message* (the external stimuli), responds on the basis of his experiences. The meaning which is attached to the message is a function of the interpretations provided by that experience. Message transmission occurs in some external physical channel; and it is sent and received through one or more of the five senses. These *channels* of transmission alter the way in which verbal and nonverbal cues are interpreted. The sender receives some *feedback* from the receiver. Even no response at all is feedback. The sender may assume that the message which was sent was not received. Through feedback and additional transmissions, the senders and receivers of messages move toward similar meanings, but it is unlikely that meanings of two people can ever be exactly the same. The more similar the sender and receiver, the more likely is the occurrence of similar meanings. Still, feedback increases understanding between two people who are highly similar. All of these processes occur within a *social context*. The social context not only has an effect on the messages which are sent, but it affects how messages are interpreted.

PROPOSITIONS

1. Communication occurs through the transmitting interpretation of verbal and nonverbal behavior.

2. Messages are interpreted on the basis of past personal experiences (with those symbols used, with the sender, with this physical context, with the channels used), the existing social context, and the channels currently employed.

3. The meaning of a message is determined by the sender and the receiver; it is not implicit in the message.

4. Feedback is an essential element in correcting a communication system.

5. Communication is dynamic.

6. Communication is continuous.

QUESTIONS FOR DISCUSSION

1. Select an occupation other than those described in this chapter and devise a system for categorizing communication that would be appropriate for that occupation.

2. What other possible goals besides mutual pleasure, catharsis, overt response, and covert response are there for interpersonal communication?

3. Lasswell's model was originally intended to represent mass media communication. How do the later models differ from it?

4. It is generally believed that an organization that allows feedback is more effective than one that does not. While the benefits of feedback, both to the organization and to the individual, are widely recognized there are some "costs" also. What are some of the "costs" either to the organization or to the individuals involved?

ENDNOTES

1. Mark L. Knapp, *Nonverbal Communication in Human Interaction* (New York: Holt, Rinehart and Winston, 1972).
2. William D. Brooks, *Speech Communication* (Dubuque: William C. Brown, 1971), 10.
3. Thomas Wolfe, *Look Homeward Angel* (New York: Charles Scribner's Sons, 1929), p. 31.
4. J. W. Black and W. E. Moore, *Speech* (New York: McGraw-Hill, 1955). pp. 162–163.
5. Studs Terkel, *Working* (New York: Pantheon, 1972), p. 494.

6. Raymond L. Gorden, *Interviewing: Strategy, Techniques, and Tactics* (Homewood, Ill: Dorsey Press, 1969), p. 90.

7. Thomas R. Nilsen, "On Defining Communication," *Speech Teacher* 6 (1957), p. 10–17.

8. Kenneth K. Sereno and C. David Mortensen, *Foundations of Communication Theory* (New York: Harper & Row, 1970), p. 5.

9. Alphonse Chapanis, "Men, Machines, and Models," *American Psychologist* 16 (1971), p. 115.

10. Dean C. Barnlund, "A Transactional Model of Communication." *Foundations of Communication Theory,* ed. Kenneth K. Sereno and C. David Mortensen (New York: Harper & Row, 1970), p. 18.

11. Harold D. Lasswell, "The Structure and Function of Communication in Society." *The Communication of Ideas.* Edited by Lyman Bryson, (New York: Institute for Religious and Social Studies, 1948).

12. Claude E. Shannon and Warren Weaver, *The Mathematical Theory of Communication* (Urbana, Ill.: The University of Illinois Press, 1949).

13. David K. Berlo, *The Process of Communication* (New York: Holt, Rinehart and Winston, 1960).

14. Frank E. X. Dance, "Toward a Theory of Human Communication." *Human Communication Theory,* ed. F. Dance (New York: Holt, Rinehart and Winston, 1967).

15. Barnlund, pp. 87–94.

16. Barnlund, p. 101.

2

Perception

In Chapter 1, Barnlund's model shows an understanding of interpersonal communication, but does not explain how those public and private cues are translated into something meaningful. As any model, Barnlund's begins with a perspective that determines its contents. In this case, the transactional viewpoint of the model emphasizes the relationship between the perceiver and his world. This interrelationship is dynamically portrayed in the diagram of his transactional model.

There is a step beyond the point that Barnlund's model has led—the relationship between the cues that one observes and the meanings attached to them. For example, questions arise as to why (using Barnlund's example) the physician and the patient in the waiting room can look at the same physical object and attach divergent meanings to that object.

The study of perception is one of the older areas of psychology. Before it was studied through psychological research, it was the object of philosophical examination. Questions about what man can know have long plagued him. Extreme empiricists argue that all universals can be known through what we experience through our five senses. On the other hand, nominalists argue that universals are not even a kind of thing. Plato differentiated between a world of phenomena and a world of forms. He accepted an objective essence which, as a universal, was intuited rather than perceived directly.

Aristotle, on the other hand, approached knowledge more empirically. He denied Plato's thesis that the phenomena and forms were separate. Things had no dual existence. Objects did not exist subjectively in this world and perfectly in a world of forms as Plato proposed. The essence of an object existed in the object itself. This Aristotelian approach is held by many philosophers in modified forms.

In opposition to the theory that deals with phenomena empirically, was the viewpoint of the skeptic. This thesis proposed that man could never be sure what reality was like. He could never directly contact the objects in his world. He is forced to depend upon light waves or sound waves that convey the image to the retina or eardrum. In the sense organs, these physical carriers of the phenomenal world are translated into neural impulses that are in turn reconstructed ideas or images that represent the world beyond us. Bishop George Berkeley's interpretation of this viewpoint suggests that man can only know ideas. In 1710, Berkeley argued that *esse* is *percipi*. The perception of phenomena is reality; the essence of objects is the perception or the ideas that we have about those objects. This viewpoint is carried to its extreme in an "idealist" position such as that expressed by Josiah Royce. While Berkeley maintained that we could, through the commonality of our ideas, know what existed in the world of phenomena, Royce viewed reality exclusively in terms of the ideas in our brains.

Neither the extreme idealist nor extreme empiricist position is particularly appropriate to our study of communication. Through the use of language, we have come to accept the actual existence of physical objects. Although we may be bound by a world of ideas so that our knowledge of reality is perceptual, we handle language as if the physical world did exist. On the other hand, difficulties with communication highlight the inadequacy of an empiricist's pragmatic approach to what can be known. Constantly, we are made aware of instances in which our boss, a relative, or a friend interpret a statement of ours differently than we intended. On occasion we may tell someone that we will arrive a little before six o'clock. For us that may mean somewhere between 5:55 p.m. and 6:00 p.m. The person to whom we made the statement may expect us before 5:45 p.m. While we can talk about a table, for example, another's description of the table will in all likelihood differ in numerous aspects from ours.

PARAMETERS FOR VIEWING PERCEPTION

The parameters for this consideration of perception are defined by three constraints. First, only subjective descriptions or characterizations that may or may not have factual foundation are of concern. That which is purely factual and verifiable is excluded. Second, perception may be viewed as primary or secondary mediation.[1] Primary mediation is the physical ability to sense phenomena in the external world (i.e., the world beyond an individual). It is the ability to see or hear. A person whose hearing, for example, is limited to a maximum of six thousand cycles per second is incapable of hearing a sound that vibrates at six thousand, five hundred cycles per second because of primary mediation. Much psychological research has been done on this subject. An example of this type of research is the determination of observable differences within one sensory modality such as the intensity of light. An early but basic study of the nature of sensory psychophysics asked subjects to make judgments about the smallest observable change in a physical stimulus such as the intensity of light. This change is called a *just noticeable difference.*[2]

Secondary mediation is the coding of connotative and denotative qualities of things. A person may sense the existence of an object through sensory experience. That is primary mediation. When the person codes that sensation symbolically, secondary mediation has occurred. The study of human information processing or perception within this chapter is concerned with secondary mediation only.

Perception is an intervening variable and therein lies the third constraint. As an intervening variable, it is somewhat analogous to learning. Learning theorists distinguish between learning (what an individual knows) and performance (what an individual is willing to demonstrate).[3] We do not observe learning; we only see performance. An individual, or a rat, in the case of the original experimental work, may have learned something, but this learning is inferred on the basis of performance.

Perception may likewise be viewed as an intervening variable. It stands between the message sent to a receiver and the response of that receiver; or it stands between the message and the meaning that a person attributes to the message. An examination of perception seeks to reveal the elements of that intervening variable in hopes of better understanding how messages that impinge upon it as stimuli are handled and how those messages are translated into meaningful units and responses. Since perception is an intervening variable, it is difficult to study. While it is easy to examine the stimuli or the responses of an animal, it is rather difficult to experimentally examine the processes that make up perception. An interesting paradox develops. As we examine perception in hope of better understanding communication, we also understand what is happening perceptually through a person's communicative responses.

Thus, three constraints limit the examination of perception. The kind of knowledge concerned here is that which is not purely factual. The study focuses on secondary mediation—the attachment of connotative and denotative meaning to sensation. And third, perception is studied as it intervenes between message and meaning or message and response.

PERCEPTION AND COMMUNICATION

Since the relationship between perception and communication is such a complex one, there is a natural tendency to consider them as one and the same, rather than to view them separately. Just as generations have been oblivious to the problems inherent in human communication, so also have they taken perception for granted. Little consideration has been given to the formation and accuracy of perception. Instead, people have generally accepted the philosophy of, "What you see is what you get," and have accepted unquestioningly that which appears to be the case.

The importance of the perceptual process and the general recognition of its importance is confirmed by the many disciplines currently doing research on it. Its significance to the individual was described by a British psychologist in terms of the informal and professional judgments of others and their effects on us. As an example of such an informal judgment he cites one's choice for marriage. Professional judgments include the selection of an individual for employment or for admission to an educational institution.[4] Soviet psychologists described its importance even more succinctly, ". . .and it is one person's capacity to perceive another (his ability to capture the rich and intricate range of expressive movements, etc.) that determines the success of mutual understanding among people and, consequently, the nature of their interrelationships."[5]

Since a person depends on his senses for perceptual data and since one individual's sensory equipment is very similar to that of another, what accounts for such glaring differences in perception? While one person may have slightly better vision than another, or more sensitive hearing, such relatively insignificant differences cannot, by themselves, be held accountable for significantly differing perceptions.

In one study of visual perception, the researchers investigated the formation of illusions, especially those involving distortions of apparent length, size, and direction. These researchers concluded that such illusions are caused by both peripheral, or physiological, and central factors. The central components included distortion from "learned patterns of information sampling and cue utilization."[6] They also found that continued inspection would clarify many such illusions. Unlike the perspective of this chapter, however, those researchers concentrated on visual perception. They balanced their consideration between physiological and psychological (i.e., "central") factors. In this chapter the physiological factors are excluded since such factors are verifiable and as such are eliminated by the constraints presented earlier.

One need not look beyond one's own experiences to document the idea that there is a difference between sensing and perceiving and that even when we do perceive an event or a person, we are often inaccurate. The automobile salesman saw the young, shoeless man inspecting the new Cadillac in the showroom and suggested that he might find something more within his budget in their used car lot. He didn't realize he had misperceived the man until the next day when he saw him pay another salesman more than eight thousand dollars in cash for the same automobile he had felt was beyond the man's budget. Thus he had sensed or saw the customer but he did not perceive him accurately.

The accuracy of the messages that are transmitted to others, whether intentionally or not, is limited by the perceptual abilities of the receivers. The individual's perceptual abilities in turn are severely curtailed by a number of restricting factors.

SELECTIVITY IN PERCEPTION

The fact that we perceive selectively limits the quantity of stimuli to which we will attach meaning. That such selectivity is necessary is obvious when one considers the thousands of stimuli one is exposed to each day. Since it is not humanly possible to attach meaning to them all, it becomes the receiver's task to select those stimuli to attend. This determination and selection are made on the basis of which ones are most meaningful to the receiver.

The phenomenon of selective perception has been confirmed through controlled research studies. Representative of such studies is one in which the selective perception of college students was investigated in the context of a presidential campaign. It was discovered that subjects recalled "acceptable" comments from the candidate of their preferred party, and they recalled unfavorable comments made by the other candidate. A second and related finding was that they ascribed statements with which they agreed to the candidate whom they preferred.[7]

An example of selective perception which most sports fans would recognize is the college football coach who, after experiencing an undeafeated season the previous year and after losing only two veteran players to graduation, tries to convince the press that this year his team will be lucky to win half of their games. A person sees only what he wants to see, in this case, the two departing players rather than the several dozen who were returning.

As a perceiver, an individual is the product of all his past experiences; these accumulated experiences naturally influence his perceptions. In an interesting study, an investigation was made of the perceptual orientation of aged persons toward the youth of today. With the rapid rate of change in the customs and behavior of the young, it might have been anticipated that the elderly would seize upon the opportunity to lament the caliber of the youth and the future of the civilized world when placed under their control. The actual evaluation by the aged of the young suggested perceptions quite far removed from what might have been expected. Instead of a blanket indictment of the young, many of the evaluations were highly positive.

The determining factor was not the age difference or changing moral codes but the relationships that the subjects enjoyed with their own children. The aged perceived the young positively to the extent that they themselves were satisfied with their present ties with their offspring. The less satisfaction they manifested, the more negatively they evaluated the young. Thus their perceptual orientation was dictated by their own experiences.[8]

STEREOTYPING

In the nineteen-twenties, columnist Walter Lippmann coined the term "stereotype." According to Lippmann:

> Stereotypes are an ordered, more or less consistent picture of the world, to which our habits, our tastes, our capacities, our comforts and our hopes have adjusted themselves. They may not be a complete picture of the world, but they are a picture of a possible world to which we are adapted. In that world people and things have their well-known places, and do certain expected things. We feel at home there. We fit in. We are members. We know the way around. There we find the charm of the familiar, the normal, the dependable; its grooves and shapes are where we are accustomed to find them. And though we have abandoned much that might have tempted us before we creased ourselves into that mould, once we are firmly in, it fits as snugly as an old shoe.[9]

It is the tendency to use stereotypes that constitutes another factor that restricts accurate perceptions. Since each individual is bombarded by countless verbal and nonverbal messages every day, some sort of screening mechanism must be employed. Personal selectivity, one such mechanism, reduces significantly the messages to be attended.

The tendency to stereotype further simplifies the individual's perceptual problems. By stereotyping, one avoids the necessity of having to recognize the uniqueness of individuals or events and instead places them in convenient prearranged categories. Thus, Susan, an attractive eighteen-year-old Georgian, is placed in the "southern belle" category suggesting that she is very feminine, not very bright, and a nonstop talker. Rob, a black student, on the other hand, was stereotyped as lazy and slow, but rhythmical, at least until he began wearing his hair in an Afro, at which time he was reclassified into the militant category.

The processing of information is greatly simplified by stereotyping and it renders the tasks of an incalculable number of occupations infinitely easier. Without stereotyping, the personnel manager might anguish for hours over which one of two equally well-prepared young men he should hire. As an acceptor of stereotypes, however, he will immediately exclude the longhaired applicant and save everyone a lot of trouble—except the rejected applicant. The person who stereotypes evaluates individuals on the basis of one characteristic, in this case, hair. Whether or not that characteristic is germane to the issue being considered is immaterial.

It is not uncommon to see stereotyping equated with prejudice nor to see it alleged that those who stereotype are prejudiced. While these statements are often true, they are not always so. There is nothing unusual about the person who uses stereotyping, for all do to a certain degree, and that degree varies with the individual as well as with the groups to which the individual belongs.

Consider the findings of a study that required college freshmen, males and females, to view photographs of males with varying amounts of facial hair and to judge the subject's masculinity. These students found a positive relationship between the amount of hair on the object person's face and their perception of him as masculine, mature, good-looking, dominant, self-confident, courageous, liberal, nonconforming, industrious, and older. The researcher found these characteristics to be consistently enhanced as the extent of beardedness increased from clean-shaven to moustache to goatee to full beard.[10]

It is interesting to speculate as to how the findings of the study would have differed had the subjects been middle-aged persons rather than college students. Perhaps the characteristics related to beardedness would have been somewhat less noble, perhaps not, but there seems to be little question that they would have differed for one's stereotyping system is determined largely by the groups, both informal and formal, of which one is a member.

Perhaps advertising man Jerry Della Femina was exaggerating when he described his image of a beer drinker:

...the man never has a shirt on. He's always in his undershirt, one of those old-fashioned undershirts, not a tee shirt. I may be wrong there, but I could swear that your typical beer drinker is proud of his beer belly. There he is, swilling beer all day long, and the only thing he has to show for it is his belly. It's his sign of masculinity. ...These guys start drinking at nine o'clock in the morning and they have their more than one by 9:05 a.m. And they drink and they drink and drink and drink, and this is the beer market.[11]

The above description clearly illustrates the process of stereotyping. Despite the fact that there exist numerous degrees of difference in beer drinking practices, in the mind of this individual they are all alike.

While the examples of stereotyping presented in this chapter may lead one to believe that only human beings are the victims of stereotyping such is not the case. Consider the picture that enters one's mind when asked to visualize a rural area. One probably conjures a pastoral scene that includes red barns, dirt roads, freshly plowed fields, and widely scattered houses. Now list the three most rural states in the U.S. based on their overall population. The first is Pennsylvania with 3.4 million people who don't live in towns and cities. The second is North Carolina with 2.8 million, and the third is New York with 2.6 million rural residents. The first and third choices certainly strain the stereotypes most often associated with them. Few perceive Pennsylvania and New York in this way. Thus, human beings are not the only objects that are stereotyped.

PROXIMITY AND PERCEPTION

The proximity of the perceiver to the object or event in question is another influential factor in the perceptual process. This proximity can be either physical or psychological. A simple example involving physical perception would be the common experience of thinking one recognizes a person from afar and not discovering the mistake until drawing close to the person, who by this time had become quite suspicious of the unsolicited attention.

Psychological proximity influences the perceiver in several ways. First, if the perceiver is somewhat similar psychologically and attitudinally, one will better understand the other. Second, such perceived psychological proximity will result in a more positive evaluation by the perceiver. In a recent study it was shown that college instructors who were attitudinally similar to the students were evaluated more positively than those who were attitudinally dissimilar. Evaluation was made in terms of such factors as open-mindedness, being stimulating and interesting, personal attractiveness, and desirability as an instructor.[12] Thus there is both better understanding and approval of those who are similar than of those who are not.

The environment in which an individual functions also exerts influence on the manner in which that individual perceives. A number of academicians may observe the same organization but may see it very differently. A sociologist may characterize it as a bureaucracy while a psychologist may focus on the pattern of rewards and punishment that characterize it.[13] A communication theorist may view it as a system of communication thermoclines.[14] The differences in such a case are traceable to the discipline in which the perceiver works for this constitutes his environment.

Although Jessor and Jessor's interesting analysis of environments is aimed at the behavioral science researcher, it is also applicable to this treatment of perception. They contend that man is always acting in multiple environments simultaneously. They state that these environments are perceivable to varying degrees and they arrange these diverse environments on a proximal-distal dimension. Distal environments are those which are more remote from the direct experience of the individual and are without immediate functional significance to him. Among their examples are such biologically "close" environments as skin color or obesity. They consider these distal since they are often irrelevant to behavior.

Proximal environments, however, are environments of perception or stimulation. They can be directly experienced and they have potential meaning for the individual. They include expectations of others and negative evaluations as examples of variables that make up proximal environments. They call those environments at the proximal end of the distal-proximal dimensions "the perceived environment."[15] It is the perceived environment that exerts force upon the individual's perception.

ROLE AND PERCEPTION

A person's role or position constitutes another restricting force on perceptions. Katz and Kahn cite the differential perceptions of supervisors and subordinates as an example of this. In a study in a utility, it was reported that 76 percent of the foremen "always or almost always" elicited ideas from subordinates in seeking solutions to job problems. Only 16 percent of the workers, however, felt that they had been so contacted.[16] Such findings lead inevitably to the conclusion that one's role strongly influences his perceptions. Not only does one's role influence the role-holder in his perceptions of another, but it also affects the other's perception of him. The findings of surveys of the National Opinion Research Council leave little doubt that there is general agreement as to the prestige of a number of occupations that are very visible in the U.S. It seems likely that the perceived prestige of these occupations is reflected to the person in one of the occupations in the form of respect, higher pay, and other such niceties and, conversely, the person in an occupation perceived as of low prestige suffers a lack of such niceties.

Recognizing the present trend of further subdividing what appears to be already highly specialized occupations, it is not surprising that investigations have begun of perceived prestige differences between specialties within a given occupation. One such study investigated the perceptions of medical doctors of prestige differences between the various specialties within the field of medicine. Twenty-two categories of specialization were identified by the 278 physicians who participated in the study and the following, which were ranked as the most prestigious specialties, are presented in descending order of prestige: 1) Neurosurgery; 2) Internal Medicine; 3) General Surgery; 4) Thoracic Surgery; 5) Obstetrics and Gynecology; 6) Opthalmology; 7) Neurology; 8) General Practice.

Of the twenty-two categories the most universally agreed upon was the one ranked twenty-second, Medical Administrator. There was near unanimity in perceiving it as the least prestigious of the specialties.[17]

The image of an individual which is held by others is the product of many factors, only one of which is the role held by that individual. What appears to the layman to be a single role, may be viewed by the insider as more than one, as was the case in the medical prestige study. In concluding that study, the researcher observed that such internal prestige differences may actually be of greater consequence to members of a given occupational group than their prestige within the larger more inclusive vocational hierarchy.

ATTRACTIVENESS AND PERCEPTION

An additional obstacle to accurate perception can be found in the attractiveness of the person being observed. To a beauty judge, whose task it is to select one girl from dozens to reign as Miss Good Posture, attractiveness is an important criterion. In many other situations, however, where attractiveness should not be a primary consideration it is weighed disproportionately. It is difficult to listen to the unimaginative comments of the sports announcer, a former major league player, without suspecting that his verbal fluency was not the primary determinant in his getting the job.

Attractiveness often constitutes a "halo" effect in that, although irrelevant, it exerts undue influence. This issue was raised in one study in the context of judging criminal behavior. It was found that the attractiveness of both victim and defendant influenced the severity with which the defendant was judged. The defendant received a harsher sentence when either the victim was an attractive person or when the defendant was an unattractive person. [18] The influence of attractiveness appears to be an especially strong factor in first impressions. With subsequent contacts it is expected to be less influential.

In another study it was shown that an attractive girl could change the attitudes of males more than an unattractive one could.[19] The "halo" effect of attractiveness apparently is not limited to females, however, for one study suggests that attractive persons will be perceived as having higher credibility regardless of their sex.[20]

A MULTI-SENSORY PROCESS

While all of the examples presented have been of visual perception, a person is not limited to only that type. Each one of a person's senses provides that person with data to which he gives meaning. Were this not so, for example, the perfume manufacturers would be faced with a sharply curtailed demand. The consumer would no longer care that "Wind Song stays on your mind" if one's olfactory system did not contribute to one's perceptions.

Auditory perception was measured in a study in which manipulated door knocks were used as stimuli. It was found that as the door knocks became louder the subjects perceived the caller to be of higher status and the message to be of greater urgency. Increasing the frequency of the knocks affected only the perceived urgency.[21] Such studies plus personal experience confirm that all sensory data contributes to one's perception; however, it is the visual avenue that is at the forefront.

There is indeed a plethora of factors that inhibit or distort perception. Among the more common of these restricting factors are: 1) the individual's selective nature; 2) the individual's past experiences; 3) the natural tendency to stereotype persons, objects, and events; 4) the physical and psychological proximity of the individual to the item being observed; 5) the environments in which perception occurs; 6) the individual's role or position; 7) attractiveness of the object of perception.

Attempts are often made to illustrate the process of perception through pictures that present several images or phrases that are misread at first inspection. While such devices fascinate, one runs the risk of oversimplifying a very complex process. Most persons need only look to past personal experiences to testify to the difficulties inherent in perception as well as to recount the high personal costs of misperception.

IMPROVING PERCEPTION

Due to the multiple factors that contribute to its complexity, there are no hard and fast rules that, if followed, will invariably result in more accurate perception. There are, however, several potential determinants of improved perception.

For one seeking to increase one's perceptivity, it is essential to recognize the role of the perceiver for what it is—an active one. Just as many view listening as a passive activity, so also do they view perception in general in that light. The active perceiver seeks as much information as possible about the subject in question. The greater the amount of information secured, the more accurate will be the ensuing perception. One experiment that confirmed this required a large number of college students to judge several persons. The amounts and types of information available on the persons being assessed was varied and it was found that accuracy was greatest when information input was greatest.[22]

Just as additional information results in more accurate perception, so also will increased proximity to the subject being assessed. Everyone has had the experience of being impressed to some extent by a person from a distance only to change that impression drastically upon closer contact. Shepherd discusses how the conceptions of persons change, for example, after working together.[23]

Creating a climate that is conducive to communication within an organization or work group leads to increased accuracy in perception also. In a doctoral dissertation, Mix found a relationship between accurate perception and interpersonal communication patterns that were perceived by the receiver as concerned and considerate and perceived by the initiator as being free of threat from the receiver.[24] Thus, a climate of trust nourishes accuracy in perception.

An awareness of the uniqueness of one's own frame of reference is a prerequisite for improved perception. Each person has his own window to the world, as well as a unique rule system in which he arranges in an orderly fashion everything he perceives. The individuality and operation of rule systems were illustrated in a study in which judges were provided with biographical data on a student and were asked to estimate the student's intelligence. While some of the judges used what were actually the most precise indicators, vocabulary and school achievement, others used much less accurate criteria.[25] The variety of approaches taken indicates the great diversity of rule systems.

Since there is an inherent tendency for all persons to be totally involved in their own perception of the world, there is a parallel tendency to believe that all share the same perception of it. By seeking maximum information, moving closer to the subject under observation, creating a more favorable climate, and recognizing the uniqueness of one's own point of view, one is able to expand his perceptions.

SUMMARY

The process of perception has long been the subject of investigation by scholars who recognize the interrelationship between perception and communication.

The consideration accorded perception in this chapter is defined by these three constraints: 1) focus is on the attachment of connotative and denotative meaning to sensation; 2) that which is factual is excluded; 3) perception is studied as it intervenes between message, meaning, and response.

Perception is selective in the sense that human receivers, being exposed to many more stimuli than can be attended, select the stimuli to which they will attend. Selection is based on past experience as well as on many other factors. Stereotyping simplifies the individual's perceptual problems by providing categories into which persons and events can be placed and thereby avoiding the necessity of recognizing the uniqueness of what is perceived. The tendency to stereotype frequently results in a misrepresentation of all parties involved.

How one perceives another is influenced by numerous factors including proximity, role, and attractiveness. By recognizing the perceiver's role as an active one and by recognizing the uniqueness of one's own frame of reference, it is possible to become more accurate in one's perceptions.

QUESTIONS FOR DISCUSSION

1. Why is that which is factual and verifiable excluded from the chapter's consideration of perception?

2. Using one or more of the communication models in the previous chapter as an example, draw a model of the process of perception.

3. The more homogeneous a group is, the more similarly the group members will perceive a given subject. Select a subject about which the class members will be in general agreement. What factors account for the shared perceptions of the class members? Select a subject about which there would be general disagreement among class members. What factors explain the dissimiliar perceptions?

4. What are some of the benefits to be derived from stereotyping? To the perceiver? To the perceived?

5. What are some examples of selective perception in which college professors have been known to engage?

6. What, if anything, can be done to minimize the influence of physical attractiveness on our perceptual processes?

ENDNOTES

1. George S. Klein, *Perception, Motives and Personality* (New York: Alfred A. Knopf, 1970).
2. Julian E. Hochberg, *Perception* (Englewood Cliffs, New Jersey: Prentice-Hall 1971).
3. James Deese and Stewart H. Hulse, *The Psychology of Learning* (New York: McGraw-Hill, 1967).
4. Mark Cook, *Interpersonal Perception* (Middlesex, England: Penguin, 1971). p. 13.
5. A. A. Bodalev et al., "New Data on the Problem of Social Perception," *Soviet Psychology* 11 (Fall, 1972), p. 87.
6. Joan S. Girgus and Stanley Coren, "Peripheral and Central Components in the Formation of Visual Illusions," *American Journal of Optometry and Archives of American Academy of Optometry* 50 (July, 1973), pp. 533–540.
7. Hans Sebald, "Limitations of Communication: Mechanisms of Image Maintenance in Form of Selective Perception, Selective Memory and Selective Distortion," *Journal of Communication* 12 (1962), pp. 142–149.
8. Arthur G. Cryns and Abraham Monk, "Attitudes of the Aged Toward the Young: A Multivariate Study in Intergenerational Perception," *Journal of Gerontology* 27 (January, 1972), pp. 107–112.
9. Walter Lippmann, *Public Opinion* (New York: Macmillan Co., 1922), p. 95.

10. Robert J. Pellegrini, "Impressions of the Male Personality as a Function of Beardedness," *Psychology* 10 (February, 1973), pp. 29–33.
11. Jerry Della Femina, *From Those Wonderful Folks Who Gave You Pearl Harbor* (New York: Simon and Schuster, 1970), p. 128.
12. Katherine C. Good and Lawrence R. Good, "Attitude Similarity and Attraction to an Instructor," *Psychological Reports* 33 (August, 1973), pp. 335–337.
13. Richard Jessor and Shirley L. Jessor, "The Perceived Environment in Behavioral Science: Some Conceptual Issues and Some Illustrative Data," *American Behavioral Scientist* 16 (July, 1973), pp. 801–828.
14. Richard C. Huseman, James M. Lahiff, and Robert Wells, "Communication Thermoclines: Toward a Process of Identification," *Personnel Journal* (February, 1974), pp. 124–135.
15. Jessor and Jessor, p. 805.
16. Daniel Katz and Robert L. Kahn, *The Social Psychology of Organizations* (New York: John Wiley & Sons, 1966), p. 188.
17. Allan M. Schwartzbaum and John H. McGrath, "The Perception of Prestige Differences Among Medical Subspecialties," *Social Science and Medicine* 7 (1973), 365–371.
18. D. Lancy and E. Aronson, "The Influence of the Character of the Criminal and His Victim on the Decisions of Simulated Jurors," *Journal of Experimental Social Psychology* 5 (1969), pp. 141–152.
19. J. Mills and E. Aronsom, "Opinion Change as a Function of the Communicator's Attractiveness and Desire to Influence," *Journal of Personality and Social Psychology*, 1 (1965), pp. 73–77.
20. R. N. Widgery and B. Webster, "The Effects of Physical Attractiveness Upon Perceived Initial Credibility," *Michigan Speech Journal* 4 (1969), pp. 9–15.
21. Herman A. Hutte and David Van Krevel, "The Perception of Door Knocks in Terms of Authority and Urgency," *European Journal of Social Psychology* 2 (1972), pp. 98–99.
22. Frederick W. Obitz and L. Jerome Oziel, "Varied Information Levels and Accuracy of Person Perception," *Psychological Reports* 31 (October, 1972), pp. 571–576.
23. J. W. Shepherd, "The Effects of Valuations in Evaluativeness of Traits on the Relation Between Stimulus Affect and Cognitive Complexity," *Journal of Social Psychology*, 88 (December, 1972), pp. 233–239.
24. Clarence R. Mix, "Interpersonal Communication Patterns, Personal Values, and Predictive Accuracy: An Exploratory Study" (Ph.D. diss., U. of Denver, 1972).
25. N. Wiggins, P. J. Hoffman, and T. Taber, "Types of Judges and Cue Utilization in Judgments of Intelligence," *Journal of Personality and Social Psychology* 12 (1969), pp. 52–59.

3

Motivation

A cursory glance at a recent newspaper revealed the following two items:

> Crotone, Italy (UPI) Rosario Gualtieri, 75, stabbed his 70-year old wife to death after learning she was unfaithful to him 34 years ago, police said.
>
> Police said Gualtieri told them his wife confided to him recently that she had committed adultery with several men in 1939 while he was serving in the army.
>
> "I killed her for reasons of honor," police quoted Gualtieri as saying.
>
> Martin, Tenn. (UPI) John Primrose, 23, rocked for four days, 20 hours and 12 minutes to take first place in the Martin Rocking Chair Competition before falling asleep in his chair. Primrose won $150.
>
> Mrs. Will Wood, 82, of Martin received a plaque for "her enduring spirit" which carried her through 66 hours of rocking competition, officials said.

As any devotee of the news media can attest, such incidents, while unusual, are reported on a daily basis. When reading of such occurrences, one naturally questions the behavior and thinking of the participants. Some will wonder why the lady revealed her secret to her husband after so many years. Others will speculate on the meaning of "reasons of honor." It is unlikely that the question, "Why did he kill his wife?" will ever be answered to the satisfaction of everyone.

On the lighter side, what prompts a twenty-three-year-old man to devote almost five days to a rocking contest? Was it solely for money? Were there other reasons? If so, what were they? Also, why would adults engage in such a frivolous undertaking? For any dedicated observer of human behavior the question "Why?" is omnipresent.

Modern society has become accustomed to regular announcements from physical scientists of their accomplishments. Almost routinely, laboratory scientists seem to discover cures for formerly fatal diseases and are researching new ones. Through laboratory research, science has overcome the obstacles to manned space flights and such scientific milestones have resulted in benefits in many diverse areas. Who, for example, would have expected the search for a heat-resistant material for space travel to result in a commercial product—teflon—now commonly used as a coating for cooking utensils?

As these breakthroughs have come to be expected, there is anticipation that soon there will be new light shed on motivation. Such hopes may be unfounded, however, for unlike research done on the prevention of diseases, or on developing heat-resistant materials, any research on human motivation must, by its very nature, center on that most amorphous of concepts, the human element. By human element is meant the uniqueness of an individual that results from the original mixture of his characteristics and qualities.

THEORIES OF MOTIVATION

Although the ultimate formula for effective motivation may never be discovered, the research continues. The findings from such research so far have provided direction to practicioners as well as to subsequent researchers.

Over the years, a wide variety of theorists have presented an equally wide variety of theories and, while many of these theories were immediately rendered untenable by cold, hard facts, others continue to be recognized as plausible and contribute to man's attempt to motivate others.

As one surveys some of the more well-known theories of motivation, one must remember that these are *theories* and, as such, are unproven generalizations. There is nothing sacred about them nor is there anything conclusive. (Perhaps, lying dormant in *you,* is the theory that will revolutionize the job of the manager. While reading the theories of others, give some thought to what your own personal theory is. There is always room for one more for there is no one "right" theory nor will there ever be.) Both Billy Graham and Don Shula are recognized for their ability to motivate others but it is unlikely that their theories of motivation are identical.

The study of motivation did not originate with the interest in the principles of effective management. As described by Luthans, it can be traced to the ancient Greek philosophers who maintained that hedonism best explained man's motivation. For many centuries thereafter, motivation continued to be explained by man's attempts to maximize pleasure and minimize pain.[1] While there have been many theorists since then, and considerable disagreement between them, most contemporary theorists acknowledge an interrelation of needs, drives, and goals in the motivation process.

Maslow

Abraham Maslow's theory of motivation is based on a hierarchial arrangement of man's needs.[2] Man's most basic needs, his physiological ones, occupy the lowest level in the arrangement. Among his physiological needs are thirst, hunger, sex, and sleep. This level of needs can be activated in order to motivate an individual until the need is satisfied. When a given level of need is satisfied, it ceases to motivate, and the next higher level of need has to be activated to motivate the individual.

According to Maslow, only after the satisfaction of the physiological needs will an individual begin to satisfy his second level needs, the security and safety needs. At this point, motivation will come from these needs to which he has just been awakened. Included in security and safety needs, is the need to be free from the fear of physiological deprivation and physical danger as well as the desire for an organized and predictable environment.

The third level in Maslow's hierarchy represents man's social needs—the needs to belong, to be accepted, and to be loved. Unlike the first two levels, however, the satisfaction of this level depends primarily on interaction with others, for it is only through the efforts of others that our social needs are satisfied.

Only after accomplishing the reasonable satisfaction of one's social needs, can one be motivated through appealing to his esteem needs. The esteem needs include such yearnings as the desire to "be somebody," to gain prestige, recognition, and status.

The highest order of need as seen by Maslow is for self-actualization. By this he means the need to realize one's fullest potential in whatever one's scope of interest happens to be. For some, this is represented by one's occupation. For others, it may be one's avocation or religion.

Although Maslow did not address himself specifically to the organizational setting, his writings have had significant effects on modern management principles. When considering his hierarchical scheme, it must be remembered that only the two lower need levels are finite and can ever be completely satisfied. Since the social, esteem, and self-actualization needs are infinite and can never be completely satisfied, an individual's awareness of any one of them only diminishes when it has become reasonably satisfied.

Herzberg

Frederick Herzberg went a step beyond Maslow, who had limited his theory to motivation in general, and applied it to the situation of work. He developed his theory as a result of research that he conducted with several hundred engineers and accountants in an attempt to learn the extent of their satisfaction with their jobs plus the factors that provided the satisfaction. In this study, a dichotomy clearly emerged comprised of those factors that are necessary to maintain a reasonable level of satisfaction but that do not strongly motivate, with a group of factors that do build strong motivation and job satisfaction. The former he called *maintenance* or *hygiene factors* and the latter he termed *motivators*.[3]

He felt that the maintenance factors operate primarily when absent as dissatisfiers of employees. Their presence, rather than providing motivation, merely maintains a reasonable level of satisfaction. Thus their potency resides in the ability to dissatisfy. Herzberg believed that many managers wrongly perceive them as motivators and that this misperception results in many managerial faux pas that could be avoided.

From his research, Herzberg concluded that there are ten maintenance factors: status; interpersonal relations with supervisor; interpersonal relations with peers; interpersonal relations with subordinates; technical supervision; company policy and administration; job security; working conditions; salary; and personal life.

Herzberg's second group, the motivators, provide motivation and satisfaction by their presence. When not present, however, there is little job satisfaction. The following six factors are the motivators or satisfiers: the work itself; achievement; the possibility of growth; responsibility; advancement; and recognition.[4]

Both Maslow and Herzberg were responsible for significant contributions to the study of motivation. Maslow's hierarchical scheme and Herzberg's recognition of the difference between motivational and maintenance factors provided a clear context in which to visualize the process of motivation. Various scholars have compared the two theories and have found them to be generally compatible with each other. Keith Davis analogized Maslow's three lowest levels to Herzberg's maintenance factors and the upper two levels to the motivational factors. One exception to this analogy which Davis notes is status, a maintenance factor that he equates with Maslow's fourth level of needs.[5]

Vroom

A more recent theory of work motivation which has met with widespread approval and publicity is that proposed by Victor Vroom. Sometimes called the expectancy theory, it is more complex than its predecessors and geared more toward explaining the uniqueness of each individual's behavior.[6]

Vroom views motivation as a process that guides the choice patterns of an employee when faced with several alternatives. His theory is structured around three concepts: instrumentality, valence, and expectancy.

The employee must initially choose among several first-level outcomes. For example, imagine that you are enrolled in an advanced accounting course and you consider an "A" in this course essential to getting a desirable job offer. Your first-level outcome alternatives range from A through F but the A outcome will assume high, positive valence because you see that outcome as a prerequisite to your preferred second-level outcome—a good job offer. Your selection of a first-level outcome will be based upon the relationship between it and possible second-level outcomes. The individual's perception of this relationship is called *instrumentality*. By valence, Vroom means the strength of an individual's desire for a particular outcome. Expectancy is the probability that a specific action will lead to particular first-level outcome. According to Vroom, an employee's motivation to perform a certain act is determined by the algebraic sum of the products of the valences for the outcomes of which instrumentality is a part, multiplied by the expectancies.

While the theories of Maslow, Herzberg, and Vroom are among the best known theories on motivation, they are far from the only ones. An example of a lesser known theory is that proposed by Jerome Kagan who views a motive as a category of ideas that can occur without any change in arousal or action. He defines motive as "a cognitive representation of a future goal state that is desired," and he thinks that motivation follows cognitive activation of a goal. He views man's primary motives as the resolution of uncertainty, hostility, and mastery.[7] Any one of these primary motives can lead to a variety of secondary motives, many of which can serve more than one primary motive. For example, the desire for affiliation with others is a secondary motive that, depending on the situation, may be traceable to any one or all three of the primary motives. Some examples of secondary motives are: achievement, dominances, and autonomy.

At this point, we have surveyed a cross section of theories and motivation each of which possesses some unique feature but all of which recognize the interrelationships between needs, drives, and goals. Let us now measure our theory and the theories of the other experts by some of the findings of objective surveys of motivation in "the real world."

MEASUREMENT OF MOTIVATION

Frequent studies are conducted to determine the attitudes of workers toward such things as their work, superiors, and coworkers. Few will question that such attitudes illustrate the level of motivation of the employees as well as their various needs. With this information, it is easier to know how to motivate them.

Recently, the Gallup polling organization conducted a survey to determine the main reason for job satisfaction and job dissatisfaction among wage earners. The reasons for job satisfaction and percentage of wage earners who included them are as follows:[8]

1. Enjoy my work   39%
2. Good pay   17%
3. Helps society   15%
4. Likes coworkers   11%
5. Interesting work   8%
6. Good working conditions   7%
7. Challenging job   5%

The main reasons for job dissatisfaction found by the pollsters are:[9]

1. Poor wages   34%
2. Boring job   20%
3. Not doing what I want   17%
4. Have to work too hard   10%
5. Being held back   9%
6. Hours too long   8%
7. Not many benefits   5%

Herzberg's theory probably lends itself most readily to a simple analysis of such factors. Of the reasons for job satisfaction, it appears that 62 percent of them (1, 3, 5, 7), are what Herzberg terms motivators. Of the reasons for dissatisfaction with one's job, 83 percent of the subjects responded with what Herzberg considers maintenance factors. Since it is the motivational factors that Herzberg says provide satisfaction to employees by their presence, and maintenance factors that provide dissatisfaction by their absence, the findings from the above poll appear to support Herzberg's thesis. It is more than likely that all of the readers will not be in complete agreement with the manner in which the reasons have been categorized to conform with Herzberg's scheme. It should also be noted again that there have been numerous such studies and there is no semblance of unanimity, neither in the findings nor in the way in which the findings are viewed by others.

In most large organizations, regular attempts are made to quantify the feelings of the employees toward their duties. One interesting study was conducted in the U.S. Navy to determine the reasons why personnel who had originally volunteered for submarine duty would subsequently "devolunteer." An individual was said to have devolunteered when he chose not to requalify for such duty, as an individual was required to do periodically, and instead sought other naval duties. The reasons given for devolunteering and some illustrative statements from the devolunteers follow:[10]

1. Motivational deficiencies—"I have lost all desire to requalify aboard this boat."
2. Dangers of submarine duty—"I no longer feel safe on submarines and the thought of going back underwater is frightening."
3. Habitability—feelings associated with the environment and its confinement and isolation and the resulting personal inconvenience.
4. Workload—long hours and protracted periods of deployment at sea.
5. Maladjustive symptoms—ranges from transient signs of frustration through somewhat morbid phobias and depressions—"I don't believe I could sanely last in submarines for too much longer. I've lain awake for many hours at night with the feeling that the walls were closing in on me."
6. Attitudes toward the Nuclear Power Program—"I no longer possess the motivation and dedication required of the Nuclear Power Program. Further, considering the loss of two nuclear powered submarines in recent years and the high turnover of inexperienced personnel, I feel that the risks involved in submarine duty are excessive."
7. Nonsubmarine interests—interests in other Navy programs
8. Family problems
9. Status incongruence—not working at job individuals were trained for, or being assigned to a job below their abilities.
10. Interpersonal problems—poor relations with peers or seniors
11. Pacifist attitudes—strong opposition to service on warship or to use of nuclear weapons.

Having access to information of this nature should provide management with insights into what causes employees to behave as they do and, in the above case, to choose not to continue in the submarine service. If management is to make use of such findings, it should be reflected in changes in its *modus operandi* with its employees and the way in which it manages them. (Armed with the above list of reasons for "devolunteering" and with your limit knowledge of Navy life how do you "read" the list and what actions would you suggest be taken?)

Now note how the above reasons given by enlisted men for "dropping out" of submarining compare with the reasons given by officers for volunteering for submarine service. While there is an obvious status difference between these two groups that would influence their perceptions of such duty, this study provides insights into what motivates individuals to undertake such duty. These are the major motives found to underly an officer's decision to volunteer for the submarine service:[11]

1. Concrete, positive benefits (good pay, food, etc.)
2. Adventure, challenge, excitement
3. Characteristics of crew (high *esprit de corps*)
4. Service to the country
5. Career and educational opportunities
6. Allows for personal fulfillment
7. Prior experience with submarines and submariners
8. Best duty in the Navy
9. Pride in a responsible job
10. Oceanographic interests

It appears that, with the possible exception of number six, none of these reasons would constitute motivators to Herzberg's way of thinking. The apparent lack of congruence between motivation theory and the above findings does not indicate that the theories are lacking in value, for the purpose served by such theories lies in the context that they provide the student to view problems in motivation.

PROBLEMS IN MOTIVATION

According to an item in the *Atlanta Journal,* an electrical union apprentice when questioned about his attitude toward his job responded with this chant: "I don't smoke, joke, use no dope, spin no wheels, or pop pills."[12] All poetic considerations aside, this type of response, in spite of its negative connotations, is representative of the sentiments of a large share of the work force today. Implicit in this statement is the view that as long as I don't break any laws, I'll hold my job. The work is viewed as a necessary evil, unworthy of mention, and the problems faced by one who tries to motivate such an individual are formidable.

As the level of sophistication and affluence rises in our society, it presents motivational problems that do not lend themselves to simple solutions. In the early decades of the twentieth century, the motivation of workers was easily accomplished in the presence of such factors as a shortage of jobs and the low educational level of most of the work force. The workers were motivated to produce in order to satisfy the basic needs and wants of food and housing. The employer was thought to have met his obligation to the workers by paying them adequately so their most basic needs could be satisfied.

The satisfaction of basic needs, however, is no longer such a significant problem. Various social programs make it possible to satisfy such needs without gainful employment if one so desires.

Also, the relatively high level of education has made the worker more independent and mobile. He is no longer bound to an employer for life, for there is usually a variety of possible jobs available. Therefore, the job of the motivator has become much more difficult, and will most likely continue in that direction, for the rewards the employer has traditionally offered have lost much of their importance to the worker.

One method used to determine the amount of job satisfaction and dissatisfaction has been to ask subjects, "What type of work would you try to get into if you could start all over again?" The findings of such a survey are presented in the following table.[13]

Note that dissatisfaction with one's job is not limited to either the blue-collar workers nor the white-collar ones. Seventy-six percent of the former apparently would not voluntarily choose the same work that they were doing and fifty-seven percent of the latter would not make the same choice again. Thus the problem of motivation permeates all levels of most organizations.

TABLE *3.1 Percentages in Occupational Groups Who Would Choose Similar Work Again*

Professional and Lower White-Collar Occupations	%	Working Class Occupation	%
Urban university professors	93	Skilled printers	52
Mathematicians	91	Paper workers	42
Physicists	89	Skilled autoworkers	41
Biologists	89	Skilled steelworkers	41
Chemists	86	Textile workers	31
Firm lawyers	85	Blue-collar workers, cross section	24
Lawyers	83	Unskilled steelworkers	21
Journalists (Washington correspondents)	82	Unskilled auto workers	16
Church university professors	77		
Solo lawyers	75		
White-collar workers, cross section	43		

APPROACHES TO MOTIVATION

A wide variety of approaches has been applied to the problem of motivation in the last several decades with varying degrees of success. One such approach has been to reduce the amount of time an individual must spend on the job. The rationale for such action is that the employee will appreciate his employer more for his increased leisure and will thus show his appreciation in better performance on the job. Some regard this notion as farfetched and unfounded. The move toward a four-day work week is an extension of this philosophy.

Increasing the wages of employees in order to motivate them has been done for a long time. Most authorities concur that such action is ineffective after an employee reaches a certain level. There is little agreement as to its effectiveness among workers who have not yet attained that level and even less agreement over the location of the level itself. The fact that salary or wage raises have diminishing impact is suggested by the ever-increasing absenteeism and the general disinclination to work overtime even while wage rates continue to rise.

Other employers strive to motivate through the liberal application of fringe benefits. Such features as employee insurance, educational assistance, planned social activities, and retirement programs are examples of fairly common fringe benefits.

Some employers try to motivate their employees by providing them with training beyond that which is clearly essential for the satisfactory performance of the job duties. Training is provided in communication or human relations to awaken the employees to the multifaceted nature of the roles that they fill and of the influence they exert in their interactions with others. Some firms provide selected employees, usually those in a supervisory capacity, with sensitivity training in order to recognize the impact that they make on others. While there is general acknowledgement of the value derived from such training when presented by qualified personnel, it is also maintained that for such training to result in more permanent improvements depends on the climate of the organization. This is dependent on the attitude of those holding the highest positions within the organization and rarely do these top employees take part with their subordinates in such training.

Herzberg calls such approaches to motivation KITA, an unsubtle acronym for the technique of motivating others through the judicious administration of kicks to the posterior of the motivatee.[14] He considers the approaches mentioned above to be positive in nature, since results are achieved through the lures of material and psychological rewards. According to Herzberg, negative KITA may also achieve results, but the appeal is directed at the fears of the consequences if the desired results are not achieved. While he does not consider either type of KITA to be actual motivation, he feels that many managers do not consider negative KITA to be motivation but do consider positive KITA to be. He attempts to explain the acceptance of positive KITA by comparing it to seduction and negative KITA to rape. He considers the positive to be even worse than the negative since, "...it is infinitely worse to be seduced than to be raped; the latter is an unfortunate occurence while the former signifies that you were a party to your own downfall."[15]

Herzberg says that there must be a "generator" within a person before that person can be motivated, and that such a person will need no outside stimulation. Some examples of motivational approaches that he does consider to be valid are: increasing the accountability of individuals for their own work; giving a person a complete natural unit of work rather than a task so minute that the contribution to the overall task seems insignificant; and, granting additional authority to employees in regard to their work activity.[16]

Most of the recent approaches to improving the motivation of workers has been based on several premises about the expectations and interests of the workers. These are:

1. Today's workers want more recognition as individuals.
2. They expect to have more control over their lives.
3. They expect there to be an actual possibility of advancement and growth for them.

In the appendix to its report entitled "Work in America," a task force to the Department of Health, Education, and Welfare documents a number of programs that leading business organizations, both in the U. S. and abroad, have initiated in order to motivate their workers.[17] Such programs were generally started in subunits that were experiencing problems rather than in the entire organization.

Some of the specific problems, which were cited as reasons for trying new techniques, were: low morale; frequent shutdowns; low productivity; excessive errors; high turnover; absenteeism; inefficiency; and general disinterest of the workers in their job. Among the techniques applied to the units experiencing problems were: organization of the workers into relatively autonomous work groups; less supervision and more job freedom for workers; rotation of employees between their factory jobs and more desirable nonfactory jobs; provision of groups with enough relevant data to allow them to set their own production quotas; and the removal of time clocks.

Some of the "human results" which were recognized as stemming from the changes were: higher morale, measured by surveys; reduction in the number of grievances; greater interest in the job, represented by increased numbers of suggestions; reduced absenteeism; and, a higher degree of involvement and committment among employees. Most of these human results were accompanied by equally attractive economic results that are also cited in the report.

For each one of the widely-publicized programs that has proved successful, it is likely that there has been at least one, if not more, failures. Since most of these techniques are of recent origin, a high rate of failure is not surprising nor does it reflect adversely on the managements involved. In light of the knowledge of the techniques that no longer serve to motivate, the unwillingness to introduce such new programs constitutes an indictment of management.

RELUCTANCE TO INNOVATE

While the above consideration of problems, techniques, and results might lead one to believe that most business organizations are deeply involved in such innovative programs such is not the case. There appears to be a general reluctance to veer from the mainstream of thinking on motivation, despite the fact that the traditional methods of motivating are recognized as decreasingly effective.

Such reluctance can be attributed to a variety of factors, no one of which would be completely explanatory. One plausible explanation is that, like most other individuals, business executives fear change and new motivational techniques represent change. Since they are more comfortable with the status quo, they may choose to persist in their present practices in which they have been somewhat successful rather than risk abject failure by initiating new practices.

The distance, both physical and psychological, by which the middle-level manager is often separated from the top executives, also contributes to this reluctance. Since the higher-ups in an organization are often far removed from the most common managerial problems, they fail to recognize the need to adapt. While the middle managers may see the need clearly, they hesitate to mention it to their superiors for fear that it may suggest incompetency on their part, or worse yet, the idea that they are "selling out" to the workers.

Such reluctance might also be explained by management's fear of losing control of their company. At first glance, such a suggestion may seem unlikely; however, the fact that most plans to motivate workers are predicated on less control by superiors and hence more freedom for subordinates, such fear is understandable. A recent study of 400 top executives in Europe indicates that they feel threatened by these new theories.[18] There seems to be no reason to believe that such feelings are unique to Europe.

CONTEMPORARY PROBLEMS

While changes in the approach to motivational problems may seem imperceptible, the same cannot be said about the problems themselves. Problems that once were of epic proportions, such as a shortage of workers educated enough to understand detailed instructions, may now be so insignificant that they have been replaced by problems that had never been anticipated. Who would have predicted the emergence of an "overeducated" work force in which many menial jobs remain unfilled because some of those looking for work consider those jobs to be beneath them?

Some of the problems that the manager of the seventies is more likely to encounter than his predecessors, involve minority group members. The Department of Health, Education, and Welfare reports that a disproportionate share of minority group members, black, chicano, Puerto Rican, or Indian, is "working at bad jobs."[19] Such a finding suggests that minority group members are more likely to encounter meaningless tasks and authoritarian environments. Thus it is to be expected that the manager's skills as a motivator will be taxed to the utmost.

For many minority group members, however, problems of discrimination will be equally important. That which a minority group member may perceive as discrimination, may be unconscious behavior on the part of the "offender." Conversely, that which a superior considers a normal, businesslike manner may be perceived by another as unnecessarily brusque. Cultural differences contribute significantly to such problems and an awareness of these differences and their effect is a prerequisite for overcoming them.

Since this age has been characterized by an easing of restrictions, whether they be laws, policies, or social norms, workers have grown to expect, and in some instances demand, a corresponding reduction of the restrictions governing their job. When increased flexibility is not forthcoming, for whatever the reason, the result is frequently alienation of the workers.

Research by social scientists has shown alienation to be comprised of four ingredients: 1) powerlessness (regarding ownership of the enterprise, managerial policies, etc.), 2) meaninglessness (with respect to the character of the product worked on and scope of the product process), 3) isolation (social aspect of work), 4) self-estrangement (detachment and boredom).[20]

Such alienation is often blamed on bureaucratic management techniques and the pyramidal structure of most business organizations. Regardless of its causes it is a fact of life for many managers and any motivational strategy that is to be viable must deal not only with its observable symptoms, but also with the underlying causes.

MOTIVATION AND COMMUNICATION

Any attempt to better the motivation of workers is destined to fail unless communication is also improved, for the processes of motivation and communication, when viewed in the context of an organization's objectives, are interdependent. The quality of one is dependent upon the quality of the other. Unless they are viewed as concomitant in importance, organizational effectiveness will be impaired. All too often, improved communication is prescribed as a remedy for any problem an organization is thought to have. Like the snake oil hawked by the fast-talking salesman of bygone days and touted as a cure for anything from sexual impotence to dandruff, so too, communication is often attributed with results that it alone is incapable of delivering. Purposeful attention must be directed at both motivation and communication for a significant benefit to result.

Stanley Peterfreund, a management consultant, recognizes the need for improved communication in companies seeking to improve worker's motivation. He contends that "having employees who feel they are well informed pays dividends in improved commitment to the company, more productive work, and more satisfaction with pay, promotions, and other working conditions." He says that this is true at every level of employment, in every type of organization. The better informed the employee, the more positive will be his attitudes. Also, he feels that improving communication improves the jobs, because it helps the workers get the information they need to do the jobs as they should be done."[21]

There are other specific ways in which communication itself can be used to motivate employees. When a company keeps its employees aware of what is anticipated, of its long-range plans as they affect employees, that company establishes a climate in which employees are most likely to grow. Such openness allows the worker to concentrate on his work, secure in the knowledge that he is a part of the organization's communication network. As a link in that network, the subordinate will also have ready access to his superior who will listen and act on his suggestions, problems, and complaints.

An employee who is thoroughly trained for his job will usually be more highly motivated than one whose training is cursory. Training must be an ongoing process and, while its initial thrust may be formal, subsequent efforts will likely be on a more casual basis. Regardless, effective training is dependent upon the regular give and take of information, on two-way communication. Such training will produce dual benefits: a more competent performance of duties; and, an informed employee who recognizes his employer's investment in him as evidence of his own worth.

The orientation of employees for change is another important function of any communication-motivation program. Such an orientation equips the employees to deal with change by facilitating whatever questions and suggestions they have about it. The motivational benefits to be derived will be accompanied by a greater willingness of the employees to accept change, since they have been made familiar with the underlying rationale.

When we attempt to get things done through others, our strategy is based on whatever assumptions we harbor about how man is motivated. The congruence of our assumptions to reality determines our success. In an organization in which provision is made for ongoing communication, the degree of incongruence will be minimal and that which there is will be fed back to the communicator through the appropriate channels. The knowledgeable and alert communicator adapts to such feedback and will continue to adapt until the desired level of motivation is achieved. Thus, when considering organizational effectiveness, the two processes are so entwined as to make concentration on one—if not impossible—extremely impractical.

SUMMARY

For a long time motivation was viewed in terms of man's quest for pleasure. This simplistic view was modified considerably as theorists began to recognize the interrelatedness of needs, drives, and goals in the motivation process.

Maslow's theory of motivation included a hierarchical arrangement of human needs. He maintained that until a person's lowest level needs, the physiological, were satisfied, that a person could not be motivated by an appeal to higher level needs and that, when satisfied, a need ceased to motivate.

Herzberg applied his theory to the work situation and recognized that existence of two distinct types of factors, maintenance factors and motivators. The absence of the former serves to dissatisfy employees but their presence will not motivate. Vroom's theory which considered valence, expectancy, and instrumentality, explained the uniqueness of an individual's behavior.

Numerous attempts have been made to measure the attitudes of workers as a means to learning what motivates them. Problems in motivation have been traced to disinterest in one's job, as well as to the availability of other jobs. The attempts made by most organizations to motivate workers have consisted of providing the workers with such features as increased leisure time, higher pay, and other fringe benefits. Such attempts have generally not been very successful.

Organizations that have tried more innovative approaches have been more successful; however, there has been a general hesitancy to innovate in this area. The success of any attempt to motivate workers is largely dependent on the manner in which it is communicated to them.

QUESTIONS FOR DISCUSSION

1. Are there any factors that neither Maslow, Herzberg, nor Vroom consider which, you feel, play a significant role in providing motivation in the work situation?

2. Do you consider Maslow's need levels appropriate? Would you add or delete any?

3. The measurement of worker's attitudes is often used to determine how best to motivate them. Are there any other measurements that might be equally appropriate?

4. List as many commonly applied techniques for motivating as you can. Which ones seem to be the most effective? Why?

5. How do you explain the reluctance of business organizations to attempt more imaginative approaches to motivation?

6. Describe one technique you would like to see tried as a means of motivating workers?

7. What problems, in addition to those described in this chapter, do you foresee as obstacles to effective motivation in the future?

ENDNOTES

1. Fred Luthans, *Organizational Behavior* (New York: McGraw-Hill, 1973), p. 389.

2. Abraham Maslow, *Motivation and Personality* (New York: Harper, 1954).
3. Frederick Herzberg, "One More Time: How Do You Motivate Employees?" *Harvard Business Review* Vol. 46, No. 1, (January–February, 1968), pp. 53–62.
4. Herzberg, p. 57.
5. Keith Davis, *Human Relations at Work* (New York: McGraw-Hill, 1967), p. 37.
6. Victor H. Vroom, *Work and Motivation* (New York: Wiley, 1964), p. 128.
7. Jerome Kagan, "Motives and Development," *Journal of Personality and Social Psychology* 22 (April, 1972), pp. 51–66.
8. *Gallup Opinion Index* Report No. 94 (Princeton, New Jersey, April, 1973), p. 10.
9. *Gallup Opinion Index,* p. 4.
10. Ernest M. Noddin, "Studies in Enlisted Submarine Motivation: Some Etiological Factors Related to Devolunteering of Submarine School Candidates, Naval Submarine Medical Research Laborary, Naval Submarine Medical Center Report No. 703, (February, 1972).
11. J. T. Giles, LT (jg.), MC, USNR, C. E. Collins, LT (jg.), MC, USNR and Benjamin B. Waybrew, Ph. D., "Characteristics of the Submarine Line Office: Patterns of Motivation for Volunteering for the Submarine Service," Naval Submarine Medical Research Laboratory, Naval Submarine Medical Center Report No. 666, (February, 1972).
12. *Atlanta Journal,* July 20, 1973, p. 1.
13. *Work in America,* Report of a Special Task Force to the Secretary of Health, Education and Welfare (Cambridge, Massachusetts: MIT Press, 1972), p. 16.
14. Herzberg, p. 54.
15. Herzberg, p. 55.
16. Herzberg, p. 59.
17. *Work in America,* pp. 188–201.
18. Harry Levinson, "Asinine Attitudes Toward Motivation," *Harvard Business Review,* Vol. 51, (January–February, 1973), p. 70.
19. *Work in America,* p. 52.
20. Robert Blauner, *Alienation and Freedom: The Factory Worker and His Industry* (Chicago: University of Chicago, 1964).
21. Judson Gooding, *The Job Revolution* (New York: Walker Pub., 1972), p. 32.

4

Language and Meaning

The cracking of secret codes has been the staple of innumerable short stories, novels, and films of the cloak-and-dagger genre. A key to effective espionage, as often recognized both in fact and fiction, is the discovery of the meaning of the enemy's code. Since it is customary to view codes as secretive and clandestine, it is understandable that many people fail to recognize that their own language is a code.

As with a code, a language is restricted to those familiar with it. To nonusers it is mysterious, indeed, often threatening. Evidence of this can be found in numerous cases in which suspicions about foreign coworkers have resulted in physical violence. News media have reported locker room fights between non-English speaking baseball players and their English-speaking teammates. These fights usually involved players of Spanish descent and the reported cause generally was that the Anglo players felt that the Latins, when conversing in Spanish, were talking about them. Like the man who quit attending football games because he was sure that each time the players huddled they were talking about him, it is common for people to be suspicious of that which they are unable to comprehend.

DIVISIVE ASPECT OF LANGUAGE

This incomprehensibility is not limited to foreign languages. It includes the sublanguages, or jargons, that have become a part of various occupations in this age of specialization. Columnist Russell Baker has facetiously written of the sublanguages which he termed Sociolojish, Pentaquack, Salesgush, Sports-gab, Journalese, Spacespeak, and Airplanish.[1] This list is far from exhaustive but all sublanguages and languages are alike in that they are restricted to a select group. When those who are excluded are exposed to the language, they often respond with suspicion and apprehension. Such is the power of mere words.

In Ireland, parents are insisting that Gaelic, a largely unused language, be taught in the schools. The Cajuns in Louisiana, hoping to keep their language alive, have gone so far as to ask for and receive government aid to provide for the importation of young people from France whose task it is to inculcate in the students their heritage and language. The government of France is so interested in the project that it is allowing interested French students and teachers to satisfy their requirement of service in lieu of conscription.[3] The extent of the interest is also evident in the Council for the Development of French in Louisiana which was founded in that state in 1967. Pressure in New York City has resulted in the schools making courses in several black dialects available to those interested.

Examples such as those should dispel the notion that language is neutral. When we treat language as a neutral medium of exchange, we leave ourselves unprotected from the ravages of semantic intruders.

Abstracting

At the core of many of our semantic difficulties lies our ability and readiness to abstract. We abstract when we concentrate on certain details at the expense of others. When a columnist refers to a political figure as a "loyal Democrat" he may consider himself accurate; however, he isn't telling the entire story. For that same person is many other things also. Among other things he may be a father, hockey fan, and reader of science fiction.

An effective communicator is one who remains aware that he is abstracting. While it should be obvious that this process is necessary, we should also recognize the high cost that accompanies it. This cost of abstracting is that we sacrifice many details, some of which may be relevant to the subject under consideration. By so doing, we alter the picture we are transmitting to the other person. Very often that other person is not aware of the alteration and acts under the assumption that he has been provided with all of the details. As serious as its effect on others is, it effects the communicator who often fails to remember abstracting and acts as though he were presenting the entire picture.

This natural inclination to abstract results in a distorted perception of reality by those who are accepting the information as gospel. The more extreme the abstraction the further astray the recipient of the information will be led. The process of abstracting is not without merit, however. One of its values is that it saves much time. Imagine trying to present your views on any subject whatever without doing any abstracting.

Another major cost is that it makes us appear to know more than we actually do. Some people of course do not consider this to be a "cost" since they enjoy this illusion of omniscience as well as the veil of mystery that enshrouds their pronouncements. Indeed, there are those who owe their present position and base their aspirations for the future on their ability to employ plenty of abstractions in their communication with the public. Politicians are an example of an occupational group that appears to flourish in direct proportion to its aptitude in abstracting. Although many would dispute this, it seems that the candidate who speaks in high level abstractions such as "democracy" or "free enterprise" is more likely to succeed then the one who chooses to become more specific. When Candidate X "levels" with his listeners and reveals that he considers the mandatory busing of students a part of his view of democracy, he will alienate those who equate democracy with the status quo as well as those who wish for things to return to "the good old days." To the politician the value of high level abstractions lies in the fact that they remain undefined. As such, the individual receivers of the information provide their own definition, one that satisfies them and in so doing tacitly agree with the mouther of the abstractions. When exposed to abstractions, we must keep in mind that something—usually much—is being left out.

Category Systems

The same kind of awareness is necessary when confronted with category systems. The tendency to categorize is every bit as human and as potentially dangerous as the tendency to abstract. We categorize when we recognize items, events, or persons as being somewhat similar to other items, events, or persons and therefore treat them as identical. When we categorize a person, on the basis of his work habits, as a perfectionist our perception of that person narrows significantly. We find ourselves looking for cues that reinforce our categories and discounting those cues that suggest that our categorization is incorrect. The moment when the traffic manager begins to view a routing problem as identical to one he encountered previously, is the moment when the probability of his selecting the best solution begins to wane.

Victims of Categorization

The problems caused to both the categorizer and the person categorized are obvious. It appears that the passive victim of categorization often resigns himself to the category into which he has been placed, and then proceeds to try to justify it or to live up to his label. The response of the office manager who is viewed as a nitpicker may be, "If they think I'm a nitpicker anyway, I'll show them what real nitpicking is" and he then proceeds to confirm their categorization.

The Women's Movement represents an attempt to break out of a category, to drop labels that have traditionally been affixed to the female role in society. Various other organizations have been founded that represent more specific attempts to break molds into which persons have been placed. The Stewardess Anti-Defamation Defense League protests the advertising campaigns of airlines that make such enticements as, "I'm Linda, Fly Me," or "She'll Serve You—All the Way."[4] The complaint of this organization is that the airlines, through their advertising, are categorizing stewardesses in the public mind into a not wholly complimentary category.

Other segments of the Women's Movement protest the fact that females have never been categorized as individuals but have always been viewed as man's silent partner. In an article entitled "One Small Step for Genkind," its authors complain that unless otherwise identified, people in general are assumed to be men and that the English language defines everyone as male. As examples they cite such terms as that by which we call the hypothetical person, the "average man," or the common person usually called the "man in the street." Another often-used term is that for an active person, "man on the move." The authors of the article feel that for too long women have been rendered invisible through this type of "semantic mechanism." They urge that henceforth "man" be used only for males and "women" for females, in other words separate but equal categories, and "gen" as a referent for both.[5]

When we allow others to categorize us, we relinquish control over the way they will respond to us. Bosmajian viewed Martin Luther King, Jr.'s career as an attempt to get blacks to stop allowing whites to define who the blacks were and are. He felt that blacks had for too long passively accepted the categories into which whites placed them, when they should have been striving to create their own categories. He also points out that the Nazis used language to redefine the Jews to the point that elimination of the "Jewish plague" seemed "reasonable" to the Nazi audiences.[6] Since it is a person's language that structures reality for him, the category system he employs is all important.

Flexibility of Categories

The flexibility of one's category systems is another major determinant of how we view the world, as well as of our ability to accept change. The individual's category system is fragile and sensitive. It requires constant attention, for it has little resistance to rigidity which, once contracted, is difficult to overcome. Such rigidity sets in when we cease to change with the times and fail to alter our categories on the basis of change. Much of Tofler's *Future Shock* is devoted to this idea. Few would deny that IBM of the seventies differs greatly from IBM of the forties or that Krupp, Inc. of Germany has changed significantly over the years, yet many of those who recognize the change in such organizations are oblivious to the same process as it occurs in one's associates and as it affects surrounding events.

Too often we treat individuals and problems as we always have, without considering the alterations called for by changing conditions. As long as a person fails to update his views, that person will remain stalled on the periphery of effectiveness as a communicator. His mental wheels will continue to spin on the foothills of the glacier semanticists call "frozen evaluation." Alfred Korzybski, the founder of general semantics, suggested that a person mentally index his general terms and in that way reduce his tendency to make such semantic errors. When we index terms, we separate them on the basis of some differences and by so doing recognize their uniqueness.

DETERMINANTS OF MEANING

While research long ago confirmed that few words have only one meaning, it continues to be routine for us to assume the opposite. In addition, we assume that the person we are trying to communicate with agrees with us on the meaning of the terms we are using. Both of these assumptions are based on the belief that somewhere there exists a repository wherein each word and its meanings are housed. The concept of such a repository is accurate, but the universality of it, alas, is not. Were it so, there would be no disagreements over meanings.

Each of us is our own repository, and we extract the meanings for words from within ourselves. Both communicator and receiver do this constantly, and the success of the interaction depends upon the similarity of the contents of the repositories. These contents are determined by those factors that shape the individuals involved—education, race, political affiliation, occupation, and personal experience, etc.

In the preceeding paragraph we are dealing with only one dimension of meaning—the denotative dimension. Denotative meaning is that which is explicit in a term, its most common definition. The fact that many often-used words have more than one denotative meaning adds a nuance that further complicates the selection of appropriate language. An example of this dilemma is found in the word "busy" which to most of us simply denotes "active" or "in use." As anyone who enjoyed Vonnegut's *Cat's Cradle* knows, however, when whispered three times by a Bokonist it is an exclamation over how "complicated and unpredictable the machinery of life really is."[7]

The second dimension of meaning is the connotative one. It refers to what is suggested by a given term, to what it connotes to an individual. While a characteristic of denotation is objectivity, connotation is subjective. While the idea of individual repositories may seem to negate the existence of a denotative dimension and, instead, suggest that all meaning is connotative, such is not the case. For denotative meaning refers to the definition generally accorded a term, but the connotative meaning is what it suggests to individuals.

When considering the meanings of a term, it is not adequate to know how it is generally defined. One must also be aware of the kinds of connotations that might be conjured up by a given group. A popular discotheque may advertise its atmosphere as "intimate." A sizable share of the population, especially that much-maligned segment over thirty, would view the same nightspot as "congested." An employee in a company's research and development department will view his department in terms of its stated function, research, and development, while to the worker on the assembly line, the term may connote a "playground for offbeat engineers."

Since there is great variance in connotations within a given population, the communicator must exercise caution in his selection of language. A term that may have positive connotations with one type of person or group may possess very negative connotations for others. Awareness of connotative meanings within certain groups constitutes a guideline to be followed in the choice and arrangement of words when dealing with members of those groups. A young Englishman discovered this after seeing his American companion bristle when, at the end of a pleasant night on the town, he told her that he would "knock her up" the following noon. Only after prolonged explanation tinged with apologies, was she convinced that his plan to "knock her up" meant that he would come to see her and that it was a common English expression.[8]

The United States has long had a reputation of opposition to socialism and socialistic institutions. Socialism has negative connotations for most

North Americans and the concept of socialized medicine has long been viewed with hostility. When it was determined that adequate health care was not within the means of all U. S. citizens, the need for a national health plan was recognized and medicare introduced and accepted. Had this program been offered to the nation as socialized medicine, it seems certain that its negative connotations would have stimulated much more opposition than actually developed. Although there are as many similarities as differences between socialized medicine and medicare, the differences were publicized much more widely than the similarities.

Great care is taken, especially when dealing with the public, to guard against making appeals in terms that have negative connotations. Market research firms survey the public to determine what a name connotes to the public before affixing the name or a certain image to a product. Occasionally, despite all of the precautions, a product will be marketed employing an appeal that will have negative connotations for many. One such example is using the deodorant soap that, according to its manufacturer "is like taking a shower in Ireland." While at another time, the prospect of showering in that location might connote freshness and cleanliness, that seems to no longer be the case. In recent years, Northern Ireland has been presented by the mass media in the United States as a battleground in which violence and bloodshed have become routine in the continuing struggle between the Irish Republican Army and the British Army.

While you can probably think of some other such examples quite readily, advertising appeals are generally presented to the public only after extensive research has validated the approach chosen. At a more personal level, however, we often not only fail to do any research on the person or persons we are trying to deal with but we also even fail to discriminate between denotation and connotation.

INTENSIONAL ORIENTATION

John Dewey cited the invention of symbols as the outstanding event in human history. Most would agree that it does merit an important position in any such hierarchy. There are many, however, who often attach too much importance on the symbols we use. Such a person is said to have an intensional orientation. Irving Lee reported some of the signs of such an orientation: 1) paying more attention to what things are called than to the facts themselves;[9] 2) responding to words as if they were more than forms of representation;[10] 3) indulging in verbal "proofs" instead of going to life facts.[11]

The intensionally-oriented individual is not content to let words shape reality; he regards words as reality. Several years ago, a headline on the front page of *The New York Times* stated, "Word 'Poverty' Faces U. S. Ban." The article described how a federal interagency committee had urged the elimination of the word "poverty" from all official reports. This type of suggestion typifies the product of an intensional orientation. The reasoning behind it seems to be that removal of the word constitutes removal of the problem. A newspaper reporter has noted the shift in terminology in government documents from "poor" to "deprived" to "disadvantaged" to "culturally disadvantaged." She observes that while the subjects remain unchanged, they are still poor, and by calling them culturally disadvantaged it sounds "as though they lacked nothing more serious than a free pass to Lincoln Center." [12] Intensionality is often characterized by a predisposition to attend to the map rather than to the actual territory. An intensional person pays more attention to feelings, thoughts, and theories than to the facts of the matter, or "reality."

Euphemisms

Intensional persons are highly susceptible to euphemisms both as senders and receivers. Since such persons are already content to ignore reality, and base their actions on internal factors instead, they accept euphemisms readily, further distorting their view of reality. A euphemism is a word or phrase that is substituted for a more offensive one. The field of advertising is probably more closely associated with the use of euphemisms than any other occupational area. Soap companies tout their products for those who wish not to "offend" when what they mean is perspire or sweat. Margarine companies compare their product to the "high-priced spread" when they mean butter.

This is not to say that advertisers are the only users of euphemisms, for their use is much more widespread than that. An analysis of your own vocabulary would most likely show that you use them extensively. No segment of society, including that which preaches "Tell it like it is," is free from euphemisms and their harmful effects. What younger people call "ripping off" is identical to what elders call theft or robbery. The military may term it a "protective reaction strike" but it remains a bombing attack, albeit one undertaken because of the possible infliction of damages if it were not. The teacher describes Junior to his parents as an "underachiever" when she means that he's a bad student. The economist uses the term "negative savers" when what he means is "those who spend more than they earn." Senator Eugene McCarthy expressed what is wrong with using euphemisms when he said, ". . .if the meaning of words is obscured, the basis for common judgment is underminded, if not destroyed."[13] Euphemisms gloss over reality and obscure it for many. They tone down facts and make the situation seem better than it is.

Inferences

An additional linguistic device which, along with euphemisms, contributes to intensionality is the inference. According to Hayakawa, an inference is "a statement about the unknown made on the basis of the known."[14] When a person makes an inference, he goes beyond the facts that he has and makes an assumption. When the annual flu epidemic comes to the campus, most professors attribute the decline in class attendance to it, some with better reason than others. The flu epidemic may be a fact, but the speculation on absenteeism is an inference.

We make many inferences each day and the extent to which we base our actions on them should depend on the probability of the inference being correct. Since it is extremely unlikely that you will suffer a heart attack today you will probably not choose to spend the day in bed nor sitting in your doctor's waiting room. If you park your car downtown at midday at an expired parking meter, however, the probability is high that you will get a parking ticket. For that reason, you will put a coin in the parking meter.

EXTENSIONAL ORIENTATION

The extensionally-oriented person is the opposite of the intensional one. Where the latter is more concerned with the map and infers readily from it, the former concentrates on the territory itself and observes. Intensionality is epitomized by the immediate, unthinking response to events. The extensional response is delayed and critical.

When we base our actions on what we observe rather than on what we infer, we are dealing with certainty rather than probability. Consequently, our resulting actions will more likely be appropriate and congruent to the context in which they occur. An observation provides a person with documentation in the way that an inference does not. This documentation may consist of either the observer's sense data or of his ability to verify it. When the Tax Foundation, Inc., found in a study that, in 1970, 14.4 million people worked for the government, this was an observation. When Mr. Average Citizen reads those figures and concludes that, "The country is going to the dogs," he is making an inference.

It is not the tendency to infer that debilitates our communicative effectiveness. It is our failure to be aware of when we are inferring rather than observing and our consequent failure to calculate the degree of probability that the inference is correct. Haney states that, since most people remain unaware that they are making inferences, they never reach the point of calculating the probability of correctness.[15] We thus treat inferential data as though it were observational, and take many uncalculated risks we might otherwise have avoided or at least have been alerted to.

The extensionally-oriented person is one who strives for objectivity and who is not content to rely on the verbal maps of others. He is predisposed to investigate the facts himself and, on the basis of those facts, to construct his own map. In 1960 many political analysts stated that a Catholic could not be elected President in the U. S. Kennedy did not accept that and proved the generally accepted maps to be inaccurate. The rapid growth of the economy motel industry in recent years is a product of someone's extensionality. At some point, a person questioned whether the public actually wanted luxurious overnight lodgings. He investigated facts, and recognized the discrepancy between the facts and the types of accommodations then available. According to *The Wall Street Journal* many economy motels now claim occupancy rates of more than 90 percent while more expensive competitors struggle to keep their rooms 70 percent full.[16]

The extensionally-oriented person recognizes the uniqueness of others as well as of himself. He views words in their proper perspective as symbols of reality, rather than as reality itself and he responds to them accordingly. He strives to further his extensionality by expressing consciousness that he is projecting his own view, through the use of such terms as "to me," "in my opinion," or "as I see it."[17] Extensional persons are creative persons also. According to Hayakawa, "...the act of bringing together the uniqueness of yourself at the moment and the uniqueness of other people's feelings at the moment into the solution of the problem is the act of creativity."[18]

SUMMARY

We are so enmeshed in the present that we grow oblivious to change. Since we perceive the territory—persons, events, and language—as unchanging, we fail to update our map. We continue to view ourselves as being in control of those factors that are largely uncontrollable. We respond to change in the manner one would expect of the French Academy, a government-authorized institution whose purpose it is to aid in the development and purification of the French language. Like the French Academy, we often engage in the futile pursuit of attempting to stabilize our ever-changing language, when we should instead be adapting to the changes.

Neil Postman facetiously proposed the establishment of a "language pollution index." As he visualized it, "Right after the weather man would come the language man. 'Thank you, Tom. Today the language pollution index rose to the danger point and the Governor had to request that a period of silence be imposed starting at 6 p.m. this evening. He lifted the ban at 10 p.m. this evening, and tomorrow's prospects for a healthier day seem quite good'."[19]

While the language man and his index may never appear on nightly television, there are practices that enable us to minimize such pollution without requiring anything as drastic as mandatory periods of silence. The recognition that language is a medium of exchange that is anything but neutral is a step in the right direction, as is the realization that, while abstracting simplifies life greatly, it cannot be done without incurring some losses in clarity. Meaning does not exist in words, but in the people who use the words and people define words in two ways, denotatively and connotatively. Our category system influences our perception of the world and, consequently, our communication about it. The practice of indexing helps us to keep our categories flexible and our objectivity operational. The intensional orientation differs significantly from the extensional one. Continuing awareness of these differences aids the individual as he strives to attain and maintain the grasp of reality that accompanies the extensional orientation.

QUESTIONS FOR DISCUSSION

1. Select an occupation and list as many examples of jargon unique to that occupation as you can. In what other ways might those same terms be defined?

2. Would communication be more accurate if everyone ceased to abstract? Why? What are the benefits to be derived from abstracting?

3. How is abstracting similar to categorizing? How is it different?

4. What factors are most influential in determing how you will interpret a word?

5. Select a public figure and a subject toward which that person is intensionally oriented. Cite examples.

6. How do you explain the widespread use of euphemisms when so few restrictions exist in regard to language usage?

ENDNOTES

1. Russell Baker, *New York Times* (Jan. 14, 1971), p. 37.
2. *New York Times* (April 16, 1971), VI, p. 36.
3. *New York Times* (May 7, 1972), p. 71.
4. *New York Times* (Dec. 17, 1972), IV. p. 3.
5. Casey Miller and Kate Swift, "One Small Step For Genkind," *New York Times* (April 16, 1972), VI, p. 36.
6. Haig A. Bosmajian, "The Language of Sexism," *ETC*, Vol. 29, No. 3, p. 305.
7. Kurt Jr., Vonnegut, *Cat's Cradle* (New York: Holt, Rinehart, and Winston 1963) p. 51.
8. Edwin A. Jr., Roberts, "Mainstreams and Others," *National Observer* (Feb. 3, 1973), p. 7.
9. Irving J. Lee, *Language Habits in Human Affairs* (New York: Harper & Brothers 1941), p. 127.
10. Lee, p. 131.
11. Lee, p. 137.
12. Grace Hechinger, "The Insidious Pollution of Language," *Wall Street Journal*, (Oct. 27, 1971), p. 22.
13. Hechinger, p. 22.
14. S. I. Hayakawa, *Language in Thought and Action* (New York: Harcourt, Brace and Jovanovich 1949), p. 41.
15. William V. Haney, *Communication and Organizational Behavior* (Homewood, Illinois, 1973), p. 222. R. D. Irwin
16. *Wall Street Journal* (Dec. 26, 1972), p. 1.
17. Wendell Johnson, *People in Quandries* (New York: Harper & Brothers 1946), p. 207.
18. S. I. Hayakawa, "The Fully Functioning Personality," *ETC*, Spring, 1956, p. 179.
19. Neil Postman, "Demeaning of Meaning," *Language in America* ed. Neil Postman (New York: Pegasus 1969), p. 20.

5

Nonverbal Communication

An executive of a large insurance company found this notice in his in-box. It was a single sheet of paper which said in toto: "This page does not apply to the following states: Missouri, Kansas, Iowa, Indiana, Arkansas." He realized immediately that he had not gotten the complete message and took steps to remedy the situation.

As members of formal and informal organizations, many individuals often fail to get the complete message. Since their lack of information is not as obvious as in the above example, however, they remain unaware of it.

Since people have a natural tendency to rely unduly on what is told to them, they are oblivious to much other information that is being transmitted simultaneously over other channels. Such extreme reliance on the spoken word places the receiver in a situation analogous to that of the insurance executive. This chapter concentrates on the many other messages, messages that are generally either perceived inaccurately or are ignored. These messages and the channels through which they are transmitted comprise what Edward T. Hall called "the silent language."[1]

Ruesch and Kees were among the first to do research on nonverbal communication and the book which resulted from their research captured the interest of many.[2] Ruesch and Kees recognized three categories of nonverbal communication, describing them as three distinct languages.

The person who uses gestures in place of words, numbers, or punctuation marks is using sign language. They cite the hitchhiker's simple gesture and the complex language system of the deaf as two extreme examples of sign language. Additional examples are the hand signals of the traffic officer as he directs heavy traffic and the catcher on a baseball team as he indicates the type of pitch he wants.

All movements that have more than a signal function constitute action language. Ruesch and Kees recognize a dual function for such acts as walking and drinking since they serve personal needs as well as constitute "statements" to anyone who perceives them. For many such actions, the only intent of the actor is to satisfy a personal need. Whatever nonverbal message is received by those in attendance is often completely unintended by the actor.

All material things, whether intentionally or unintentionally displayed, comprise the object language. Such items as clothing, books, and buildings are all a part of it. All such items transmit cues to any observer and as such constitute a language.

It was the research of Ruesch and Kees and others that led to the acceptance of the idea that the linguistic message is but one of many that humans transmit and receive. In *The Silent Language* Hall categorizes ten different "message systems," only one of which involves language.[3] This certainly suggests that considerable meaning is transmitted nonverbally. Mehrabian found that only seven percent of a message's effect is carried by words and that the listeners receive the other ninety-three percent through nonverbal means.[4] It is these nonverbal means to which this chapter is devoted. Most nonverbal messages that an individual receives come through one of these message systems: 1) environmental; 2) appearance; 3) facial; 4) tactile; 5)vocal; and 6) motile.

ENVIRONMENTAL MESSAGES

In *The Territorial Imperative* Ardrey discusses man's tendency to identify with an area over time and to willingly defend it against aggressors.[5] This concept of territoriality is evident in the ways in which man handles space. Proxemics is the term that refers to its study.

Hall related speaking distances to the shift in voice level and to its relationship to the nature of the information being transmitted. A distance of three to six inches between interactors is used for relaying top secret information in a soft whisper. Eight to twelve inches suggest very confidential information and this is usually transmitted in an audible whisper.[6]

In his category system, Hall extends the ranges progressively outward, recognizing the voice level appropriate for a given distance as well as the nature of the information involved. Thus an observer is able to attach meaning to such factors as distance and voice levels, factors previously considered to be free of content.

Hall's research on the meaning of distances was done in the United States and his findings would not be universally true. As pointed out by Hall and others, the use of space in largely influenced by one's culture, so the meaning attributed to such differences would vary accordingly.

One need not look only at national boundaries, however, to identify differences in the use of space. Consider how differently urbanites perceive and use space as compared to those from rural areas. City dwellers are often described as alienated from their surroundings. They are less inclined to initiate interaction with their coworkers or with others whom they encounter frequently. Despite the fact that cities and their office buildings teem with crowds, feelings of loneliness are routine. Although city dwellers are often forced into close proximity with others, there is a reserve and a psychological distance that is maintained. The following describes a scene familiar to any commuter:

> Very few people talk on the bus going home. Sort of sit there and look dejected. Stare out the window, pull out their newspaper, or push other people. You feel tense until the bus empties out or you get home. Because things happen to you all day long, things you couldn't get rid of. So they build up and everybody is feeding them into each other on the bus. There didn't seem to be any kind of relief about going home.[7]

Such feelings of isolation are rarely mentioned as characteristics of life in small towns. Instead, there is cited an openness and freedom lacking in the urban setting. Thus in the crowded city, where close proximity to others is unavoidable, individuals rely on other means of seeking privacy. As in the example of the commuter, by staring out the window or holding (not necessarily reading) one's newspaper one makes it clear that no interaction is desired. Sleeping or pretending to sleep is another means of being left alone on public conveyances.

Formal Space and Status

A person need only look at the blueprints for a collection of offices in order to ascertain the status of the intended occupants. Size as well as location suggests status. The office that is against an outer wall and has a window usually is intended for a person of higher status than that office located in the center of the floor. In those organizations that occupy several floors of a high-rise building, persons with higher status occupy the higher floors. The type of partition separating one office from the next is also indicative of status. Permanent walls suggest more status than do temporary partitions; an office with a door more than a doorless one. One large company reassigns those parking spaces closest to its office each month according to which of its salesmen made the most sales during the previous month. Mehrabian has studied the relationship between status and space and he believes that those with more status "control" space and those with less respect it.[8]

Furnishings and Functions

While considerable thought usually precedes the selection and arrangement of furnishings in one's home or office, most such decisions are based on "eye appeal." Perhaps one could create an environment more conducive to communication by attending to relevant research findings. Certain kinds of furniture arrangements appear to facilitate better communication than do other kinds.

In a study conducted in a doctor's office it was found that desk placement had a significant effect on the tension experienced by the patient. With the desk separating the two parties, only ten percent of the patients were reported to be at ease. After the desk was removed from between them, fifty-five percent of the patients were perceived as being at ease.[9]

In a more recent study, four different seating arrangements were evaluated to determine their desirability for counseling sessions. Four photographs of different seating arrangements for a counselor and a client were shown to the subjects. They were: 1) two chairs placed side by side at a forty-five degree angle; 2) two chairs placed directly opposite each other with a table alongside; 3) two chairs placed at a forty-five degree angle with the corner of a table intervening; and 4) two chairs placed opposite each other with a desk between. Administrators preferred the position with the desk between the interactors and the counselors chose the two chairs at a forty-five degree angle. The clients, however, favored the two chairs with the intervening table corner.[10] Studies such as these have had a noticeable effect on the way in which business environments are being designed.

For many years, it was felt that the desk had to be the central point in any office since it symbolized work and business. No longer does this feeling pervade all work environments. Evidence of this is found in the new styles of office arrangements in which desks have been recognized as barriers to communication and have been deemphasized. The purpose of the desk is now viewed in terms of intended function—that being to provide a surface for writing. This relegation has been accompanied, in many instances, by moving the desk to a less conspicuous location. In the offices of many modern executives today, the desks have been placed with their front against the wall. Such an arrangement gives the executive more openness and more immediate access to anyone entering the office. In this less formal setting, interviews become more conversational and there appears to be less of a status difference between superior and subordinate.

In addition to the desk there are other office trappings that transmit environmental messages to all who are exposed to them. Such furnishings as carpets, paneling, and type of nameplate each provide information of special interest to other organizational members since it is they who are familiar with the code system within the organization and are thus able to accurately interpret the message.

Within some business and governmental organizations, the differentiation between different job levels extends to the office furnishings. Even when an individual attains a level high enough to warrant a private office, the furnishings allocated to him will proclaim his status. To an outsider the furnishings will be mute testimony to the individual's allegiance to the employer. To the knowledgeable insider, however, the furnishings announce the occupant's income level, degree of responsibility, and probable future with the company.

Color/Time/Temperature

An important aspect of any environment, whether task or social, is its color scheme. In one study an attempt was made to relate colors to specific moods. Table 5.1 presents the findings of this study.

In the United States, people are very conscious of time. People are always aware of it and are prone to regulate their lives according to it. Most are awakened by an alarm at a specific time, measure their rate of progress in the morning traffic rush by the frequent time checks provided on the car radio, and announce their arrival at work by inserting their time card into a timeclock that, in turn, prints their arrival time on the card while greeting them with an appreciative click.

According to Toffler, a person devotes approximately twenty-five percent of his time to his work.[11] The person who said that time is money was voicing the feelings of many. The importance of the subject of time management also suggests the value placed upon it. A factor that greatly influences our perceptions of others is the way in which they use their limited budget of time. In one study, time was related to status and it was found that the longer it took a person to respond to a message the higher his status was perceived as being and the greater was the discrepancy between the status levels of the two parties.[12]

Hall points out that the handling of time differs according to region within the United States, and that the northwest views it somewhat more

TABLE *5.1 Colors and Moods.*

Mood tone	Color	Frequency of times chosen
Exciting-Stimulating	Red	61
Secure-Comfortable	Blue	41
Distressed-Disturbed-Upset	Orange	34
Tender-Soothing	Blue	41
Protective-Defending	Red	21
	Brown	17
	Blue	15
	Black	15
	Purple	14
Despondent-Dejected-	Black	25
Unhappy-Melancholy	Brown	25
Calm-Peaceful-Serene	Blue	38
	Green	31
Dignified-Stately	Purple	45
Cheerful-Jovial-Joyful	Yellow	40
Defiant-Contrary-Hostile	Red	23
	Orange	21
	Black	18
Powerful-Strong-Masterful	Black	48

L. B. Wexner, "The Degree to Which Colors (Hues) Are Associated with Mood-Tones," *Journal of Applied Psychology* 38 (1954), 432–435. Table from *Nonverbal Communication in Human Interaction* by Mark L. Knapp. Copyright © 1972 by Holt, Rinehart and Winston, Publishers. Reprinted by permission of Holt, Rinehart and Winston, Publishers.

casually than do the other regions.[13] Throughout this society the meaning and importance of time is introduced to a child at a very young age. From that child's first plaintive query of "Are we almost there?," directed at his father who, at this point, has driven the first twenty miles of their planned trip from Chicago to Denver, to the day when his rate of pay is determined by the number of widgets he can produce in an hour, the concept of time assumes increased importance.

Multiple meanings are attached to time. The duration of one's meeting with a superior suggests one's status within the organization. The longer the meeting the more importance is attached to the individual as well as to the subject of discussion. The executive who instructs his secretary to show Mr. Snitch in as soon as he arrives is making a public statement about Snitch's importance.

In many parts of the country, the person who can get an appointment with a doctor within several days of his request is either a very important person or else deathly ill. The time at which an individual starts and ends his work day is meaningful, for the person who works "banker's hours" has indeed arrived. One of the nicest compliments you can pay a person is to say, "He's got time for everyone."

Temperature is another environmental factor that influences human behavior and makes certain types of behavior more likely than other types. By manipulating the temperature in a laboratory experiment, Griffit and Veitch were able to confirm this and to show that a higher room temperature would be accompanied by more negative feelings toward others.[14]

Any office worker especially can testify to the effect of temperature on an individual's performance and on sociability. A manager of a branch office of a large midwestern company has a theory regarding the temperature maintained in typing pools. He asserts that whenever four or more typists are gathered in one room, the group will invariably include one who is comfortable only with a temperature of sixty-five or lower and another who is chilly if the temperature dips below eighty degrees.

In factory settings, temperature is often beyond the control of anyone, since a specific manufacturing process and a certain temperature level may be unavoidable. In an office environment where climate is controllable, it is the reason for many interpersonal conflicts.

APPEARANCE MESSAGES

If one were to accept unequivocally the testimony of clothing manufacturers found in their advertisements in such periodicals as *Playboy, Gentleman's Quarterly,* and *Cosmopolitan* one would be convinced that an individual's social and professional progress is determined by the individual's choice of clothes. Were one to then read the claims made by the makers of beauty aids and cosmetics, both men's and women's, one might enlarge his category of progress determinants to include such products. Few deny the importance of appearance and the messages it transmits, through such factors as dress, hair, and various types of personal adornments.

Dress

While clothing may not "make the man" it does influence the way in which others perceive him. A person's style of dress provides the observer with many bits of information about that person. One gets many occupational clues from clothing. An obvious example is anyone who must wear a uniform on the job. When one sees a young woman wearing a white uniform and white shoes and stockings one could be correct in assuming that she is employed in the health care area. When one sees a distinguished looking man wearing a three-hundred-dollar Brooks Brothers suit, it is generally a safe bet he is not a college professor.

Considerable research has been done on the relationship between clothes and other factors. Hoult found that the clothing worn by a stranger did influence the judgments made about the stranger.[15] In a study conducted in England, it was shown that middle-class subjects disclosed significantly more personal information to a market researcher when he was wearing a tie than when he was not. Working class subjects did not differentiate in that way.[16]

In the United States there appears to be a growing inclination to dress as one chooses with less regard for the occupational image that was formerly expected. It might be assumed that fewer evaluations of others would be made on the basis of clothing worn. This has not yet been shown to be true.

Several differences were detected in the responses of passers-by to individuals who were trying to get signatures on an antiwar petition in a downtown area. One group wore hippie attire and the other was more conservatively dressed. The hippie attire seemed counterproductive in obtaining signatures in that they were considerably less successful. Also, while the conservatively dressed person received polite or reasoned refusals from nonsigners, the hippies received evasive verbal responses or were physically avoided.[17] It appears that many do indeed judge others by their clothing.

Hair

The growing number of hair products indicates its value in this society. There have actually been fights, divorces, and killings brought about by differing opinions on it. Of course, some engagements and marriages may have been initiated in part by one or the other's beautiful hair.

Hair has become an emotional topic and feelings run strong on it. One product urges the consumer to comb the gray away, while another will give gray hair a bluish sheen. The woman who has the blahs is urged to change her future by changing her hair color. The person who considers his hair unsuitable or whose hair has departed, need only buy a hair piece to improve his life.

As cited in Chapter 2, Pellegrini found a positive relationship between the amount of facial hair a male has and the positive qualities attributed to him.[18] In another study which also used college students as subjects it was shown that a bearded man was perceived more favorably than his nonbearded counterpart.[19]

There have been frequent complaints made to various government agencies alleging discrimination in hiring or promotion due to hair length. An equally appalling type of bias was revealed in a study in which one-half of a group of psychology undergraduates rated the personal problems and clinical symptoms of a long-haired young man. The other half of the group rated a short-haired young man and a significant difference was detected. The students evaluated the short-haired man as being more sick and they were more willing to make broad inferences from limited contact and data.[20]

While there certainly is no universal meaning attributed to a particular hair style nor to beardedness, there are some prevalent assumptions. This is true of hair color also, and stereotypes have long existed about it.

Personal Adornments

In addition to clothing itself, the objects with which a person adorns his clothing and himself should be considered. Students wear emblems that indicate their allegiances to social, civic, or atheletic organizations. Employees of a given organization are given pins to recognize their years of service. While a five-year pin may rarely be worn by its owner, a twenty-five year pin will probably be displayed more because it is less common and it represents a more significant contribution on the employee's part.

Very often a person's occupation will dictate the type of clothing to be worn. It is in the personal artifacts which that person selects that the observer gets insights into the person's personality.[21]

Glasses have long been regarded as indicative of an individual's personality. Whether "Men seldom make passes at girls who wear glasses" is true or not hasn't been proved; however, in a study in 1944, Thornton found higher ratings in intelligence and industriousness for people who wore eyeglasses.[22]

OTHER MESSAGES

Facial

Of all the sources of nonverbal information the face provides us with the most information about another. When meeting someone for the first time, one especially concentrates on the person's face and receives many cues from it about that person. The tendency to rely on facial cues was confirmed in a study when it was shown that the subjects weighed facial cues more heavily than vocal cues, and the latter more heavily than lexical content in inferring the attitude of one person toward another.[23]

Since one is much more aware of the impact of one's facial expressions one learns to "fake" an expression of feeling when not actually experiencing it. Thus the student sits through a boring lecture, with interest written all over his face, while he thinks about the approaching weekend. The personnel interviewer conducting his twentieth screening interview of the day strikes an interested appearance as he asks the same questions he has asked countless times. The person who finds himself in a social or occupational rut may grow numb to the sameness of the routine and feel forced to offer feigned interest and attention since the actual ingredient is unavailable.

Mehrabian found that many subjects were unable to produce sarcastic messages for audio recording because they could not produce an appropriate tone of voice.[24] They had a tendency to rely on facial cues to transmit the message and, when placed in a situation in which their face was not visible, they were ineffective.

One of the problems in attempting to identify a person's facial expression and its related emotion lies in the idiosyncratic behavior of an individual. An individual's personal mannerisms may lead the receiver to misinterpret facial cues. There is some evidence, however, that certain emotions are perceived more accurately than are others.

Osgood found the following emotional clusters to be the most accurately perceived: 1) annoyance, disgust, contempt, score, and loathing; 2) silent laughter, quiet pleasure, and complacency; 3) joy, glee, and worried laughter. The following emotional clusters were found to be the least accurately perceived: 1) physical pain, dread, and anxiety; 2) acute sorrow, pity, dreaminess, sadness, and sulkiness; 3) cynical bitterness.[25]

Of all the elements in one's face it is the eyes that provide the observer with the most information. The eyes have aptly been described as the windows of the soul.

There has been considerable research done on this subject and much of it should interest the student of interpersonal communication.

Steady eye contact has often been associated with integrity; however, such a relationship has never been proven. We are taught to be suspicious of one who doesn't look us in the eye. The job applicant who continues to avert the interviewer's eyes is unlikely to get the job.

It has been proven that a person will maintain more eye contact with a subject that is pleasing. We look more at people we like and seek to minimize eye contact with those we don't like.[26] Another study identified personality differences on the basis of which direction a person looked in when asked a thought-provoking question.[27] One's eye behavior has also been identified as related to one's level of anxiety with a higher rate of blinking indicating a high degree of anxiety.[28]

A final aspect of facial behavior that warrants consideration is the smile. Whether or not empirical evidence is thought necessary to show the importance of smiling in making friends, it is available.[29] In an interesting experiment using Eskimo and Indian high school students as subjects, it was shown that exhibiting personal warmth toward the students resulted in their improved performance on intelligence tests. This warmth was communicated through physical closeness and smiling.[30]

Only a small number of the findings of studies on facial and eye expression have been cited. They should provide the reader with a sense of the type of research being undertaken as well as a respect for its importance. It would be difficult to read of such studies and to recall one's own personal experiences in interpreting nonverbal messages without agreeing with Libby and Yaklevich that the face does "leak" information regarding one's personality.[31]

Tactile

For many years there was a popular bath soap sold with the assurance that the regular use of it would give the user "the skin you love to touch." It retained the same advertisement for a long time because it was so successful. Today various skin cleaners are billed as giving the user "baby-soft skin." There is something appealing obviously about such skin, especially for females, and it is desired because others will derive pleasure from touching it. Tactile communication plays a more significant role in our lives than is generally recognized.

Probably the most obvious example of tactile messages is that received by users of braille. For the blind, it actually constitutes a means of verbal communication; however, it is included here simply to illustrate the untapped potential of tactile communication.

It is through the sense of touch that an infant is first introduced to his environment. For the first six months, the confines of his world and the confines of his crib are one and the same. During this period, the infant's sensory awareness is steadily developing as he becomes able to differentiate between such characteristics as shapes and textures of the immediate surroundings.

While the infant's education progresses in this manner as he continues to extend his reach to new stimuli, he is also the recipient of much tactile stimulation. Through stroking, nuzzling, and hugging, the family and observors are introduced to the new member. During this tender stage, the infant learns the pleasure of such physical contact and also masters those plays that will insure him of an almost unending supply of such attention.

With childhood there comes a deemphasis of such activity and verbalization is thought to replace it as a medium of exchange. The need experienced by all for greater touching belies this thought, however. In one study the subjects interacted with another person under three different conditions: visual only, verbal only, and touch only. Following all three conditions the subjects described the interactions in this way: *verbal*—"distant, noncommunicative, artificial, insensitive, and formal"; *visual*—"artificial, childish, arrogant, comic, and cold"; *touch*—"trustful, sensitive, natural, serious, and warm."[32]

With the growing interest in sensitivity training and encounter groups as a means of facilitating openness, there is an increased awareness of the importance of tactile communication. In one study it was found that physical contact in an encounter group setting will reduce barriers between people and increase their self-disclosure.[33]

It does not require empirical studies, however, to illustrate the high rewards and low costs to be experienced through tactile communication in an interpersonal setting. We all can testify to the friendliness transmitted in a handshake, the frivolity in a well-placed pinch, and the reassurance in a pat on the back.

Vocal

While the primary function of the voice is the conveyance of audible language, another function is encapsuled in the term *paralanguage*. Paralanguage concerns the *way* in which something is said rather than *what* is said. Trager divides paralanguage into four categories: voice qualities; vocal characterizers; vocal qualifiers; and vocal segregates.[34] Pitch, rate, and volume are included among the qualities. Vocal characterizers include conditions like laughing and clearing one's throat. Pitch and volume variations that are momentary in nature are known as qualifiers. Vocalized pauses such as "ah" and silent pauses comprise the vocal segregates.

Upon recognizing the all-encompassing nature of paralanguage, one can see the countless cues that affect one's choice. The meaning of any verbal message can be contradicted in a wide variety of ways as evidenced by the frequency with which simple statements are misconstrued. Consider all of the possible interpretations of a request by an executive to his secretary, "Oh Miss Jones, could you work a little overtime tonight?"

Trager's qualities, characterizers, and qualifiers, while often subtle, are not as subtle as the vocal segregates, especially the silent pauses. Although

Helmut Mossback was dealing with nonverbal communication in Japan his illustration is apt for describing the meaning of silence in any context:

> An American professor at a Japanese university with an excellent command of Japanese language told me the following:

> One day he had attended a faculty meeting where he fully partici-pated in the lengthly discussions, using Japanese throughout. On leaving the meeting, he remarked to a Japanese colleague that, in his opinion, the meeting had finally arrived at a particular conclusion. Had not Professor X spoken in favor? His Japanese colleague agreed. And other professors, too? (going down the list one by one). Again, his Japanese colleague agreed, but finally remarked, "All this may be so, but you are still mistaken. The meeting arrived at the opposite conclusion: You have correctly understood all the words spoken, but you didn't understand the silences between them.[35]

Although the vocal cues are but one ingredient in the total message transmitted by an individual, these cues are significant. In fact Mehrabian and Weiner found that when exposed to an inconsistent message, the impact of facial expression is greatest, vocal expression second, and verbal expression has the lowest impact.[36]

Motile

One man can walk across a crowded room and look as though he's completely in control of his destiny and the destiny of others. Another man, of approxi-mately the same age and dressed similarly, will cross the same room appearing hesitant and misdirected, rather like an accident looking for a place to happen. The difference lies in the messages transmitted through one's move-ments, gestures, and posture.

Ekman and Friesen recognize five different types of body expressions: 1) emblems, 2) illustrators, 3) regulators, 4) affect displays, and 5) adapt-ors.[37] Emblems are those gestures that are equivalent to verbal messages because their meaning is recognized by those involved.

A veteran steelworker used an emblem in this encounter he had with a young foreman. This occurred shortly after the worker had received a deduction in pay due to an earlier argument between the two:

> The guy comes over and smiles at me. I blew up. He didn't know it, but he was about two seconds and two feet away from a hospital. ...He was just about to say something and was pointing his finger. I just reached my hand up and just grabbed his finger and I just put it back in his pocket. He walked away.[38]

Grabbing the foreman's finger constituted an emblem. No further communication was required.

Illustrators complement the verbal cues that are being sent and reinforce that message. The pedestrian trying to "flag" a cab with his arms is illustrating his plea of "Taxi!" Regulators control oral interaction by providing the communicator with some instructions. The executive, constantly looking at his wrist watch while his secretary tells him of her vacation trip, is using a regulator. The secretary who intentionally drops her pencil while her boss dictates a letter is seeking to regulate the pace of the dictation. Affect displays are largely unconscious emotional responses that are generally facial in nature. The reddening of the sales manager's complexion as his salesman explains how he lost an account is an example. Adaptors are learned actions that have an instrumental purpose. The sender is often not conscious he is performing such an action and, therefore, it can be very meaningful to an alert observor. Stifling a yawn often falls in this category.

Additional information about an individual can also come from a careful observation of that person's posture. The person who slouches reveals his attitudes toward the subject being considered as well as toward those with whom he is interacting. Mehrabian showed, for example, that when a person leans toward one he is addressing it indicates positive feelings toward that person.[39] The research done by Mehrabian and others has revealed a relationship between various postural cues and such qualities as warmth, status, inclusiveness, and deception.

As communicators, most individuals are derelict in the sense that they misperceive or ignore many information-loaded messages. The coverage of messages included herein is not exhaustive but it is cues from the environment, appearance, face, voice, and motion that comprise most of the nonverbal signs that, if recognized, would significantly improve one's interpersonal communication.

NONVERBAL COMMUNICATION: A PERSPECTIVE

Although this chapter has remained in the shallows on the subject of the nonverbal, it has exposed the reader to a representative cross section of relevant research findings. After this consideration of the various categories of nonverbal messages the reader should be aware of the countless stimuli to which one is exposed daily. Throughout this chapter the ideas have been presented from the perspective of the receiver. This is not to infer, however, that the sender is impotent in terms of the nonverbal image he transmits. In his excellent analysis of nonverbal communication, Knapp makes an important point to this effect. "The self-image is the root system from which all of our overt communication behavior grows and blossoms. Our overt communication behavior is only an extension of the accumulated experiences that have gone into making up our understanding of self. In short, what you are, or think you are, organizes what you say and do."[40]

An individual's verbal messages are dwarfed by the magnitude of the nonverbal ones. For the person whose verbal and nonverbal messages are congruent, there are built-in redundancies that serve to clarify for the receiver. Such congruency serves the receiver well as he receives inputs that are consistent over multiple channels. When there is incongruency between the verbal and the nonverbal, however, the meaning to be derived is left up to the receiver. Since the receiver has access to many more nonverbal messages than verbal ones, the accuracy of the nonverbal will usually be assumed.

The fact that nonverbal communication is less controllable by the sender will serve to reinforce its validity in the mind of the receiver. An individual will mentally edit his message before he speaks just as he has the opportunity to edit a letter before sending it. Not only is there no such option available in nonverbal communication, the process is an unending one. A person thus transmits nonverbal information regardless of the intensity of his desire, at times, not to do so.

There is general acceptance of the idea that a code of nonverbal communication does exist and there is a significant degree of agreement as to the meaning of routine nonverbal messages.

The ability to interpret nonverbal cues accurately varies with the individual and is also dependent upon the nature of the sender.

> . . .Accurately perceiving and judging another is a complex task which is affected by many variables. Cues can be covert or overt, verbal or nonverbal—but in either case ease in decoding them can range greatly on a continuum of difficulty depending on the transparency or opaqueness of the person being judged.[41]

The nonverbal messages transmitted, either consciously or unconsciously, by an individual, significantly influences the image another holds of him. When one attempts to interpret nonverbal cues, there is always a possibility of rank injustice occurring. One must not, therefore, select a single nonverbal cue and define the sender accordingly for that is stereotyping of the lowest level.

The more thoroughly one analyzes the entire context in which the interaction occurs, however, the less likely such an event becomes. An understanding of the principles of nonverbal communication plus the mental alertness to recognize exceptions to those principles will result in new dimensions of meaning for the concerned individual.

SUMMARY

Much of the meaning attributed to an individual is transmitted nonverbally. Most nonverbal messages which an individual receives come through one of these message systems: 1) environment; 2) appearance; 3) face; 4) touch; 5) voice; and 6) motion.

Included in environmental messages are such factors as the use of space and types of furnishings. The receiver attaches meaning to such factors as well as to such other environmental messages as color, time, and temperature.

Dress, hair and personal adornments exemplify appearance messages. Of the various nonverbal message systems, it is generally thought that facial messages provide the alert receiver with the most information about others. Touch, paralanguage, and motion messages transmit additional information about the individual.

An individual transmits many more nonverbal messages than verbal ones. By attending to nonverbal cues, the perceptive receiver will recognize that the "silent language" is oftentimes loud and clear.

QUESTIONS FOR DISCUSSION

1. Define nonverbal communication. What are the criteria that determine whether a message is actually nonverbal?

2. What evidence can you cite that nonverbal communication is being recognized and accepted more readily in business organizations?

3. What nonverbal cues should a professor "trust" when seeking a student in class who is prepared to discuss the concept being taught?

4. What nonverbal cues do you consider unique to the North American culture?

5. Since relations between the press and industry are sometimes strained, some business consultants are hired to train businessmen to transmit the firm's point of view more accurately and with greater sincerity. What

advice regarding nonverbal communication would you offer businessmen who wish to project more sincerity?

ENDNOTES

1. Edward T. Hall, *The Silent Language* (New York: Doubleday, 1959).
2. J. Ruesch and W. Kees, *Nonverbal Communication: Notes on the Visual Perception of Human Relations* (Los Angeles: University of California Press, 1956).
3. Hall, p. 174.
4. Layne A. Longfellow, "Body Talk/The Game of Feeling and Expression," *Psychology Today* (October, 1970).
5. R. Ardrey, *The Territorial Imperative* (New York: Atheneum, 1966).
6. Hall, p. 163.
7. Studs Terkel, *Working* (New York: Pantheon, 1972), p. 31.
8. A. Mehrabian, "Significance of Posture and Position in the Communication of Attitude and Status Relationships," *Psychological Bulletin* 71 (1969), p. 363.
9. A. G. White, "The Patient Sits Down: A Clinical Note," *Psychosomatic Medicine* 15 (1953), pp. 256–257.
10. R. F. Haase and D. J. DiMattia, "Proxemic Behavior: Counselor, Administrator, and Clinet Preference for Seating Arrangement in Dyadic Interaction," *Journal of Counseling Psychology* 17, pp. 319–325.
11. Alvin Toffler, *Future Shock* (New York: Random House, 1970), p. 337.
12. A. Mehrabian, "Significance of Posture and Position in the Communication of Attitude and Status Relationships," *Psychological Bulletin* 71 (1969), p. 363.
13. Hall, p. 145.
14. W. Griffit and R. Veitch, "Hot and Crowded: Influences of Population Density and Temperature on Interpersonal Affective Behavior," *Journal of Personality and Social Psychology* 17 (1971), pp. 92–98.
15. R. Hoult, "Experimental Measurement of Clothing as a Factor in Some Social Ratings of Selected American Men," *American Sociological Review* 19 (1954), pp. 324–328.
16. W. Paul Green and Howard Giles, "Reactions to a Stranger as a Function of Dress Style: The Tie," *Perceptual and Motor Skills* 37 (October, 1973), p. 676.
17. Charles B. Keasey and C. Tomlinson-Keasay, "Petition Signing in a Naturalistic Setting," *Journal of Social Psychology* 89 (April, 1973), pp. 313–314.
18. Robert J. Pellegrini, "Impressions of the Male Personality as a Function of Beardedness," *Psychology,* 10 (February, 1973), pp. 29–33.

19. Charles T. Kenny and Dixie Fletcher, "Effects of Beardedness on Person Perception," *Perceptual and Motor Skills* 37 (October, 1973), pp. 413–414.

20. Ted L. Rosenthal and Glenn M. White, "On the Importance of Hair in Student's Clinical Inferences," *Journal of Clinical Psychology* 28 (January, 1972), pp. 43–47.

21. William D. Brooks, *Speech Communication* (Dubuque: William C. Brown, 1971), p. 107.

22. G. Thornton, "The Effect of Wearing Glasses Upon Judgments of Personality Traits of Persons Seen Briefly," *Journal of Applied Psychology* 28 (1944), pp. 203–207.

23. A. Mehrabian and S. Ferris, "Inferences of Attitudes from Nonverbal Communication to Two Channels," *Journal of Consulting Psychology* 31 (1967), pp. 248–252.

24. A. Mehrabian, "When Are Feelings Communicated Inconsistently?" *Journal of Experimental Research in Personality* 4 (1970), pp. 198–212.

25. C. Osgood, "Dimensionality of the Semantic Space for Communication via Facial Expressions," *Scandanavian Journal of Psychology* 7 (1962), pp. 1–30.

26. A. Mehrabian, "Significance of Posture and Position in the Communication of Attitude and Status Relationships," *Psychological Bulletin* 71 (1969), p. 365.

27. M. E. Day, "Eye Movement Phenomenon Related to Attention, Thought, and Anxiety," *Perceptual and Motor Skills* 19 (1964), pp. 443–446.

28. Paul Watzlawick, Janet Beavin, and Dan Jackson, *Pragmatics of Human Communication* (New York: W. W. Norton & Co., 1967), p. 173.

29. A Mehrabian, "Verbal and Nonverbal Interaction of Strangers in a Waiting Situation," *Journal of Experimental Research in Personality* 5 (1971), pp. 127–138.

30. J. S. Kleinfeld, "Effects of Nonverbally Communicated Personal Warmth on the Intelligence Test Performance of Indian and Eskimo Adolescents," *Journal of Social Psychology* 91 (October, 1973), pp. 149–150.

31. William L. Libby and Donna Yaklevich, "Personality Determinants of Eye Contact and Direction of Gaze Aversion." *Journal of Personality and Social Psychology* 27 (August, 1973), pp. 197–206.

32. J. P. Bardeen, "Interpersonal Perception Through the Tactile, Verbal and Visual Modes," (Unpublished paper presented to International Communication Association, Phoenix, Arizona, 1971).

33. Cary L. Cooper and David Bowles, "Physical Encounter and Self-Disclosure," *Psychological Reports* 33 (October, 1973), pp. 451–454.

34. G. L. Trager, "Paralanguage: A First Approximation," *Studies in Linguistics* 13 (1958), pp. 1–22.

35. Helmut Morsbach, "Nonverbal Communication in Japan," *Journal of Nervous and Mental Disease* 157 (October, 1973), pp. 262–277.

36. A. Mehrabian and M. Wiener, "Decoding of Inconsistent Communications," *Journal of Personality and Social Psychology* 6 (1967), pp. 109–114.
37. P. Ekman and W. Friesen, "The Repertoire of Nonverbal Behavior: Categories, Origins, Usage, and Coding," *Semiotics* 1 (1969), pp. 63–92.
38. Turkel, xxxiii.
39. A. Mehrabian, "Communication Without Words," *Psychology Today* 1 (1968), p. 54.
40. Mark L. Knapp, *Nonverbal Communication in Human Interaction* (New York: Holt, Rinehart and Winston, 1972), p. 74.
41. Victor B. Cline, Jon Atzet, and Elaine Holmes, "Assessing the Validity of Verbal and Nonverbal Cues in Accurately Judging Others," *Comparative Group Studies* 3 (1972), p. 393.

6

Communication and Conflict

The assumption that conflict is inevitable in any human organization has gained wide acceptance in recent years. Whether it takes overt form, as in a dispute between two secretaries over one new typewriter, or covert form, as with a production supervisor struggling to adopt a "Theory Y" style of leadership, while his peers deride his emphasis upon participative management, conflict is a pervasive force in every organization.

Given, then, that some level of conflict is inevitable, it becomes important for the manager to discover methods not only for identifying conflict, but also for channeling it in ways beneficial to his organization. The major purpose of this chapter is to examine the interrelationships between communication and conflict. As will become evident, a communication problem is often a cause of organizational conflict. Yet, communication may paradoxically serve as a preventive and curative factor in dealing with conflict as well. First, the nature of conflict in organizations will be briefly considered; next, the critical role of perception in conflict will be discussed; and finally, the specific relationship between communication and organizational conflict will be examined in detail.

THE NATURE OF CONFLICT

There exists, of course, a real diversity of definitions and explanations of the term "conflict." One of the most useful of these is Walton's definition of interpersonal conflict, that includes both "a) personal disagreements over substantive issues, such as differences over organizational structures, policies, and practices, and b) interpersonal antagonisms, that is the more personal and emotional differences which arise between interdependent human beings."[1] Conflict can be viewed, then, as having the aspects of both issue and personality.

Conflict involving *issue* could arise, for example, when a group of workers collectively demands pay increases from management, and management simply and perhaps arbitrarily refuses. Conflict of this type could also emanate from management's introduction of new production quotas, such quotas being perceived by the workers as much too demanding.

A common form of *personality* conflict is that between a manager and his immediate subordinates, all of whom view him as dictatorial and unfair in his dealings with them.

Finally, some conflict situations contain both issue and personality, as where the promotion policies in a given company are perceived by its employees to be fraught with favoritism, personal loyalties, and other forms of subjective criteria.

A convenient perspective from which to examine issue and personality conflict is what Pondy has termed the "conflict episode."[2] A conflict episode, according to Pondy, consists of five distinct stages:

1. *Latent Conflict* deals with underlying *sources* of organizational conflict. Among those sources are competition for scarce resources (e.g., materials, money, manpower), drives for autonomy, and differing subunit goals within the organization.

2. *Perceived Conflict* can supposedly occur in either the absence or the presence of latent conflict. When no latent conflict exists but conflict is nevertheless perceived, such conflict is said to be a result of the parties' misunderstandings of one another's true position. When latent conflict exists but fails to reach the level of awareness, it is not because such conflict is not actually perceived, but rather, because certain individual defense mechanisms tend to suppress it.

3. *Felt Conflict* may also be termed the personalization of conflict, because it is at this stage that the conflict actually affects the individual directly. Felt conflict is normally a function of either: a) individual anxieties created by organizational demands that the individual perceives to limit his individual growth; or, b) total involvement of the individual in a relationship, such involvement making him necessarily more aware of the occurrence of conflict.

4. *Manifest Conflict* is identified simply as the actual occurrence of conflicting behavior. It may range from open aggression to apathy or even extremely rigid adherence to rules, with the intention of frustrating another party to the relationship. So long as both parties perceive a specific behavior to be conflicting, and so long as the party indulging in the behavior persists in doing so, a clear case of manifest conflict has developed.

5. *Conflict Aftermath* is a function of how well the entire episode or sequence of episodes have been resolved. Perhaps this stage will reveal that bases for a more cooperative relationship have been established; or it may suggest how newly perceived problems might be handled, or if the latent conditions were merely suppressed instead of resolved, then they may emerge at this time to foster more serious difficulties. The aftermath stage suggests the dynamic nature of conflict; that is, a conflict relationship between or among two or more individuals in an organization is not likely to consist of only one conflict episode, but is rather made up of a sequence of such episodes, each one resulting from the resolution of conflict in the previous episode.[3]

Thus far, then, conflict has been described as involving either (or both) issue and personality. Additionally, a means of tracing the development of conflict (the conflict episode) has been presented. A final consideration in the nature of conflict in organizations is its utility.

For a number of years, management theorists tended to view conflict solely as a destructive force within the organization. More recently, however, some have proposed that not all forms of conflict are as destructive as was once believed. Huseman provides an enlightening historical summary of what surveys of managers, for example, have revealed about the perceptions of the usefulness of conflict. He divides them into three groups:

1) Early surveys where managers would not even admit conflict was present in the organization, 2) surveys where managers admitted that conflict may be present, but it was viewed as an evil to be eliminated, and 3) more recent surveys of organizational managers where managers not only admit that conflict is present, but moreover, that conflict can sometimes serve a positive function.[4]

Thus, conflict is perceived by present theorists as both functional and dysfunctional, and some of the more common terms they use to describe this dichotomy are productive versus destructive,[5] beneficial versus destructive,[6] and natural versus unnatural.[7] And the really crucial decision the contemporary manager must make is not whether conflict exists in his work group, but rather, if conflict exists, is it dysfunctional or is it functional?

The answer to this question is predictably and unfortunately not an easy one. Suppose for a moment that the manager of a retail department store decides to hold a sales contest (with some suitable rewards) among his employees in order to increase the store's sales. Several days after the contest begins, two of his appliance salesmen enter his office and complain that a third salesman is "stealing" some of their customers. Obviously, the conflict episode is well under way, and at first glance it appears to be a dysfunctional one. The manager, however, examines the appliance department's sales record and finds that total sales have increased dramatically since the contest began.

At the risk of oversimplifying this situation, the manager is confronted with a dilemma: On the one hand he can take a human relations kind of approach and attempt to resolve the differences among these salesmen. On the other hand, however, he can assume a more task-oriented position and tell the complaining salesmen that what he is interested in are increased sales—he doesn't care how they come about.

Choosing the first approach in this case assumes the conflict episode to be dysfunctional, one that should be immediately resolved. Selecting the second, task-oriented approach assumes the conflict to be functional, perhaps a simple manifestation of heady competition. Not surprisingly, some managers would opt for the second approach.

Whether the conflict described in this illustration is actually functional or dysfunctional is beyond the realm of this discussion. What is important is that the manager in the illustration is employing his *own* value system to determine the utility of the conflict. His primary consideration should have been the value systems of the conflicting parties (the three salesmen). Was the conflict functional or dysfunctional to them?

The critical implication here is that before one can be sure he has actually identified "good" or "bad" conflict, he must determine on *what* and *whose* bases the "goodness" or "badness" is determined; that is, *what* is the value system at work and *whose* value system has determined the criteria for "good" or "bad"?

Consider the fact that on any given work day, each salesman in the appliance department might be able to state the primary goals of the company in relationship to his department. Given that all men in the department have been exposed to the same information (and are equally capable of recalling that information), it is suggested here that each salesman may possess an individually unique understanding of those goals as a function of his particular value system.

Furthermore, upon asking the head of that department the same question, it is expected that his understanding may be quite different because of his position in the organization, as well as his personal value system.

Given, finally, the same group of individuals questioned about any subject (their company softball team, the new summer help, or the recent conflict between Shipping and Sales), it is expected that each individual's story will be influenced not only by the subject matter, but also by his personal value system as well.

Ultimately, then, the potential manager must remember that no matter how careful his analysis of the situation has been, and how confidently he feels the sources and effects of the conflict episode have been isolated, *if* he has not taken the necessary time to learn and understand others' viewpoints (manifested through their separate value systems) on the situation, he may well be in danger of underestimating a more complex and serious episode or perhaps run the risk of completely missing the crux of the episode.

In summary, conflict in organizations, involves issue or personality, and typically occurs in episodal form. It may be functional or dysfunctional, functionality residing in the value systems of the parties involved. The ensuing discussion of the relationship between perception and conflict will hopefully provide a suitable means for analyzing those value systems.

PERCEPTION AND CONFLICT

Working from the basic premise that conflict within an organization is inevitable, it is expected that any one member of an organization could easily identify sources of conflict he himself has experienced as a member of that organization or has observed occurring within, between, or among the sub-units of the organization. By accepting the proposition that the individual can and does identify sources of conflict, two constant determinants of the existence and degree of conflict emerge: 1) What is viewed as a source of conflict to one person may not be seen as a source of conflict to another. Thus, *who perceives* the source of conflict is essential to any useful analysis of a conflict episode. 2) Closely linked to the influence of one's perceptual processes is the possibility that *anything* can be a potential source of conflict. Each of these two determinants will be discussed in more detail below.

The Perceptual Process

Haney defines perception as "the process of *making sense out of experi-ence—of imputing meaning to experience.*"[8] This definition seems to point to the personal nature of perception. Each individual has his own unique physiological and psychological make up that affects his perceptual processes and that, in turn, determine his experience. The following illustration suggests how one's physiological and psychological make up can influence what it is he perceives and is ultimately capable of experiencing.

Imagine a machinist who has worked a number of years in an area of continuous loud noises. From this overexposure to excessive noise levels, he has developed a hearing impediment (physiological influence) that allows him to withstand his son's loud stereo music; in effect, he has been immunized to the stimuli of excessive loud noises. His wife, however, who has not suffered any loss of hearing, cannot withstand the loud music and is forever telling her son to turn down the stereo. In effect, the machinist's hearing impediment has limited his perceptual processes; a certain level of sound waves no longer impinge on his perceptual processes and consequently will never be experienced.

On the other hand, however, the machinist, realizing that he has lost some of his hearing, is very aware of the predicament this places him in while driving a car. Because he cannot hear police sirens or ambulance sirens, he consciously places certain restrictions on his driving habits: he always remains in the outside lane, so as not to hinder the passage of an emergency vehicle; he is constantly checking his rear view mirror and his side mirror so that he can see an approaching emergency vehicle even if he cannot hear the siren. In effect, the psyiological limitations placed on his perceptual processes have been compensated for by this psychological preparedness while driving a car.

While it cannot be said that all physiological limitations will be compensated for by improved psychological factors in one's perceptual make up, that both physiological and psychological factors of an individual's perceptual process are closely related is an important fact to be realized.

Take again the example of the machinists's wife. Her physiological make up cries out, "If that loud music is not turned down, I am simply going to lose my mind!" And eventually because the stereo is forever blasting, her friends and family begin to hear her say, "That rock music is the worst noise there ever was. How can they call it music!" One wonders if her psychological disposition to rock music might be different if she had been permitted to listen to the music at the moderate levels her physiological system is equipped to handle But because she has not, she will not be afforded the experience of the contemporary sounds.

Thus, when one considers the process of perception in the modern organization, he should remember that there are both physiological and psychological factors contributing to what a person perceives and how it is that he perceives it. Therefore, it is not difficult to see how "experience" is a very personal event, unique from one individual to another.

Means of Analyzing Perception and Conflict

While it is important to understand the reasons for differences in perception, it is just as important to find ways to analyze the nature of the perceptual process as it is likely to operate within individual members of an organization. Especially critical are means of analyzing perception as it operates in creating conflict situations. Working from the basic assumption that conflict, whatever variety it might be, must be *perceived* by those involved in order to, in fact, exist, the following means of analyzing perception is set forth:

From the eyes of the designated perceiver:

1. intra-*individual conflict:* conflict experienced by the designated perceiver within himself. This conflict may be a result of job responsibilities or personal responsibilities. The point is that the conflict this individual feels is within himself and has some potential or current, direct or indirect, impact upon his job performance.

2. inter-*individual conflict:* conflict that the designated perceiver experiences with another individual within the organization. While it is not essential that the other party necessarily perceive the conflict, it is important that the perceiver who identifies the conflict recognizes the potential or current, direct or indirect, impact upon his job performance.

3. intra-*group conflict:* conflict that the designated perceiver experiences or identifies within his immediate group in this organization. The idea of a primary group usually refers to one's department or particular work team, but it could also be used to designate a much larger group, such as an entire union. The important thing is that the designated perceiver is a member of group in which he perceives conflict to exist. He may be either deeply involved in the conflict issue or only superficially aware of the situation, but he does perceive the conflict, and it does have some potential or current, direct or indirect, impact upon his job performance.

4. inter-*group conflict:* conflict that the designated perceiver experiences or identifies between his immediate (primary) group and another group within the organization. Again, the designated perceiver may be either deeply involved in the conflict issue or only superficially aware of the situation, but he does perceive the conflict, and it does have some potential or current, direct or indirect, impact upon his job performance.

5. *organization-environment conflict:* conflict that the designated perceiver sees or identifies between the organization of which he is a member and the environment of which it is a part. Again, the designated perceiver may be either deeply involved in the conflict issue or only superficially aware of the situation, but he does perceive the conflict, and it does have some potential or current, direct or indirect impact on his job performance.

   Environment here refers to anything from the city in which the organization resides to the country or the world, for that matter. If faced with the situation in which the organization has a home office and a number of branches, such an analysis may place each branch as an organization within its own environment or the entire organization (home office and branches) within the environment of one state (if home office and branches are within one state) or the country or the world. Faced with the decision of defining organization-environment boundaries, the analyst will certainly formulate his definition in a manner that will best facilitate his purpose and take into account all the relevant factors.

To illustrate these five levels of analyzing sources of conflict, one can imagine the case of Mr. A, a foreman for fifteen years who has recently been promoted to department head. In making his decision as to whether or not to accept the promotion, he was greatly concerned about the extra demands upon his free time that the position would require (intra-individual conflict). Second, Mr. A's good friend, Mr. B, was also a foreman within the same department. Because Mr. B had been with the company for seventeen years, Mr. A was aware that there was a potential for conflict between himself and Mr. B over the promotion (inter-individual conflict). Third, Mr. A was acutely aware of the furor that had been created within production because of the employment of female line workers (intra-group conflict). Fourth, it was again time to renew the contract, and because labor was expected to make several demands likely to be unacceptable to management, a long period of contract negotiations was expected (inter-group conflict). Fifth, pollution standards required that new equipment be installed in order to cut down on pollution within the highly industrial surroundings of Mr. A's plant. The time required for installation and the extra cost on the company for the equipment has been felt by every department and employee within the organization (organization-environment conflict).

The following chart summarizes the five levels of analyzing the various sources of conflict with which Mr. A was faced in deciding whether or not to accept the new position. While all the cells in the chart will not be filled through the example of Mr. A, it is easy to imagine other examples that would provide illustrations for the empty cells.

Having provided a means of analyzing an individual's perceptual process in the evaluation of a conflict situation, the discussion will now turn to how communication can cause, prevent, or cure conflict.

COMMUNICATION AND CONFLICT

It was earlier indicated that the major purpose of this chapter is to describe the role of communication in conflict. A convenient perspective from which to view this relationship is to visualize communication as a causal factor, as a preventive factor, and as a curative factor in conflict situations.

First, of course, the manager should be familiar with the nature of communication as described in Chapter 1. In terms of its relationship with conflict, effective communication may be usefully defined "as existing between two persons when the receiver interprets the sender's message in the same way the sender intended it."[9] Once his definitional framework is established, the manager is prepared to examine the communication-conflict interface.

TABLE 6.1   A Chart of Conflict. Designated Perceiver: Mr. A

Perceived Source of Conflict	Perceived Impact of Source of Conflict			
	Direct (Impact Seen on Job Performance)		Indirect (Impact Seen on Extra-Org. Concerns)	
	Current (Operating Now)	Potential (Likely to Operate)	Current	Potential
1. intra-individual	Mr. A thinks about impending decision while on the job.			Possible loss of time with family
2. inter-individual		Conflict with Mr. A and Mr. B over promotion		Strained relationship with Mr. B.
3. intra-group	Concern over the furor created in his dept. over the hiring of women line workers.	Foreman to replace Mr. A will be unfamiliar with the individuals in the dept. and make the intragroup conflict even worse.	Reservations for the company picnic show evidence of the conflict in the department.	
4. inter-group		Forthcoming contract negotiations may create problems in meeting work schedules.		
5. organization-environment	New equipment has made the job more difficult for some of the line workers.	Production is likely to drop if environmental demands continue to come at such a rapid and time-consuming rate.		Costs for new equipment may make the pay raise that accompanies a department headship slow in coming

Communication that Causes Conflict

Redding, in his comprehensive survey of contemporary thinking concerning communication within organizations, typifies the role of communication as a causative factor: "The communication climate of the organization should be one which deliberately allows for, and even encourages, a tolerable level of disorder and conflict."[10] Thus, while this discussion suggests that some kinds of communication may cause conflict, whether or not the conflict that actually occurs is "good" or "bad" must be decided by those involved in the situation. However, if an organization recognizes the inevitable nature of conflict, it will be prepared to channel the causes of conflict to productive ends.

Communication Overload

One way in which an organization may be prepared to channel potential conflict is by recognizing that organizations inherently tend to produce communication overload. Communication overload "denotes primarily an excess of '*in*put' over the ability of the message-receiver to 'handle' such input."[11] Essentially, what this concept suggests is that a human being can handle only so much information at one time. Information, in this case, may refer to anything from extra-organizational responsibilities to seeing that the work order for each day is completed on time. A problem will arise, however, if the demands placed upon the individual become too great. Such may be the case when an employee is concerned with family difficulties, does not understand exactly what his superior expects of him, or feels that he does not have sufficient time to complete adequately the demands of his job. If such situations become more than the individual can handle, results such as errors, emotional strain, dissatisfaction, interpersonal conflicts, or any other means of coping with the overload experienced might occur. Recalling the means of analyzing perception and conflict, one can see how communication overload can create conflict at all levels of the organization. While the organization, through its organizational chart and job descriptions, does reduce *some* of the overload, the alert manager will be aware of the possible conflicts likely to result from communication overload.

Persuasive Communication

A second means by which communication may engender conflict is when it is perceived to be persuasive in nature: "Evidence has been accumulating to support the conclusion that increased communication—and especially increased *persuasive* communication—can easily lead to greater rather than to lesser conflict."[12]

One common misperception among some managers, for example, is that an effective means for indoctrinating employees is to employ persuasive devices when communicating with them. Thus, house organs, company meetings, and even memoranda are built around or have included in them some "block buster" formula for persuading employees. The item in the company newsletter that describes how "everybody" is signing up for the new series of training programs illustrates bandwagon techniques. A supervisor who uses participative decision making as a human relations tactic may be covertly attempting to increase his level of interpersonal influence over employees.

The point here is not that persuasive communication is inimical to effective management-labor relations. Rather, it is when employees perceive themselves to be in a "win-lose" situation with management that persuasion tends to effect an increase in conflict:

> In so far as such a relationship [win-lose] is *perceived* by either party, persuasive efforts are likely either to fall upon deaf ears or actually to produce a boomerang or backlash effect. That is, the target of the persuasion frequently ends up in a position *more* opposed to that of the persuader than he was before the persuasion ever started.[13]

Persuasive communication, therefore, especially in perceived "win-lose" competitive situations, may serve only to foster greater conflict than that which had previously existed.

Ambiguity in Communication

Ambiguous communication is a third means by which communication may foster conflict. Consider the district sales manager who receives a memorandum from his immediate supervisor that states simply, "Get sales straightened out." The district manager could readily interpret this message to mean that: a) his total sales are too low; b) his salesmen are mishandling clients' accounts; or, c) he needs to fire several of his salesmen.

Ambiguous situations such as this occur frequently in day-to-day encounters between supervisors and subordinates. The foreman who instructs a line worker to "clean up that mess over there" may well return in an hour to discover the "mess" has not been touched. When he pointedly asks the worker why his orders were not carried out, the subordinate may respond "Oh, I thought you meant for me to do it before I left work today."

Communication that is ambiguous, then, can readily create a conflict situation. Such conflict may occur because one party unintentionally (or perhaps intentionally) misunderstood another's communication.

Overload, persuasiveness, and ambiguity in communication, are three causal factors associated with organizational conflict. Other principles associated directly with the nature of communication are also potential causes of conflict. Redding, for example, cites three:

1. *Meanings are not transferred:* "the receiver really *creates* his own meaning from the incoming messages he perceives, based upon his total life experiences up to that moment."[14]

2. *Anything is a potential message:* "there are no boundaries limiting the range of phenomena which potentially can arouse meaning in the head of some observer or receiver."[15]

3. *The message received is the only one that counts:* "the only message which a person can act upon is the message which he *receives* . . . And in many instances the message received is quite different from the one sent."[16]

By its very nature, therefore, communication may effect conflict as well.

Communication that Prevents Conflict

Since communication is a primary causal factor in organizational conflict, it is important to understand how the concept may simultaneously serve also as a preventive factor.

Communication Climate

Perhaps the most useful approach to preventing the occurrence of conflict is the fostering of a supportive and participative climate within the organization: "Seriously destructive conflict would rarely occur if in fact the organizational climate is one of a) trust and confidence, b) an "everyone wins" approach, and c) openness and candor in the airing of differences."[17]

In simple terms, when the parties to a relationship, be they a superior and subordinate or peers in the organizational hierarchy, openly trust and have confidence in one another's communicative behavior, then destructive conflict is likely to be inhibited. Likewise, when a "win-lose" atmosphere does not dominate the relationship, and when an optimum degree of openness and candor characterize the expression of ideas and feelings, dysfunctional conflict will not likely occur.

Communication that Cures Conflict

Once conflict occurs, management's function becomes finding ways to resolve it. A number of communication processes exist for this purpose.

Group Problem Solving

Especially if the parties to conflict are not so much opposed that confrontation would serve only to further alienate them a problem-solving conference (as described in Chapter 8) might effectively alleviate the conflicting behavior.

An important criterion in considering this form of conflict resolution is the perceived gravity of the problem. Quite often, problems involving overlapping responsibilities, scarce resources, and ambiguity can be resolved through direct interaction between parties.

Another criterion is the amount of ego involvement that apparently characterizes each party's position. Even supposedly minor problems, such as competition between two retail departments for storage space, may have associated with them a high level of ego involvement, should the conflicting parties perceive status in increased storage area.

A final aspect of group problem solving is perceived distance, in terms of agreement, between the opposing parties. As we indicated earlier, if it seems that the factions have not assumed diametrically opposing positions, then perhaps group problem solving, a "low-key" form of conflict resolution, might function effectively.

Mediation

This second method for resolving conflict involves the introduction of a third party who, in essence, mediates the opposing factions. It is important to remember that the mediator renders no decisions in the dispute; rather, he serves in a liaison function, clarifying positions and issues and attempting to enhance the flow of cooperative communication between parties.

His position in the conflict is twofold. First, he serves as chairman in whatever face-to-face confrontations occur. Second, because such confrontation is not always conducive to conflict resolution, he serves as messenger between the parties.

Obviously, mediation is intended to be utilized in conflict situations that are more serious than those for which group problem-solving is employed; that is, the gravity of the problem, the ego involvement, and the distance between parties are more pronounced.

Arbitration

This final form of conflict resolution is used when it is obvious that neither group problem solving nor mediation will effect the desired outcome. Unlike the mediator, an arbitrator has complete decision-making power. Whether he is a department head settling disputes between two first-line supervisors, or a federal official resolving a management-labor conflict, the arbitrator listens to both sides, weighs the evidence and arguments, and renders a binding decision.

Because arbitration is actually the final alternative in resolving conflict, its use is limited to those situations where the gravity of the problem, ego involvement, and agreement distance are most severe. Arbitration is a win-lose method and, as such, is a last resort.

SUMMARY

Conflict can be viewed as a dynamic process that functions in organizations in both constructive and destructive ways. Whether a particular conflict episode is dysfunctional depends heavily upon whether it is, in fact, perceived and how the individual chooses to evaluate his perception. Communication, finally, is a significant feature in conflict process, not only as a causative factor, but also as a means for preventing and curing conflict.

QUESTIONS FOR DISCUSSION

1. What are some of your own *unique* physiological and psychological characteristics that would affect your perception in a conflict situation?

2. One of the factors described in the latent stage of the conflict episode was a divergence of subunit goals. What are some examples of these goals that you think might foster conflict?

3. What are some examples of organizational conflict that may be functional?

4. What are some specific behaviors that you think would characterize a win-lose climate and an "everybody wins" climate?

5. Which of the forms of conflict resolution do you think is most suitable to you personally? Why?

ENDNOTES

1. Richard E. Walton, *Interpersonal Peacemaking: Confrontations and Third-Party Consultation* (Reading, Massachusetts: Addison-Wesley, 1969), p. 2.
2. L. R. Pondy, "Organizational Conflict: Concepts and Models," in *Management of Change and Conflict*, eds. John M. Thomas and Warren G. Bennis (Middlesex, England: Penguin Books, 1972), pp. 360–366.
3. *Ibid.*
4. Richard C. Huseman, "Conflict in Modern Organizations," in *Readings in Interpersonal and Organizational Communication*, 2d ed. eds. Richard C. Huseman, Cal M. Logue, and Dwight L. Freshley (Boston: Holbrook Press, 1973), p. 195.
5. M. Deutsch, "Productive and Destructive Conflict," in Thomas and Bennis, *op. cit.*, pp. 391–398.
6. Henry Assael, "Constructive Role of Interorganizational Conflict," *Administrative Science Quarterly*, XIV (December, 1969), pp. 573–582.
7. T. C. Laughlin and D. P. Kedzic, "Role of Conflict," *Best's Review*, LXXII (May, 1971), p. 96.
8. William V. Haney, *Communication and Organizational Behavior* 3rd edition, (Homewood, Illinois: Irwin, 1973), p. 56.
9. David W. Johnson, "Communication and the Inducement of Cooperative Behavior in Conflicts: A Critical Review," *Speech Monographs*, XLI, 1 (March, 1974), p. 77.
10. W. Charles Redding, *Communication Within the Organization*, (New York: Industrial Communication Council, 1972), p. 23.
11. *Ibid.*, p. 87.
12. *Ibid.*, pp. 210–211.
13. *Ibid.*, p. 212.
14. *Ibid.*, p. 28.
15. *Ibid.*, p. 30.
16. *Ibid.*, p. 37.
17. *Ibid.*, p. 214.

part
two

Interpersonal Perspectives

7

Listening

One of the most demanding, yet unfortunately least emphasized, aspects of the communication process is listening. Consider first that almost one half of the time one spends in communicating with others through reading, writing, speaking, and listening is consumed by the listening process.[1] Given this significance of listening in communication, then, it is surprising that so little attention is devoted to it in either high school or college training. Courses in reading, writing, and speaking are offered and often required; yet few students are exposed to more than a brief examination of listening skills.

Consider second the fact that the average person speaks at a rate of from 100 to 200 words per minute. An average listener, however, can adequately process no fewer than 400 words per minute.[2] Given this differential between what is normally heard and what can potentially be processed, it is little wonder that people tend to "tune out" during political speeches, small group conferences, and even sermons. Mental tangents are the obvious product of this differential,[3] and the manager who believes that subordinates are listening intently to every word he utters is deluding himself.

Consider finally the findings of research that indicate that the retention rate of orally communicated messages is approximately fifty percent immediately after the message is transmitted and only twenty-five percent two months later.[4] Given this low rate of retention which seems to characterize the average individual, it should therefore not surprise a manager when orders are forgotten or carried out incorrectly. He may well have issued those orders succinctly and coherently. Unfortunately, his subordinates simply did not retain what was said.

The purpose of this chapter, therefore, is to examine the listening process as it relates to effective management. Attention will be given the nature of listening, barriers to successful listening, and several suggestions for improving this vital facet of the total communication process will be made.

THE NATURE OF LISTENING

At first glance, listening might appear to be nothing more than the mere hearing of oral messages. Adopting this frame of reference, however, would necessarily commit one to the position that listening ability is a function of his physical, aural processes. Such a position is, in part, a valid one; yet listening is a much more complicated activity.

Perhaps an appropriate perspective from which to view the listening process is to conceive of it as consisting of three basic parts: 1) attention, 2) reception, and 3) perception. As will become evident, these three sub-processes are interrelated and interdependent; however, examining them separately will enhance one's understanding of the total listening process.

Attention

Attention, simply defined, is the process of exposing oneself to certain stimuli in the environment. Obviously, there are innumerable such stimuli present in one's immediate environment—so many, in fact, that an individual is incapable of attending to all of them. Thus, attention is a selective process whereby one entirely ignores some stimuli, gives partial attention to others, and devotes full attention to still others. A manager, for example, while involved in a correction interview with one of his subordinates, may be carefully attending to the subordinate's explanation of his reasons for committing a particular error. Simultaneously, however, other stimuli that may be impinging upon the manager's attention process could include a noisy, malfunctioning air conditioner, the telephone ringing in his secretary's office, and the sound of an ambulance or police siren in the street outside the building.

Notice that the hypothetical stimuli are directed toward the supervisor's aural attention process. Still others could be demanding the attention of his other senses (e.g., sight and touch). Hence, though attention can be described as a factor in the listening process, it should not be conceived of as limited to that process alone.

That the process of attention is a selective one can be further illustrated in five basic principles of attention cited by Thayer:

1. People will attend to stimuli that they think are relevant to their own goals or objectives.[5] Thus, a subordinate who is interested in a promotion will likely listen carefully when his supervisor discusses opportunities and techniques for advancement in the company.

2. People will attend to stimuli that serve to satisfy the needs of their "conceptual/evaluative" system.[6] One critical component of this system, according to Thayer, is the self-concept. To illustrate the principle, a subordinate with an extremely low self-concept may listen carefully, during performance appraisal, to his supervisor's positive remarks concerning his performance. Such activity satisfies his need for an improved self-concept. However, when the manager begins discussing his weaknesses, the subordinate may well "tune out," as any such information is incongruent with the needs of his conceptual/evaluative system.

3. People will disattend to stimuli that disconfirm their own models of the world.[7] The retail salesman, for example, who believes that females are poor sales people will tend to avoid information that demonstrates that a saleswoman in his department is selling more merchandise than her male counterparts. Conversely, should the sales manager post a sales report that indicates that her sales are lowest in the department, the salesman will attend carefully to that information.

4. People will attend to stimuli that are unexpected.[8] Typically, individuals possess expectations about what they will hear. When these expectations are contradicted by actual messages, people will attend more carefully.

5. The ongoing relationship between people and their environment plays a significant role in their attention process.[9] Thayer illustrates:

> A subordinate is differently "tuned in" to his boss than he is to his fellow workers. At the same time, he will be differently calibrated (communicatively) to the utterances of those of his peers he likes and admires than he will be to those he dislikes or those he simply does not know.[10]

Generally, then, listening is, indeed, a selective process by which the listener exposes himself in varying degrees to stimuli in his environment.

Reception

In terms of the listening activity, reception can be described as the process of actually receiving those stimuli to which one exposes himself. While attention was depicted primarily as a psychological, selective process, reception may perhaps be best viewed as a physical one. Naturally, it would be hazardous to assume that reception occurs only through use of one's aural processes, since the other senses are also important; however, in terms of *listening*, one may presume that the primary activity is hearing.[11]

If the primary reception process is the physical act of hearing, then, the nature of reception should be heavily dependent upon one's physiological hearing ability. To a large degree this is true. An individual will receive aural stimuli only to the extent that he can hear them. Yet it was indicated earlier that the processes of attention and reception overlap. In this case, the level of attention will also affect the quality of reception as well. If the supervisor in the earlier correction interview example is devoting more attention to his secretary's telephone or to the sirens outside the building, then his ability to receive crucial information from the subordinate will consequently be hampered. Hence, reception is a function of both an individual's hearing ability and the degree of attention he is directing toward a specific stimulus.

Perception

Perception is the third critical process in the listening activity. Simply defined, it is the assignment of meaning to whatever stimuli are received. Like attention, perception is a psychological process, and like reception, it is dependent upon the level of attention devoted to particular stimuli.

Because the nature of perception was treated in detail in Chapter 2, it will be considered only briefly here. Its importance in the listening process, however, should not be considered lightly. Assignment by the receiver of meanings to messages similar to those intended by the sender is a major goal of the communication process. Perception serves, as the next section shows, as both an inhibitor and a facilitator of effective listening.

Listening, in summary, can be described as the process of attending to, receiving, and perceiving primarily aural stimuli in the environment. Consequently, the manager who attends carefully to what his subordinates say, who is capable of receiving their communication adequately, and who perceives their messages as the subordinates intended them to be perceived, can be called an effective listener.

BARRIERS TO EFFECTIVE LISTENING

It should be obvious from the discussion of attention and reception that certain inhibitors of effective listening are inherent in the two processes. As was exemplified in the five principles of attention, the selective aspect of attention presents an initial barrier. That one's hearing ability may somehow be physiologically impaired constitutes an example of a second barrier—this one associated with reception.

Some of the most formidable barriers in the listening process, however, occur during the perceptual stage, the facet of listening where meanings are assigned. The ensuing discussion of barriers to effective listening will therefore focus upon a number of problems associated with perception. These problems, moreover, may be viewed as a set of principles similar in structure to those relevant to the selectivity of attention.

1. People will perceive stimuli according to their own frame of reference. This principle is typified in the communication cliché "Meanings are in people." The essence of the principle, moreover, is that a message is composed of nothing more than aural and visual stimuli. Despite the fact that the speaker may intend to convey certain meanings in a particular message, whatever meaning is actually assigned to the message depends upon the listener's frame of reference, i.e., "his total life experiences up to that moment."[12] Thus, although speaker and listener may share similar meanings through a given message, it should be remembered that at no time will those meanings be identical.

2. People perceive stimuli according to their own expectations.[13] Suppose, for a moment, that a particular line worker in a manufacturing plant believes that he is being harassed by his immediate supervisor. He has, indeed, been experiencing difficulty completing his work adequately; yet, almost daily the foreman passes his work station, examines his work, and makes some sarcastic comment about the quality of his production. Despite the absence of a climate of supportiveness in this relationship, the line worker strives to improve. Then, one morning, his supervisor again approaches his station, inspects his work, smiles, and says simply, "Good job." The line worker is bitter, and he resigns that afternoon.

Actually, in this example, the foreman's smile and utterance of "Good job" were intended to be complimentary. Finally, he thought, his subordinate was performing satisfactorily. Yet the line worker, because his *past experiences* indicated to him that communication from his supervisor was universally sarcastic and uncomplimentary, perceived even the foreman's praise as further criticism.

Expectations, then, are based upon past experiences in similar situations. As Barker indicates, "The listener's past communication climate has helped condition his perception of the immediate listening setting, the speaker, and the message being transmitted."[14]

3. People will perceive stimuli according to their own attitudes and beliefs. Most individuals possess an almost uncanny ability, at times, to distort information so that it "fits" their model of the world. This is the process of selective perception, and it applies to the listening activity in the same manner as it is associated with perception in general. A subordinate, consequently, who firmly believes that his performance is quite adequate may well tend to "filter out" criticisms from his supervisor, reminding himself that there is really no sound reason to question his work. Selective perception thus often serves as a protective device against incongruous aural stimuli.

4. *The ongoing relationship between speaker and listener plays a significant role in the perception process.* This principle is particularly relevant to superior-subordinate relationships. Not only will a subordinate give closer attention to a credible supervisor's comments, but he will also be more conscious of how he interprets communication from that supervisor. If, however, that supervisor is perceived to have low credibility or little power, then the subordinate may likely attach little significance to what he says. The nature of the relationship, then, affects the meaning assigned to messages.

GUIDELINES TO EFFECTIVE LISTENING

The literature of listening is, of course, filled with suggestions concerning how one might improve his listening skills. The remainder of this chapter will be devoted to describing several of what seem to be the most significant of these guidelines. Employed conscientiously, they can potentially serve to enhance a manager's ability to communicate effectively with both his subordinates and his own supervisors.

Awareness

This initial guideline to effective listening involves an individual's being aware of the problems that are inherently associated with the processes of attention, reception, and perception. Selectivity of attention, physiological impediments to reception, and distortions of meaning can be precluded or alleviated if one is first aware of their existence. Thus, an effective listener analyzes his own listening process, concentrating upon the factors of attention, reception, and perception and how they influence his listening behavior.

Motivation

As should be obvious from the earlier discussion of attention, an individual is motivated to listen in varying degrees to a variety of messages. Simultaneously, however, he is "demotivated" from listening for many of the same kinds of reasons.

An effective listener, however, is one who is continually, consciously motivated to listen. From his viewpoint, if another person wishes to communicate with him, then whatever that individual wants to say is important. Though at first it may appear that nothing of any great value may be gained through listening in some situations, the listener consciously strives to disprove his expectations. He becomes what Barker terms a "selfish listener," one who looks for "potential economic benefits, personal satisfaction, or new interests and insights."[15] Nichols describes his behavior:

> Whenever we wish to listen efficiently, we ought to say to ourselves: "What's he saying that I can use? What worthwhile ideas has he? Is he reporting any workable procedures? Anything that I can cash in, or with which I can make myself happier?"[16]

Motivation, then, is the second factor in effective listening.

Concentration

It will be remembered that there exists a significant differential between average speaking rate (100 to 200 words per minute) and a listener's ability to process messages (400 words per minute). Such a differential, it was indicated, provides opportunities for mental tangents. The average listener therefore tends to tune in and tune out of conversations. As a consequence, he sometimes never hears what the speaker deems the important contents of a message.

Concentration is the key to avoiding such counterproductive tangents. "The listener should be aware of the difference between the rate of speech and the rate of thinking and should use the time lag effectively rather than letting it destroy the listening process."[17] In terms of informal, dyadic interaction, there are several tactics a listener can use to facilitate concentration:

1. *Anticipate what the speaker will say next.*[18] Whether or not one's anticipations or expectations are confirmed, such activity serves to focus the listener's attention upon the subject at hand.

2. *Focus on the message.* Such tactics as weighing the speaker's evidence[19] and searching for deeper meanings, especially connotative ones, in the speaker's words[20] will help fill the "idle time" created by the speech-thought differential.

3. *Review previous points.*[21] This activity involves recapitulating in

one's mind the major points the speaker has already covered. The value of reviewing is that it can help one learn information by reinforcing ideas.[22]

Concentration, then, consists of successfully managing the time lag between speech and thought. Certain tactics can be employed both to maintain attention on the speaker's message and to facilitate retention.

Empathy

One of the perceptual problems earlier associated with listening was the principle that people will perceive stimuli according to their own frame of reference. Such a limited perceptual basis naturally inhibits an individual's capacity for comprehending the meaning a speaker intends to convey in a particular message.

The essence of empathic listening is that the listener attempts to perceive messages from the speaker's frame of reference. "It means feeling yourself into, or participating in, the inner world of another while remaining yourself."[23] The value of efforts to empathize is that if the listener is, indeed, capable of understanding the speaker's frame of reference, then he will more likely be able to assign meanings to messages that are congruent with the speaker's intentions. In so doing, he enhances the effectiveness of communication between himself and the speaker.

Questions

In dyadic communication, such as between a superior and subordinate, asking questions may often be an effective listening tactic. Such activity serves two purposes: First, it encourages the speaker by demonstrating to him that one is, indeed, actively listening;[24] second, questions can clarify and develop points, thereby enhancing the listener's chances of clearly understanding the speaker's message.

Probes are a highly useful type of question to pose in improving one's listening capabilities. Here the listener simply asks questions that build upon a speaker's utterances. The reader is encouraged to examine the various types of questions (including probes) developed in the discussion of interviewing in Chapter 11.

Objectivity

Objectivity is a crucial element in effective listening. Lack of objectivity can not only result in the assignment of distorted meanings to messages, but may also deleteriously affect the relationship between speaker and listener. In terms of objectivity, an effective listener:

1. *Minimizes the impact of emotionally-laden words.* Quite often, a listener's perceptual process goes awry simply because the speaker utters a word or phrase that arouses an automatic, emotional response in him. Words and phrases such as "sex," "reduction in force," "strike," and "grievance" can sometimes engender feelings of hostility and anxiety in a listener. When such feelings arise, his ability to think clearly and logically may be severely hampered.

2. *Judges content, not delivery.*[25] Too often, listeners are prone to disattend to messages largely because of some purportedly distracting characteristic in the speaker's tone of voice, rate of delivery, or pronunciation. Such subjectively derived impressions of the value of messages seriously endangers one's listening efficiency. An effective listener, therefore, focuses his attention upon what is said, not how it is communicated.

3. *Reacts fairly and sensibly.* One of the most difficult listening functions is to avoid reacting too soon to what one hears. Consider the example of a department head who, when informed by his plant manager that his staff must be reduced by two people, responds immediately and in a defensive manner. Rather than wait for an explanation or justification from his superior, he plunges into the conversation, amassing every reason he can imagine for not cutting back the number of people in his department. His defensiveness begets defensive behavior in the plant manager, and hostile feelings are created.

An effective listener "waits his turn." He allows others sufficient opportunity to communicate satisfactorily their position or ideas. By adhering carefully to the prescript of "turn-taking," the listener becomes a more effective communicator.

SUMMARY

In general, then, listening can be viewed as the process of attending to, receiving, and perceiving aural stimuli in the environment. Attention involves selectively exposing oneself to certain stimuli; reception, the physiological process of receiving the stimuli; and perception, the assignment of meaning to those stimuli. Certain perceptual barriers to effective listening were presented, together with suggested guidelines for improving one's listening skills. Good listening, finally, requires that one remember: "Nature gave man two ears but only one tongue, which is a gentle hint that he should listen more than he talks."[26]

QUESTIONS FOR DISCUSSION

1. What are some of the criteria that you personally employ in evaluating "good" and "bad" listeners.

2. Which of the processes (attention, reception, perception) do you think is most critical to effective listening? Why?

3. Which of the barriers to effective listening do you think is most critical? Why?

4. Think of a person you know who is, in your perception, a good listener. What is it about him that makes him effective?

5. When you are in conversation with someone, do you normally pay more attention to aural or visual stimuli? How does this affect your listening process?

ENDNOTES

1. See, for example, Ralph G. Nichols, "Do We Know How To Listen? Practical Helps in a Modern Age," *Speech Teacher*, X (1961), 118–124; Ralph G. Nichols and Leonard A. Stevens, *Are You Listening?* (New York: McGraw-Hill, 1957), 6–10; and D. Bird, "Teaching Listening Comprehension," *Journal of Communication*, III (November, 1953), pp. 127–130.

2. Ernest G. Bormann, *et al.*, *Interpersonal Communication in the Modern Organization*, (Englewood Cliffs, New Jersey: Prentice-Hall, 1969), p. 197.

3. *Ibid.*

4. Ralph G. Nichols, "Do We Know How to Listen?" in Joseph A. Devito (Ed.), *Communication: Concepts and Processes*, (Englewood Cliffs, New Jersey: Prentice-Hall, 1971), pp. 207–208.

5. Lee Thayer, *Communication and Communication Systems*, Homewood, (Illinois: Richard D. Irwin, Inc., 1968), 51.

6. *Ibid.*, pp. 51–53.

7. *Ibid.*, pp. 53–54.

8. *Ibid.*, p. 54.

9. *Ibid.*, pp. 54–55.

10. *Ibid.*, p. 54.

11. Larry L. Barker, *Listening Behavior*, (Englewood Cliffs, New Jersey: Prentice-Hall, 1971), p. 30.

12. W. Charles Redding, *Communication Within The Organization*, New York: Industrial Communication Council, 1972, 28.
13. Barker, *Listening Behavior*, p. 38.
14. *Ibid.*
15. *Ibid.*, p. 74.
16. Nichols, "Do We Know How to Listen?", p. 209.
17. Barker, *Listening Behavior*, p. 75.
18. See Barker, *Listening Behavior*, pp. 75–76, and Bormann *et al.*, *Interpersonal Communication*, p. 199.
19. Keith Davis, *Human Behavior at Work* 4th edition, (New York: McGraw-Hill, 1972), p. 395.
20. Barker, *Listening Behavior*, p. 75.
21. *Ibid.*
22. *Ibid.*
23. Alfred Benjamin, *The Helping Interview*, Boston: Houghton Mifflin Company, 1969, p. 50.
24. Davis, *Human Behavior at Work*, p. 20.
25. Nichols, "Do We Know How to Listen?" p. 209.
26. Davis, *Human Behavior at Work*, p. 396.

8

The Small Group Conference

A common perception of management's role is that it involves fulfilling certain functions. These functions are generally considered planning, organizing, directing (or leading), and controlling.[1] Central components in each of the functions are the elements of problem solving and decision making.

Problem solving is "thinking which results in the solving of problems,"[2] and decision making is "thinking which results in the choice among alternative courses of action."[3] The foreman, for example, who is faced with a morale problem must, as part of his leadership function, isolate and alleviate causes of the inadequate morale. In organizing a small company, its board of directors may well be concerned about the relationship of one department to another. Will problems arise, for instance, if both Production and Shipping are situated beneath a single department head? If so, then what are the alternatives to this arrangement that might preclude the occurrence of such problems?

An effective method for solving problems and making decisions in organizations is the small group conference. Some managers unfortunately believe that a primary responsibility of their positions is individual decision making. While decision making is important, it is not an individual responsibility when the manager possesses inadequate knowledge or expertise to render an effective decision. There are, indeed, advantages to group (as opposed to individual) decision making, just as there are certain benefits to be derived from the use of computer technology in making decisions.

The purpose of this chapter is to examine the small group as a format for decision making and problem solving in organizations. Though the conference may readily serve other distinct purposes (e.g., briefing, or the transmission of information down through the organizational hierarchy, and brainstorming, or creativity sessions devoted to the stimulation and expression of new and useful ideas), its widespread use by management warrants careful consideration of its nature and processes.

THE NATURE OF CONFERENCE DECISION MAKING

Purpose

Normally, the problem-solving or decision-making conference is *ad hoc* in nature; that is, the meeting is held for the specific purpose of alleviating some problem or selecting a desirable course of action with respect to some issue.

Participants

Members of a problem-solving group can come from all levels of the organizational hierarchy. Such a group may be composed only of peers (e.g., a selected number of department heads), or it may be comprised of individuals from a vertical slice of the hierarchy (e.g., a department head, two second-line supervisors, and three first-line supervisors). The major criterion for selecting or appointing members of the group is the nature of the problem. The question is what individuals possess the necessary expertise to deal successfully with a specific problem? Other criteria for small group conference membership do exist, however, and they will be discussed shortly.

The optimum *size* of a problem-solving group has been the subject of considerable research. Generally, it has been discovered that groups of five persons seem to perform best, provided that these five possess the necessary skills for handling a specific problem.[4] Actually, more than five persons may enhance the quality of the group's decision, but factors such as member satisfaction, coordination, and team spirit tend to suffer in larger groups.[5]

Advantages and Disadvantages of Group Decision Making

It was earlier indicated that some managers avoid the use of problem-solving conferences simply because they perceive the responsibility for decision making to be theirs alone. Thus, a plant manager, when confronted with a severe drop in production, might tend to attempt to analyze the problem and derive a satisfactory solution on his own. If, indeed, he is capable of successfully making such decisions in all cases, then perhaps his is the best course of action; however, research into group problem solving and discussion has pointed to a number of sometimes secondary outcomes, both advantageous and disadvantageous, that tend to accrue from employing small group methods. The practicing manager would do well to be aware of them.

Advantages

If the conference method of problem solving is utilized, then the manager can often expect the following outcomes:

1. *Quality Decisions.* Research has demonstrated that frequently a group decision, because it involves interaction and corrective feedback among group members, is superior to the decision of an individual working alone.[6] The presumption here, of course, is that those individuals involved in the decision making possess sufficient expertise to render a good decision. A plant manager who requests that a group of his first-line production supervisors decide on a new air filtration system for the plant is likely assuming too much about their expertise.

2. *Acceptance.* On many occasions, a decision made by subordinates will experience greater acceptance among them simply because they have been an integral part of the decision-making process.[7] Maier, in fact, poses the interesting and compelling argument that if good quality is not the major criterion for an effective decision, then perhaps the manager might consider involving his employees in the decision-making process.[8] A simple illustration may help clarify his point. An appliance department manager in a retail store is concerned that all three of his full-time salesmen have requested the same week for their vacation. Knowing that he can free only two of the salesmen for that week, the manager must decide who should be required to reschedule his vacation. Decision quality is not a critical factor in this case, as any one of the three salesmen could perform adequately during the absence of the other two. If the manager renders the decision, then he can readily create hostility among his subordinates and between the unlucky salesman and himself. If, however, he asks the three salesman to work out a suitable arrangement, then each has the opportunity to discuss his points with the others. Chances are greater here that all the salesmen will accept the decision.

3. *Commitment.* Closely tied to the advantage of acceptance is the element of commitment. The logic supporting this advantage is that if individuals are directly involved in analyzing a problem and selecting a solution for it, then they will experience a greater sense of commitment for effectively implementing the decision. Supporters of such logic would argue, then, that a company considering various motivational programs (e.g., job enrichment, wage incentives, profit sharing) would do well to involve employees in the selection of an appropriate program. Even though *both* management and labor might arrive at the

same decision (e.g., job enrichment), commitment to the success of the program would be greater if the employees were involved.

4. *Status.* Some experts maintain that the responsibility and interaction involved in group decision making engenders a sense of status and recognition to the participants.[9]

Other purported advantages of group, as opposed to individual decision making include greater attitude change[10] and opportunity for discovering group standards.[11]

Disadvantages

Unfortunately, group decision making can effect certain disadvantages as well. Several of these disadvantages are often enough to entirely preclude the use of problem-solving conferences.

1. *Time.* Perhaps the greatest barrier to using groups to solve problems and make decisions is the expenditure of time, both in terms of an individual's preparing for a conference and in terms of the actual time consumed in the decision-making process.

2. *Cost.* Associated with the time factor is the element of monetary expenditure. Taking employees away from their regularly assigned duties obviously results in loss of monies that, in individual decision-making situations, would not have occurred.

3. *Conformity.* Unlike the first two disadvantages, the problem of conformity is not inherent to the group decision-making process; however, its frequent occurrence warrants its consideration as a major disadvantage. Consider the case where a small group conference is dominated by one participant whose aggressive personality falsely conveys superiority in knowledge and expertise to the other participants. In situations such as this, the advantage of increased inputs and, hopefully, better decisions is precluded because most members of the group are either unwilling or perhaps unable to contribute their ideas, no matter how useful they might be.

Other disadvantages also characterize the group decision-making process. These include hidden agendas, groupthink, and the risky shift, all to be discussed in detail in the following chapter on group problems.

Generally, then, the problem-solving conference is normally an *ad hoc* small group, composed ideally of roughly five members. Utilization of this method of decision making is contingent upon management's perception of the attractiveness of certain advantages and the gravity of specific disadvantages that might possibly occur.

THE PROCESS OF CONFERENCE DECISION MAKING

If management opts to employ the conference method in its decision-making process, then all participants, and especially the leader, should be cognizant of certain processes inherent in group problem solving.

The Decision Process

Common to every small group conference is some format, or agenda, that is intended to guide the participants to a successful decision outcome. A number of such formats exist; however, most of the effective and widely used contemporary agendas rely heavily upon John Dewey's Reflective Thinking Process.[12] The six-step format presented here is an example.

Step 1: Defining and Analyzing the Problem

Generally, this initial stage of the conference involves specifying the precise nature of the problem to be solved and searching for the underlying causes for that problem. Suppose for a moment that a small retail firm has been experiencing what seems to be low morale, a definite drop in sales, and an unusually high turnover rate. The leader might begin the conference by describing these factors, supporting them with whatever facts he has available. By concisely depicting the present state of affairs, he is defining the problem.

When it can be safely assumed that each conference participant understands the nature and scope of the problem, the group is prepared to investigate potential causes. This is the crux of the first step in problem solving. As different group members offer their perceptions of what could be creating the morale, sales, and turnover problem, these perceptions are discussed, modified (if necessary), and recorded by the leader or someone appointed by him. Perhaps the group in this illustration came up with four potential causes: 1) lack of communication between superiors and subordinates; 2) poor motivational programs; 3) conflict between the sales and delivery departments; and 4) insufficient advertising. For some reason, such as attitude surveys or information derived from grievance and exit interviews, the group decides that the major cause of the problem is inadequate motivation. Once the problem is defined and the suspected cause is isolated, the group is prepared to move to Step 2.

Step 2: Establishing Criteria for a Solution

First, it should be remembered that the *location* of this step in the problem-solving sequence is optional. As will become evident, the criteria step may be postponed until solutions are actually evaluated.

Suppose, however, that this group is capable of setting up certain criteria that any potential solution must meet. In this case, the criteria might be: 1) the solution must involve all nonmanagement employees; 2) it must become effective within no more than two months; and 3) it should cost the company no more than two percent of its gross profits.

These criteria are derived, of course, through interaction among the conference members. Some suggested criteria are rejected outright; others are altered slightly. In any event, this group has selected three and is ready to begin Step 3 of the process.

Step 3: Proposing Possible Solutions

Essentially, this step is a brainstorming process. The focus is on suggesting as many potential solutions as possible. Each participant attempts to propose solutions that meet the specified criteria. Critically, *no* solutions are evaluated during this stage, although members may amend the solutions offered by others. Again, the leader or his appointee keeps a record of these possible solutions.

Suppose that this group conceived of five potential solutions: 1) wage incentives; 2) profit sharing; 3) increased commissions; 4) a fringe benefit package; and 5) a sales contest. They are now prepared for Step 4.

Step 4: Evaluating Possible Solutions

It was indicated previously that in some decision-making situations, the proposing of criteria for useful solutions may be delayed until this step. Additionally, it may be beneficial for participants to add new criteria as the evaluation process progresses.

This step proceeds with the conference participants evaluating each of the proposed solutions. Every solution is weighed, of course, against the criteria outlined in Step 2 and other criteria that have been proposed. The group essentially attempts to define both the advantages and disadvantages of each solution. The wage incentives, for example, might be perceived to be applicable to all nonmanagement employees, easily set up within two months, but too costly. Additionally, such incentives, some members of the conference think, will be useless in motivating salesmen who work solely on a commission basis.

After the advantages and disadvantages have been assigned to each solution, the group is ready to begin Step 5.

Step 5: Selecting a Solution

It is critical to remember first that the group is under no obligation to select only one of the proposed solutions. A combination of two or three of them or an altered version of only one might comprise the most effective decision.

At this stage of the conference, however, a final decision is made concerning how the problem should be solved. The precise details of the solution should also be decided. Suppose, in this instance, that the group opts for increased commissions and a sales contest. More specifically (but hardly specific enough for a real-life situation), they decide to increase commissions by one percent across the board. Also, a sales contest, lasting three months, will be held between the hard and soft lines divisions. Winners will receive money bonuses and gift certificates. The group is now prepared for the final step in the problem-solving sequence.

Step 6: Plotting a Course of Action

This step involves deciding how best to employ the solution. Before the conference can be terminated, the members must agree upon a specific, detailed method for taking appropriate action on the solution. Sometimes, participants will volunteer to assume responsibility for various aspects of the solution. On other occasions, the leader may assign members specific tasks. In any case, until agreement has been reached, the problem-solving process has not been completed.

Suppose, in the example, two department heads have volunteered to direct the sales contest. Together, they will work out the details and report to the store manager in one week. Finally, the store manager indicates that the one percent commission hike will become effective at the beginning of the next month. He will compose a memorandum to that effect. The conference is concluded.

In summary then, a problem-solving format is composed of six distinct stages:

1. Defining and Analyzing the Problem
2. Establishing Criteria for a Solution

3. Proposing Possible Solutions
4. Evaluating Possible Solutions
5. Selecting a Solution
6. Plotting a Course of Action

The Leadership Process

A central role in every problem-solving group is that of the leader. Unfortunately, many assume that the leader's function is merely to guide the group to an acceptable decision. Realistically, however, his responsibility is much more complex. As will become evident, what he says and does during the conference invariably has a pronounced and unmistakable impact upon the quality of the group's decision, upon the level of personal satisfaction members derive through participation, and upon the interpersonal relationships among these members, both while the conference is in progress and when participants return to their regular activities. For these reasons, it is important to examine certain key functions for which the group leader is responsible.

Task and Human Relations

The terms "task" and "human relations" have been borrowed from general management theory to show that, like the supervisor in his day-to-day activities, the group leader's primary function is to achieve a proper balance between completing the task and maintaining a spirit of teamwork and harmony among group members.

Research by Robert Bales at Harvard University has demonstrated that two types of leaders tend to emerge in small, problem-solving groups: a task leader and a socioemotional leader. The former will be interested in solving the problem and arriving at a decision as quickly as possible, while the latter will be primarily concerned with interpersonal relationships among group members.[13] The actual group leader's function is not so much to attempt to serve in both the task and human relations (socioemotional) roles, as the two are somewhat incompatible, but rather to foster a climate in which behaviors corresponding to the two types gain acceptance.

Achieving a balance between task and human relations, then, means here that the small group leader encourages task accomplishment, while simultaneously emphasizing healthy social relationships among group members. Unfortunately, the proper "balance" need not be fifty-fifty; rather, it varies with group composition and the difficulty of the task.

Neutrality

A second important leadership function is to remain neutral. Oddly enough, many individuals believe, because they have been appointed group leader, that they have an increased responsibility to offer their attitudes and opinions. Such is hardly the case. Consider the situation in which a department head calls together a group of first-line supervisors to solve a particular problem. The status associated with his position in the organizational hierarchy, together with the additional status he derives simply from being group leader, affords him an unusual amount of influence in altering (at least on the surface) the attitudes of the members of the group. Thus, should he volunteer his perception of what constitutes the most attractive solution to the problem, then it would not be surprising for the group members to immediately adopt his proposal. Consequently, the problem-solving conference becomes an occasion for the development of "yes-men," an insidious phenomenon in contemporary management.

Theoretically, the rationale behind maintaining neutrality is this: When management opts for a small group, problem-solving conference composed of individuals from different levels of the hierarchy, the power to render decisions is simultaneously and implicitly delegated downward. This is not to say that management is turning over control of the organization to a group of subordinates. Rather, management is ostensibly seeking assistance in making sound, creative decisions. Any outright attempts to influence the direction of a group's thinking, then, will be counterproductive to the central purpose of a problem-solving conference.

There is, however, an important exception to the neutrality guideline. Sometimes, in the course of the discussion, the members will turn *directly* to the leader and request his ideas. Obviously, the department head in this case possesses a certain level of expertise. If the members of the group, therefore, ask for his opinions, then he has an obligation to respond.

In summary, the group leader remains neutral unless the members specifically and directly request opinions from him.

Completing the Agenda

This third function of a group leader is closely tied to the maintenance of neutrality. Very often, an inexperienced group leader will become deeply concerned about exactly what is expected of him if he is not permitted to become voluntarily involved in debates over issues before the group. Overseeing the completion of the agenda, is, in fact, his new obligation.

Such an obligation has two aspects. First, the leader should make sure that the members do not deviate from the six-step sequence described earlier. Any time consumed in human relations or socioemotional behavior is, of course, a deviation; yet, because this type of activity is both acceptable and, in fact, necessary, the leader is generally not deeply concerned about its occurrence. What he does want to avoid, however, are tangential or improperly sequenced discussions. It is not uncommon, for example, for some group members to begin proposing and evaluating solutions as soon as the problem is defined. Remarks such as, "Well, I think the cause of our problem is pure laziness. What we need around here is some close supervision. I'm willing to try it, too, if the rest of you are" possess the potential for destroying the step-by-step sequence of the agenda. In general, then, the leader strives to move the group *systematically* through the problem-solving format.

The second aspect of his obligation to complete the agenda is to ensure that the *entire* format is completed during the conference. Too often, groups dedicate themselves tenaciously to discovering causes for problems. Once they have accomplished this aspect of the problem-solving sequence, they feel their work is ended. Still other groups will progress only through Step 5 in the sequence, thinking then that their responsibility is satisfied. The leader's obligation here is to inform the group of its function and to direct the group through the entire sequence.

Decisions

A fourth function of the small group leader is to direct the actual voting and rendering of decisions. A number of different types of decisions can emanate during a conference. The first of these is consensus, or a unanimous decision. Here, unanimity means that no one in the group is strongly opposed to the decision. One or two members may not support the decision completely, but neither are they convinced the decision is incorrect or inadequate. Consensus may also mean, of course, that all group members wholeheartedly support the decision.

A decision by majority is the second decision type. Here, obviously, more than half the group members favor a particular decision.

The third major kind of decision rendered in small groups is one by authority[14] or power.[15] Such a decision is normally made for the group by one person who possesses most of the power in the group (e.g., the leader).

The presence of these three types of potential group decisions raises an important issue in conference leadership. Obviously, the leader wants to avoid decisions by authority. But which is the better decision—by majority or consensus? The answer to this question provides an unfortunate dilemma for the group leader.

First, a decision by majority vote will invariably result in the presence of a sometimes dissatisfied and even disgruntled minority segment of group participants. Given this situation, the earlier discussed advantages of acceptance and commitment may well accrue for only a portion of the group members.

Yet, associated with decision by consensus is the disadvantage of time. Especially when the decision is an extremely critical one and the debate surrounding it heated, the group can easily consume almost unrealistic quantities of time simply working toward total agreement. Additionally, a leader who adopts a policy of "consensus on everything" is simultaneously fostering an atmosphere conducive to conformity behavior. Some participants, simply to avoid the trauma of argument or the excessive expenditure of time, will modify their positions in order to guarantee a consensus decision. Associated with decisions such as this, however, are hidden agendas that render the consensus decision no more effective or representative than a decision by majority.

Perhaps the most useful tactic the group leader can employ is to *strive for consensus*. Here his explicit purpose is to attempt to reach consensus on every important decision. Should it appear, however, that consensus cannot be achieved without impractical sacrifices of time and potential conformity, then a majority decision is used. So long as the group members understand his attitude toward consensus decisions, and so long as the group leader is willing to recognize the existence of a minority opinion even after the decision is rendered, striving for consensus can be an effective decision-making tool.

Summaries

A final leadership function is the provision of summaries. First, the group leader provides what are termed "internal summaries" during the course of the discussion. He summarizes contributions (especially lengthy ones) of group members and major issues before voting occurs, as well as at the end of each step in the problem-solving sequence.

An "external summary" is also offered at the conclusion of the conference that normally reviews the process by which the group reached its decision, the decision itself, and the plan of action for carrying out the solution.

Too much emphasis cannot be placed upon the utility of summaries. They are critical first because members often tend to "tune out" sporadically during the discussion. As in any interpersonal communication situation, carefully attending to all that occurs is a difficult task. Consequently, participants must be periodically advised by the group leader concerning, for example, arguments for and against certain issues.

Summaries are useful too because they provide clarification of issues and positions members have adopted. The group leader who states, "Let's see, Jim . . . it seems to me you're saying that the problem is really a motivational one" is not only summarizing Jim's position for the group, but also giving Jim a chance to elaborate if, indeed, the leader's perception of his position is inaccurate.

Finally, summaries can stimulate thinking. Often, the conference will seem to have reached some sort of stalemate. An uneasy silence may permeate the room, as each participant waits for someone else to initiate the discussion again. In situations such as this, a group leader's first inclination is frequently to offer his own opinions or attitudes; however, doing so, as was pointed out earlier, may elicit immediate conformity behavior from the group members, perhaps even enhancing the likelihood of an authority decision. Yet an internal summary of whatever issues or arguments have effected the stalemate may well provoke further thinking about those issues, prompting participants to continue their interaction. A summary in this case is not a substitute for a solution but it could prove to be a useful tactic.

This discussion of leadership functions has sought to highlight several of the major obligations a conference leader must meet. Satisfying only these obligations does not guarantee effective leadership. The group leader must also mediate arguments, involve reticent members, do sufficient preplanning, and remain objective throughout. His is a demanding and sometimes traumatic task. But the benefits to be derived for the company, the conference participants, and the leader himself usually justify his efforts.

The Participant Process

Though the leader's role is central in a problem-solving conference, the participants, because they are collectively responsible for a quality decision, have certain specific functions for which they are responsible as well.

Assisting the Leader

Until recent years, a common perception among some writers was that there were certain leadership "styles," to be adopted intentionally or unintentionally by a conference leader. Popular delineations of these styles included the authoritarian (or autocratic) leader, the democratic (or participative) leader, and the laissez-faire (or free rein) leader. Associated with these styles, furthermore, were certain characteristic activities. The authoritarian leader, for example, tended to employ authority decisions and to rule the problem-solving process with an iron hand, while the laissez-faire group leader was inclined to sit back and allow the participants to control the discussion, often to the point where, because of role conflicts over leadership and confusion about responsibilities and procedures, nothing was accomplished. The democratic leader was considered the ideal form of leadership. In fact, many of the leadership functions described earlier are derived from principles inherent to the democratic style of leadership.

The important point, however, is that group leadership is no longer considered to be the function of a single individual as much as it is a role to be assumed at various times by different members of the group.[16] Hence, the performance of those leadership functions cited earlier is the responsibility not only of the designated group leader, but also the participants in the discussion.

Assumption of such a responsibility, of course, can lead to interpersonal conflict, especially in a small group where a predetermined (by the organization) hierarchy exists. Consequently, conference participants in such situations should direct their efforts toward *assisting the leader* with his primary functions.

First, it has already been pointed out that no one person can assume both roles of task and human relations leader. Thus, because the role a person assumes in a small group is generally determined by a combination of his own and others' perceptions of the role he should play,[17] each participant can contribute toward achieving that critical task—human relations balance—by attempting to assume certain roles himself and helping others to work out their role conflicts as well. Responding favorably to a tension-relieving anecdote, for example, may readily enhance the fostering of a more informal, cooperative climate during periods of group stress.

Additionally, a group member can be prepared to assist the conference leader in properly completing the agenda, summarizing, involving other participants, and mediating disputes among other group members. By doing so, he can facilitate the group's arriving at an effective decision, while achieving satisfaction, responsibility, and other important group rewards for himself.

Thus, the conference participant is an *ex officio* group leader. He may not possess the formal authority of the designated leader, but he can exercise an abundance of power in helping the leader perform his functions.

Interaction

As Gerald Phillips observes, "Interpersonal communication is the group's primary activity."[18] Interaction with others, then is the major function of a conference participant. Unfortunately, interaction skills vary among group members as widely as do physical and psychological attributes. A productive group member, in short, is cognizant of his own and others' interaction capabilities. The higher his degree of skill, furthermore, the greater is his emphasis upon:

1. *balanced participation:* a conference participant neither ignores nor dominates the discussion. He is actively involved in the problem-solving process, but not to the point where he infringes on the opportunities of others to contribute;

2. *brevity:* no one of his single contributions is either so lengthy or multifaceted that other participants have difficulty understanding his position;

3. *objectivity:* the small group conference is not a public debate, nor is it an arena for competing for promotions, liking or appreciation from superiors, or closedmindedness; and

4. *listening:* the participant listens to others as much as he expects or wishes them to listen to him.

SUMMARY

Three general processes characterize the functioning of a small, problem-solving group: decision, leadership, and participation. The six-step format patterned after John Dewey's *Reflective Thinking Process* is designed to improve the decision process. In addition to the many obvious obligations that accompany leadership, there are interpersonal requirements that the leader must satisfy if the group is to achieve maximum success. While the participants lack the formal authority of the designated leader, a large extent of the group's accomplishment depends on the attitudes and abilities of the participants. The following chapter will examine certain problems associated with small groups at both the individual and group levels. Each of those problems will, of course, be relevant to the processes previously described.

QUESTIONS FOR DISCUSSION

1. Does *frequent* use of the small group conference indicate that you as a manager are inherently incapable of making decisions on your own? Why or why not?

2. Some managers maintain that it is acceptable practice to use the small group conference to guide subordinates to a predetermined (by the manager himself) decision. Why do you think they support such a practice? Do you agree or disagree with it?

3. What are some advantages and disadvantages of making the "establishing criteria for a solution" stage of the problem-solving process a compulsory second step?

4. Do you agree with the shift away from leadership as the function and responsiblity of a single individual toward a viewpoint of leadership as a role to be assumed at various times by different group members? What are some advantages and disadvantages of this shift?

5. Which of the leadership functions do you think is most crucial to facilitating a successful discussion? Why? Why *didn't* you choose one of the other functions?

6. Two participants in a small group conference are involved in a heated debate over an issue. One of them turns to you, the lender, and says, "OK, who's right?" What responses *could* you give to this question? What response do you think you *should* give? Why?

7. In addition to the advantages and disadvantages of group (as opposed to individual) decision making, what are some other criteria that you think are relevant to whether or not you employ a small group, problem-solving conference?

ENDNOTES

1. See, for example, J.B. Poe, *An Introduction to the American Business Enterprise* (Homewood, Illinois: Richard D. Irwin, Inc., 1972), p. 127.
2. Donald W. Taylor, "Decision Making and Problem Solving." Chapter 2 in *Handbook of Organizations.* Edited by James G. March (Chicago: Rand McNally, 1965), p. 48.
3. *Ibid.*
4. A.C. Filley "Committee Management: Guidelines From Social Science Research," *California Management Review,* XIII (Fall, 1970), pp. 13–21.
5. *Ibid.*
6. Wayne N. Thompson, *Quantitative Research in Public Address and Communication* (New York: Random House, 1967), pp. 97–104.
7. Howard H. Martin, "Communication Settings," in *Speech Communica-*

tion: Analysis and Readings, ed. by Howard H. Martin and Kenneth E. Anderson (Boston: Allyn and Bacon, 1968), pp. 70–74.

8. N.R.F. Maier. *Problem-Solving Discussions and Conferences* (New York: McGraw-Hill, 1963), pp. 3–19.

9. Martin, *op. cit.,* pp. 70–74.

10. Thompson, *op. cit.,* pp. 97–104.

11. Martin, *op. cit.,* pp. 70–74.

12. John Dewey, *How We Think* (Boston: D.C. Heath, 1933).

13. Robert F. Bales, *Interaction Process Analysis* (Cambridge, Massachusetts: Addison-Wesley, 1950).

14. John Keltner, *Interpersonal Speech-Communication* (Belmont, California: Wadsworth Publishing Company, 1970), p. 302.

15. Gerald Goldhaber, *Organizational Communication* (Dubuque, Iowa: Wm. C. Brown, 1974), p. 225.

16. *Ibid.,* p. 218.

17. Ernest G. Bormann, *et al. Interpersonal Communication in the Modern Organization* (Englewood Cliffs, New Jersey: Prentice-Hall, 1969), pp. 55–57.

18. Gerald M. Phillips. *Communication and the Small Group* (Indianapolis: Bobbs-Merrill, 1966), p. 38.

9

Problems with Groups

The wag who described a committee as "a group of the unfit appointed by the unwilling to do the unnecessary," was voicing a sentiment with which many would agree. While the benefits of group efforts have long been extolled, the problems inherent in the group situation are often minimized if not completely ignored.

The presence of other persons activates social motives in the individual that are not relevant when one works alone, and it is these social motives that lead to problems. Many of these problems, if not anticipated and recognized, have the potential to result in a group experience that is personally dissatisfying, nonproductive, and perhaps, counterproductive. It is in order to prevent such eventualities that this dimension of groups is investigated. These problems can be divided into two categories: problems of group members and problems within the group itself.

A SENSE OF BELONGING

Effective group functioning is facilitated by individuals who are cooperative, efficient, and profound. Among the problems that confront participants of groups and thus inhibit these characteristics, one of the most significant is the extent to which an individual feels a part of the group. A group has the potential to help safisfy the social needs of the group members who truly feel

---

*H.R. Smith, Chairman of Department of Management, University of Georgia, is a co-author of this chapter.

that they do belong and who share a camaraderie with the other participants.

The fact that a person has been appointed or selected to a given group does not insure that one will experience this sense of belonging. It is frustrating when one participates in any group over an extended period of time without ever feeling that he belongs; however, this is especially true if the group is one to which an individual has a formal commitment, such as having been elected by one's peers or selected by one's employer. In a voluntary group setting, if one still lacks the feeling of belonging even after considerable exposure to the group, that individual will usually cease to be active in the group. Where a formal commitment exists, however, one customarily recognizes a responsiblity to persist and does so until the obligation ends. An individual cast in such a role will usually regard his interaction with the group as a drudgery, and this feeling of not belonging will generally be reflected in his minimal contributions to the group as well as in his observable lack of enthusiasm for its activities.

Having acknowledged the individual's need to belong, it would seem logical to assume that any member who is satisfied with his group would be content to blend into it and become one with it. Logic is not a good tool for evaluating the human element, however, for while a sense of belonging is desirable, the loss of one's identity is not.

When a member of a group feels that he is sacrificing his individuality to the group, he will usually begin to seek a better arrangement, and that will often entail breaking ties with the group. A study that illustrated the positive effect of identity on motivation showed that undergraduates had fewer errors on a dull lecture when told to listen as if they were "A students," than others not so motivated.[1]

STATUS AND ROLE PROBLEMS

Closely related to belonging, from the standpoint of the individual, are the dual problems of status and role. Even though a group member may feel that he does belong to the group, a question often remains in the member's mind as to what status he enjoys within the group. It is the other group members who determine the status to be accorded an individual, and by their actions also identify the member's standing with respect to such other qualities as power, leadership, and attractiveness.

A group member will experience status problems when the member feels that his actual worth is unrecognized by others or that others do not show him proper respect. Oftentimes, a distinction is made between status that is ascribed and status that is achieved. The former concerns that which is attributed to an individual through no merit or fault of his own, while the latter is based on an individual's success or failure. Regardless of which type is attributed to an individual, however, it is based on the perceptions of the group members. After the status hierarchy has been established, it influences both the flow and content of communication within a group. The low-status individual remains aware of his status because the group members will direct less communication to him than to those of higher status.[2]

As with status, the role one fills in a group is also determined by the other members of one's group. Ernest Bormann compares the interaction of members of a new work group to the "shakedown cruise" that a ship or aircraft must undergo prior to being put into regular service. Group members audition for preferred roles, and their success is determined by the response they get from the other group members.[3]

In many cases an individual will make several unsuccessful attempts for roles before gravitating to one that the other group members acknowledge as appropriate. Such a sequence of events partly explains how an individual who initially views himself as a likely leader for a given group may well find himself in a less visible role such as clarifier, or procedural specialist.

Problems may arise when an individual is unhappy with the role he ultimately fills, and feels he has been miscast by the other group members. Another source of problems may be the fact that while a group member is content with the role he fills, he may be unhappy with the status that the other group members have accorded it. The participant experiencing role or status problems will be of less value to the group of which he is a part.

The basic need for being liked also exerts influence on the manner in which an individual functions in a group. When one feels that his coworkers like and enjoy him, a member is more likely to remain attuned to the best interests of the other group members and enthusiastic toward the goals of the group.

PROBLEMS WITH THE INDIVIDUAL

Another problem often experienced by new members of a work group can be traced to an unawareness of group processes. In order for a member to be productive as well as satisfied with his group experience, he must develop awareness of all the forces that shape one's experience with a group and also those that shape the group as an entity. Such awareness will better equip the individual to operate within the group.

Through research it has been confirmed that the sheer amount of talking one does is influential in forming the impression others hold of that person.[4] Thus a group member, especially one who joins an already intact group, is often torn between becoming more vocal and risking a *faux pas* and maintaining a low profile and, hopefully, appearing knowledgeable. A study done in Norway suggests that one will be more effective by actively seeking information when faced with an unfamiliar task.[5] Another study showed that the less time it takes an individual to initially begin speaking, the greater his participation would be.[6] A person's unawareness or misperception of the expectations others harbor for him often results in tentativeness and hesitation on that person's part and, as a subsequent result, a negative impression of him by others.

The various sources of uncertainty surrounding a new group member will produce anxieties that are largely dysfunctional to the group effort. In one study, when members of a problem-solving group were exposed to high levels of anxiety, men were found to make more errors.[7] As with all of the problems that have been related to the individual, there are repercussions for the group also.

Another source of problems is found in the incongruent values held by many. Bales described it: ". . .individuals typically have multiple values, and often conflicting ones, so that single individuals are not singleminded in their desires.[8] When one member has conflicting values regarding his group's task, his value to the group will be limited.

PROBLEMS WITHIN THE GROUP

Although not completely separated from the problems within the individual, are the problems within the group. While they vary in scope, some of them are similar in principle.

The situation in which an individual interacts with a group is a complex one with a wide variety of forces in operation. Since, very often, the output of a group is somewhat remote to individual behavior the interaction among participants is the source of most satisfactions to the individual.[9] For that reason, the previously mentioned problems to which an individual may be prone are especially deleterious to the effective functioning of a group.

Although there is a general tendency to associate pressure to conform with formal organizations, such pressure is as influential in informal groups. Informal pressures are called *norms* and members of a group behave accordingly for the rewards or sanctions that will result from their behavior.

Norms may be either explicit or implied, and an individual's willingness to operate within norms is also determined by the group's attractiveness to the individual. The more attractive the group, the stronger is an individual's desire to remain in the group, and hence the greater his acceptance of rigid norms. It has also been shown that there is a relationship between a person's perceived acceptability as a group member and his willingness to conform to group norms. Those rated average in acceptability are most likely to conform, and those rated high less likely to do so.[10] Group norms are a major factor in determining the extent to which individuals will interact productively in a work group.

Just as the determination of one's identity is vital to the individual, so also is it important to the group. A group will act more purposefully and smoothly if its function is clearly defined and if there is general agreement as to its task. Ideally, such agreement will extend well beyond the subject of task and will also encompass procedural matters and questions of decision-making authority. What steps is the group to follow? What is its exact assignment? Is it to solve a problem or is its capacity one of fact finding? Mutual agreement between members on the answers to such questions will provide the group with a clearly defined identity.

Group Composition

As an ongoing group develops, a hierarchy of the members becomes more apparent and also more rigid. Such a hierarchy is shaped by the various roles of the members and the status attached to each role. In turn, the hierarchy helps shape the channels of communication, the degree of interdependence between certain members, and the subgroups that gradually evolve. During the process establishing the hierarchical system, the structure will be the source of problems and conflicts with which the group must cope.

The size of the group is also a significant determinant in a group's productivity and efficiency. As such it presents a problem for a group. Most authorities state that four to seven members is a good range of participants in a work group, and five is the number most often identified as the ideal. An increase in a group's size over seven, for example, is usually accompanied by less personal satisfaction to the participants who feel that they suffer a loss of personal influence. Therefore, allegiance to one's group wanes as that group grows. A.W. Wicker made this point in an interesting comparison of the contribution of time and energy by members of smaller churches as compared to larger churches.[11]

Just as excessive group growth debilitates the operation of a group, so also does undermanning. A group with too few participants may lack adequate resources to accomplish its goal. If members of a group feel they are undermanned, they may begin to consider their task futile or of little importance and may grow apathetic. While such factors as the requirements of the task and the available resources will, in part, dictate the optimum size of a group, the personalities and expectations of the participants must also be considered. Size affects motivation of participants as well as group productivity.

The failure to maintain equilibrium with a group represents another obstacle to effective functioning. As with all social systems, it is vital that a balance be maintained. As long as the task and social dimensions of a group are both receiving adequate attention, there will be equilibrium. When undue emphasis is placed on one dimension, however, an imbalance will result, and it will be accompanied by an increase in the dissatisfaction of members and in a corresponding decrease in the group's ability to function.

The presence of hidden agenda prevent many groups from reaching their full potential. Hidden agenda are comprised of the personal attitudes and emotions of an individual. Unlike the agenda for a meeting that is apparent to all of the participants, an individual's hidden agenda may remain unnoticed for any number of meetings. A person's hidden agenda may be his ulterior motives for having joined the group, or his desire to make another group member look bad. Such a hidden agenda may retard the progress of a group until it is given a full airing. Since such agenda often remain unverbalized and other members consequently remain oblivious to them, feelings of frustration may envelop the group and further limit its accomplishments as well as weaken its ties.

One of the most frequently mentioned advantages to using groups to accomplish goals or to solve problems is that of having access to a variety of points of view. Often, in the same breath, one will repeat the adage about two heads being better than one. A consequence of the growth of organizations is that the problem of coordinating an organization's affairs has become much more complex. The individual mind is therefore less and less adequate for processing all of the information needed to carry collaborative efforts forward.

Groupthink

Of all of the problems faced by any collection of individuals functioning as a group, one of the most threatening is the condition that prevails when critical thinking is hindered by the wish for concurrence. Irving Janis has termed this difficulty "groupthink" and it often results in highly knowledgeable and even experienced decision makers making decisions that turn out poorly. As an example, it is suggested that the year-after-year continuation of the Viet Nam ground war was a groupthink decision.[12]

When one recognizes that a decision made by a group is "bad," one is often right in suspecting that some aspect of the group process went awry. Very often the group members will realize in retrospect why the group met with failure. When groupthink prevails, however, that is not the case, for even after group members recognize a decision as being inferior, they would still most likely express satisfaction with the process. It is not a paradox that a "good" decision process may produce "bad" decisions, for these are separate and very different.

When group members are extremely satisfied with their interaction among the other group members, even though they may have misgivings about the group's accomplishment of the task, they are willing to trade off actual accomplishment for satisfaction. Recognizing that continued satisfaction depends on group cohesion, cohesion becomes all-important.

Groupthink does not occur instantaneously, but through gradual phases during which the group leader seduces the members by reserving positive feedback only for those suggestions that conform to his own way of thinking. Each time the Sales Manager responds coolly or indifferently to the suggestions of the new salesman, the probability that he will continue to offer such suggestions shrinks and the likelihood of groupthink grows. While a group leader seldom finds all of the suggestions of the members to be equally acceptable, by failing to reinforce the members who offer suggestions, the possibility of groupthink grows.

Symptoms

The following list of the symptoms of groupthink supports the hypothesis most likely forming in the reader's mind—getting along too well is a major contributor to groupthink.

1. An illusion of invulnerability, shared by most or all the members, which creates excessive optimism and encourages taking extreme risks;

2. Collective efforts to rationalize in order to discount warnings that might lead the members to reconsider their assumptions before they commit themselves to their past policy decisions;

3. An unquestioned belief in the group's inherent morality, inclining the members to ignore the ethical and moral consequences of their decisions;

4. Sterotyped views of enemy (or opposition) leaders as too evil to warrant genuine attempts to negotiate, or as too weak and stupid to counter whatever risky attempts are made to defeat their purposes;

5. Direct pressure on any member who expresses strong arguments against

any of the group's sterotypes, illusions, or commitments, making clear that this type of dissent is contrary to what is expected of all loyal members;

6. Self-censorship of deviation from the apparent group consensus, reflecting each member's inclination to minimize to himself the importance of his doubts and counterarguments;

7. A shared illusion of unanimity concerning judgments conforming to the majority view (partly resulting from self-censorship of deviations, augmented by the false assumption that silence means consent);

8. The emergence of self-appointed mindguards—members who protect the group from adverse information that might shatter their shared complacency about the effectiveness and morality of their decisions. [14]

Although the concept of groupthink sounds somewhat sinister and alien, it is but a natural progression of those forces that structure the larger society in which we live. It would be impossible to maintain a complex society without the individual's willingness to sacrifice his narrowly personal outlook in favor of a larger public interest; thus, the tendency toward groupthink has become a natural one.

Power

The presence of power within a group also contributes to groupthink. The greater the power differential is between members, the more likely it is that a move toward groupthink will ensue. Leaders who forget how subtly influential their behavior is likely to be, may find that the group members look for cues from them before taking a stand on an issue. Thus "yes-men" develop and people who may otherwise be quite strong find themselves surrendering to the pressure exerted by close proximity to power. Moral integrity and professional judgment are modified as those who have surrendered say "yes," when in circumstances less constraining they would have said "no."

Group Attraction

Understandably, groups and individuals often do not equally attract one another. Thus a group may want a member who is indifferent to it. Conversely, an individual may seek a greater role in a group than the members deem desirable. In either case, frustration results.

The Exceptional Participant

The exceptional participant is a major contributor to the ongoing problems faced by groups. Examples of this are the shy individual, and the member who is aggressive by contrast. Such members will typically be semi-isolates within a larger group and their relationship to that larger group may be complicated by the clique phenomenon. A clique is a small, close-knit group within a larger, less cohesive network of relationships. As a clique grows stronger, the exceptional participants become more isolated.

Shyness in a group, where it is a problem, suggests that someone is not contributing what he might. At one extreme, the individual and the group give up on one another; and the group problem is resolved by dissolving the group, or the group may discard the individual and continue with one fewer marginal member.

Another option is for the group to intensify its efforts to integrate their shy comrade more securely into the group. Here the group resolves its problem by broadening itself, concentrating on inclusiveness rather than exclusiveness.

The overly aggressive individual seeks to use the group for his own ends and the group, in its impatience, may discard him. Of course, the individual may take this step first. If what he wants is not readily available, perhaps he can find a more congenial environment elsewhere.

Here also the group could attempt to solve the problem by drawing the aggressive individual closer to the group. This requires extra effort from the members and is accomplished through broadening the group.

Cohesion

Cohesion means, most literally, clinging together. Members of cohesive groups are more trusting of one another than of others and the willingness of members to give of themselves to the group is characteristic of high cohesion.

It follows that groups would not function as well where people are joined together who do not strongly feel the need of being together. It is a fact of life that people who do not get along together cannot always steer clear of one another. Some groups, such as the P.T.A., must be open enough to attract an extremely diverse assortment of individuals. A work group that is necessarily comprised of members representing various areas of specialization is another example, as are civic associations. The committee is a format in which such operations must be advanced and individual differences often constitute a formidable barrier to such advancement.

While some groups must face the problem of securing greater cohesion, a group under the influence of groupthink is able to capitalize on that which is available. Both groups generate similar problems since they are at different stages of an identical process. The cohesive group has completed its selection process and has achieved a comfortable equilibrium. The group low in cohesion is trying to attain that level by pressuring members to conform.

Limitations of Conflict

In both cases there is a systematic limiting of conflict and, therefore, the benefits of differing outlooks are excluded.

Group leaders must not allow the human preference for pleasantness to become necessary for consensus. Participants must not be allowed nor encouraged to take refuge in a group rather than responsibility for its decisions.

Risky Shift

Just as one need not look beyond one's personal experience for examples of groupthink, one can also readily observe the phenomenon of the *risky shift*. Simply put, the risky shift is the tendency of groups to take riskier actions than individuals would do. Although it was first observed under laboratory conditions in which subjects were to imagine themselves in a hypothetical setting, it has since been repeated and observed in more realistic settings.

The risky shift was found in a set of survival problems administered to airmen at a survival training school,[15] as well as in actual group betting situations.[16] It was found to be operative in an even more naturalistic setting—one common to everyday experience—that of choosing the type of long distance phone call to make to a third person under various probabilities of successfully completing the call.[17] Thus the risky shift is more than a phenomenon found in only one setting. It may emerge in any type of group and, therefore, represents a universal threat to effective group functioning.

The decision-making group appears especially susceptible to the risky shift. Consider the implications of this for business decision making. Since decisions in business frequently require the selection of alternative courses of action—one product over another, or one contract over another—the decision will be riskier if made by a group. For major decisions, this would suggest that a change be made in the decision-making procedures used in most organizations.

The implications of the risky shift are especially forboding as they pertain to governmental situations, especially those that concern crisis situations, such as the determination of military strategy. In doing research on this subject Wallace, Kogan, and Bem concluded:

> It is presumed that the staff of experts, communicating about the meaning of incoming information, will thereby have a conservative, check-and-balance type of influence on one another. Yet, as our experience has demonstrated, conditions may be present which generate diffusion of responsibility and thereby increased risk taking.[18]

One would expect that, as a natural consequence of their positions, individuals in situations of crisis would experience extreme anxiety and stress. Lieblich's finding that the tendency to take risks increases under conditions of stress,[19] makes the risky shift effect even more worthy of attention.

The research findings on the risky shift should not be interpreted to mean that in all cases the group will reach a riskier decision than the individual. They do, however, indicate a reasonable supposition that this tendency exists. When one considers the potential consequences of certain decision making they should be taken into account.

Fostering creativity has always been a matter of concern in all types of organizations, and groups have frequently been viewed as tools for increasing it. The traditional and conservative nature of most organizations, however, can hurt creativity because of the apprehension of the group members concerning the consequences of their suggestions. The risky shift phenomenon has implications for creativity as creative behavior bears a close relationship to risk.

> One of the primary determinants of a climate conducive to creativity is the degree to which executives are willing to commit themselves to risky decisions or responses. To the extent that such a condition exists among personnel capable of creative responses, the conservative bias implicit in our traditional models of organization will tend to be counterbalanced.[20]

Problems concerning a lack of creativity might be alleviated by lessening the responsibility of the participants for the consequences of their creativity. One study revealed that individuals assigned to an advisory capacity generated riskier responses than those who were still held responsible for their own actions.[21] Thus the diffusion of responsibility that may lead to disastrous solutions in problem solving may increase creativity when that is viewed as desirable.

On the subject of bargaining and negotiation, research findings on the risky shift suggest that since groups engage in riskier negotiating behavior than individuals, they are more likely to produce bargaining sessions that result in deadlocks and withdrawals.[22]

Research on the risky shift also has implications for the creation of attitude change in groups. Not only has it been shown that the attitudes of group members will shift toward extremity in the direction of the dominant group opinion, but it appears that this attitude shifts may be lasting in its effects.[23]

Thus the phenomenon of the risky shift has implications for any type of group. It, along with the other group problems, always looms as a probable disruptive element.

NOMINAL GROUP TECHNIQUE

Now that problems inherent in small group communication have been presented, a question arises as to how to overcome or alleviate them. Richard Huseman suggests the *nominal group procedure* as a means of identifying problems and generating solutions. This method minimizes the disadvantages of the interacting group while enhancing its advantages.[24]

When using this procedure, the participants assemble in groups but are told not to speak to each other. Since the members are in a group setting but are not allowed to interact, the groups are nominal—in name only. Each person is then asked to write down what they view as the advantages and disadvantages of the proposition under consideration. Following the individual listing of the advantages and disadvantages, the group compiles two master lists, one of advantages and one of disadvantages, without allowing any duplicity of items.

The individuals then rank the advantages and the disadvantages separately on paper without consulting any other member of the group. In this way, priorities are established.

There are several characteristics of the nominal group technique that uniquely enable it to minimize many of the problems discussed in this chapter. These are:

1. Because no verbal interaction is allowed, there is less of an opportunity for powerful individuals to control the group. In many groups such a tendency results in important dimensions of the problem never emerging in the group because some individuals will only contribute an idea if it is well-developed and completely thought out.[25]

2. Since no verbal interaction is permitted while all dimensions of a problem are being identified there will be no evaluation made at this time and hence there will be a freer climate. When evaluation is done prematurely some dimensions of a problem may be ignored.

3. Since each individual must identify dimensions on his own, aspects which never would have been considered are more likely to be considered. In a normal interacting group some participants prefer to confine their participation to reacting to the ideas of others. Since this is not an option available to the participants of nominal groups, a greater number of ideas will probably be aired than would otherwise be true. In an interacting group the dimensions identified first are the most obvious ones and, quite often, the group does not progress beyond them. In the nominal group balanced participation insures a greater breadth of ideas.

The nominal group technique has the potential to reduce the magnitude of group problems because it embodies those characteristics that are essential for that goal to be accomplished. It provides for balanced participation. There is no evaluation during the process and hence the climate will not be a threatening one. The group is not allowed to dwell on the most obvious aspects and, therefore, a diversity of suggestions is usually forthcoming. Used in conjunction with the problem-solving steps, the nominal group technique will result in greater group productivity as well as more satisfaction to the participants.

SUMMARY

While there are many benefits to be derived from the efforts of groups, there are also problems inherent in the group situation that must be alleviated if the group is to be effective. These problems may reside within an individual member or within the group.

When a group member feels that others do not recognize his worth, or that the role he must fill is inappropriate for him, his dissatisfaction will be reflected in the degree of his involvement with the group. While such problems may appear to be limited to an individual, they affect the entire group and its operation.

The status hierarchy within the group, as well as the number of members, in part, determines productivity and efficiency. The hidden agenda of the members will also influence the progress of the group toward its goal.

Another significant problem that occurs in groups is that known as "groupthink"—when concurrence-seeking overrides critical thinking. The desire for power or for proximity to power contributes to the attractiveness of the group to the individual and helps explain why members relinquish their individuality rather than deviate from the group.

The phenomenon of the risky shift describes the tendency of groups to take riskier actions than individuals would do. This tendency to take risks comes about under conditions of stress. The nominal group technique is suggested for identifying problems and for generating solutions. Through its use, it is possible to minimize the disadvantages of the interacting group while enhancing its advantages.

QUESTIONS FOR DISCUSSION

1. What are the criteria that should determine whether a situation is appropriate for group or for individual problem solving?

2. The more attractive a group is to its members, the closer the members will adhere to its norms. What are the differences between a situation in which members rigidly adhere to group norms and the situation called groupthink?

3. What steps might a group leader take to alleviate problems of status or role that group members might experience?

4. What characteristics should one look for in a group in order to determine its susceptibility to groupthink?

5. In what ways can the members of a group that is low in cohesion attempt to break this cycle?

6. From your knowledge of history or of current events, describe a decision made by a group in which you suspect that the risky shift phenomenon was operating.

7. What approaches, other than the diffusion of responsibility, might foster creativity in groups?

ENDNOTES

1. John B. Cullen, "Social Identity and Motivation," *Psychological Reports*, 33(1) (August, 1973), p. 338.
2. Barry E. Collins and Harold Guetzkow, *A Social Psychology of Group Processes for Decision-Making* (New York: John Wiley, 1964), p. 172.
3. Ernest G. Bormann, *Discussion and Group Methods* (New York: Harper & Row, 1969), p. 262.
4. Donald P. Hayes and Leo Meltzer, "Interpersonal Judgments Based on Talkativeness: I. Fact or Artifact?", *Sociometry*, 35(4) (December, 1972), pp. 538–561.
5. Geir Kaufmann and Kjell Raaheim, "Effect of Inducing Activity Upon Performance in an Unfamiliar Task," *Psychological Reports*, 32 (1973), pp. 303–306.
6. Don Willard and Fred L. Strodtbeck, "Latency of Verbal Response and Participation in Small Groups," *Sociometry*, 35(1) (March, 1972), pp. 161–175.
7. Jerry Tomasini, "Effect of Peer-Induced Anxiety on a Problem-Solving Task," *Psychological Reports*, 33(2) (October, 1973), pp. 355–358.
8. Robert Freed Bales, *Personality and Interpersonal Behavior* (New York: Holt and Rinehart, 1970), p. 172.
9. Collins and Guetzkow, p. 209.

10. James E. Dittes and Harold H. Kelley, "Effects of Different Conditions of Acceptance Upon Conformity to Group Norms," *Journal of Abnormal and Social Psychology*, 53, pp. 100–107.
11. A. W. Wicker, "Size of Church Membership and Members' Support of Church Behavior Settings," *Journal of Personality and Social Psychology*, 13 (1969), pp. 278–288.
12. Irving L. Janis, *Victims of Groupthink: A Psychological Study of Foreign Policy Decisions and Fiascoes* (Boston: Houghton-Mifflin, 1972).
13. Janis, Chapter 5.
14. Janis, pp. 196–197.
15. R. C. Ziller, "Four Techniques of Group Decision Making Under Uncertainty," *Journal of Applied Psychology*, 41 (1957, pp. 384–388.
16. A. I. Teger and D. Pruitt, "Components of Group Risk Taking," Journal of *Experimental Social Psychology*, 3 (1967), pp. 189–205; N. Kogan and M. Zaleska, "Level of Risk Selected by Individuals and Groups When Deciding For Self and Others," proceedings of the 77th annual convention of the American Psychological Association (1969), 423–424; D. G. Marquis and H. J. Reitz, "Uncertainty and Risk Taking in Individual and Group Decisions," *Behavioral Science*, 14 (1969), pp. 281–288; J. Davis, H. Hoppe, and J. Hornseth, "Risk Taking: Task, Response Pattern and Grouping," *Organizational Behavior and Human Performance*, 3 (1968), pp. 124–142.
17. Neil Malamuth and Seymour Feshbach, "Risky Shift in a Naturalistic Setting," *Journal of Personality*, 40 (1972), pp. 38–49.
18. Michael Wallach, Nathan Kogan, and Daryl Bem, "Diffusion of Responsibility and Level of Risk Taking in Groups," *Journal of Abnormal and Social Psychology*, 68 (1964), p. 274.
19. Amia Lieblich, "Effects of Stress on Risk Taking," *Psychonomic Science*, 10 (1968), pp. 303–304.
20. Larry Cummings and Gary Mize, "Risk Taking and Organizational Creativity," *Personnel Administration*, 31 (1968), p. 41.
21. Larry Cummings and Gary Mize, "Risk Taking Propensity and Cognitive Set," *Journal of Social Psychology*, 79 (1969), pp. 277–278.
22. Arnold Kohn and John Kohls, "Determinants of Toughness in Dyadic Bargaining," *Sociometry*, 35 (1972), p. 307.
23. M. A. Wallach, N. Kogan, and D. J. Bem, "Group Influence on Individual Risk Taking," *Journal of Abnormal and Social Psychology*, 65 (1962), pp. 75–86.
24. Richard C. Huseman, "The Role of the Nominal Group in Small Group Communication," in *Readings in Interpersonal and Organizational Communication*, 2nd ed., eds. Richard C. Huseman, Cal M. Logue, and Dwight L. Freshley (Boston: Holbrook Press, 1973), pp. 411–420.
25. Donald W. Taylor, Paul C. Berry, and Clifford H. Block, "Does Group Participation When Using Brainstorming Facilitate or Inhibit Creative Thinking?" *Administrative Science Quarterly*, 3 (1958), pp. 23–47.

10

```
┌─────────────────────────────────────┐
│  ┌───────────────────────────────┐  │
│  │                               │  │
│  │      Interview Types          │  │
│  │                               │  │
│  └───────────────────────────────┘  │
└─────────────────────────────────────┘
```

The interview is a highly useful management tool. Just as it assists reporters in gathering information for news stories and physicians in obtaining medical information from patients, so also can the interview serve the manager in a variety of useful capacities by helping him hire, train, counsel, discipline, and even terminate employees. Whether he is a foreman attempting to counsel one of his line workers, a department store manager hiring new salesmen, or the owner of a small business trying to correct or discipline one of his employees, the supervisor who lacks training in the interview process is unquestionably at a severe disadvantage in performing critical functions associated with his job.

This chapter will focus on the several types of interviews a manager has at his disposal. While it takes more than reading to becoming a genuinely skilled interviewer, the information offered here will hopefully provide a basic understanding of the purposes and principles inherent in the various interview types. By building upon such fundamental knowledge through actual practice, a person may significantly improve his ability to deal with people in organizations—a primary requisite of effective management.

THE NATURE OF INTERVIEWING

Before considering the types of interviews, it is important to gain an appreciation for those unique defining characteristics that distinguish the interview from other forms of interpersonal communication. All interviews share these distinctive attributes, and examination of them will provide a useful frame of reference for the later discussion of interview types.

Purpose

The first distinguishing characteristic of an interview is that it involves *purposeful*, or *goal-directed* communication. Bingham and Moore, for example, indicate that an interview is "a conversation directed to a definite purpose other than satisfaction in the conversation itself."[1] Hence, like a small group, problem-solving conference, an interview possesses a specific purpose, whether it be the hiring of an accountant in an employment interview, the advising of a subordinate in a counseling interview, or the reprimanding of a worker in a correction interview.

Conversely, an interview is unlike informal social conversation in that its purpose is normally predetermined, explicit, and formal. The managers of a production and a sales department who pause in the hall to exchange ritualistic "Hello's" and "How-are-you's?" are not engaged in what is usually thought to be the interviewing process, even though their conversation might turn to some problem of planning or coordinating within the organization. Though it is obvious that one party to an informal conversation might have a predetermined and explicit purpose in mind, there is a formality about the purpose of an interview that helps distinguish it from mere social conversation.

Participants

An interview is often labelled "dyadic" (two-person) interaction. Consequently, when one visualizes himself involved in a performance-appraisal interview, for example, he generally thinks in terms of two individuals: the interviewer and the interviewee. Such is not always the case, however. A foreman conducting a grievance interview in a unionized plant will almost invariably be confronted by the presence of the shop steward, a union representative who accompanies the dissatisfied employee into the interview. Thus, the interview becomes a three-party interaction. The foreman can be sure that the shop steward will be present for any correction interviews, as well. It is not uncommon, moreover, for some employment interviews to involve more than one interviewer.[2]

Therefore, though an interview is normally considered to be a form of dyadic interaction, it should be remembered that it can involve more than just two persons.

Structure

A third defining characteristic of an interview is that it possesses a definite structure. Just as there are certain stages through which a problem-solving discussion should progress, so also are there specific stages that engender structure to the interview: 1) opening, 2) body, and 3) closing. Each of these stages will be treated in detail in the next chapter. Presently, it should be obvious that such structure readily distinguishes the interview from informal, social communication.

Context

Commonly associated with the concept of interviewing is the situation or environment in which the interview occurs. Because it is a kind of formal interaction, each type of interview is usually conceived as taking place in a certain location, be it a personnel director's office for an employment interview or the floor of a department store for a sales interview. Thus, like a problem-solving conference, with which one associates a certain context, and unlike informal social conversation, that is normally context-free, the interview characteristically occurs in a specified environment.

Exchange of Information

Though it is not a *distinguishing* characteristic of the interview process, the exchange of information is an important defining characteristic of the interview. As will be evidenced in the following chapter, the term "information" is not limited to mere facts; rather, it is intended to include also a variety of feelings, values, attitudes, and perceptions. Whatever information is exchanged, moreover, is usually relevant to the purposes of the interview or some subpurpose associated with a specific stage or aspect of the interview.

Given these defining characteristics, then, an interview may be conceived to be *goal-directed communicative behavior between or among two or more individuals who, through direct, structured interaction in a given environment, exchange information*. With this basic frame of reference established, it is appropriate to consider the various types of interviews.

THE EMPLOYMENT INTERVIEW

It has been estimated that at least 150 million employment (or selection) interviews occur in the United States each year.[3] Such figures confirm the fact that almost every one of us, at one time or another, has been subjected to the screening by another individual upon whose judgment rests the direction of our future.

Unfortunately, however, the figures belie one of the critical problems associated with the selection process. The employment interview is not necessarily as valid or reliable as its widespread use might indicate ("valid" here means that the interviewer is successful in hiring persons actually appropriate for specific jobs; "reliable" means that two different interviewers who interview the same applicant will render identical selection decisions). A number of empirical studies have demonstrated this.[4] There are also some rather chilling anecdotes concerning how some interviewers make their selection decisions that attest to the aura of suspicion which, for many experts, surrounds the practice of employment interviewing. One personnel director, for example, was not averse to basing his decision entirely upon the firmness of an applicant's handshake. A sales manager, when hiring, would place two chairs in his office, one next to his desk and the second several feet across the room. When the applicant entered the room, he was instructed merely to sit down. If he chose the chair nearest the interviewer, then he was considered to be an aggressive, outgoing individual, certainly material for the selling profession. If, however, he selected the chair farther away, then he was obviously shy and withdrawn—ill-equipped to become a successful salesman.

Such stories of gimmickry, together with actual research findings concerning the interview's validity and reliability, should make one aware that the selection interview is not an uncomplicated, perfunctory kind of process. Indeed, some researchers have spent years attempting to identify methods for improving this type of interview. Among their suggestions for enhancing its predictive capability are: 1) a high degree of structure (specific, preplanned, direct questions)[5]; 2) extensive and systematic interviewer training, coupled with feedback on actual selection decisions made[6]; and 3) the development of standards for a particular job, so that the interviewer might compare the applicant to those standards, rather than to other applicants.[7]

Thus, the employment interview is hardly a perfect management device. Fortunately, some organizations have taken steps to improve the quality of their employment interviewers. The interview is sometimes used to complement other selection devices, such as aptitude and skill tests, biographical questionnaires, and self-descriptive personality inventories. Used in this manner, it can be an invaluable tool.

Purposes

Many assume that the sole purpose of the employment interview is to screen applicants for a specific job. Such is hardly the case. The selection interview, in fact, has at least three major purposes. First is the screening process. The organization's ultimate purpose is to gain sufficient knowledge about the applicant in order to determine whether or not a job offer should be extended.

A second purpose, however, is to provide the applicant with needed information about the company and the position for which he is applying. Equally as burdensome as screening, is the interviewer's responsibility for shaping the expectations of the applicant with respect to both the job being considered and promotional opportunities. It is difficult to conceive that an individual applies for *a* job; rather, he is applying for a *number* of future jobs within the organization. The selection interview can be crucial in clarifying and realistically stating these future possibilities.

Third, the selection interview should establish or promote good will for the organization. Obviously, not all applicants for a particular job are hired. Those who are not invited to join the organization may disseminate either favorable or unfavorable information concerning a company based solely upon two factors: 1) their not being hired, and 2) their impressions gathered during the interview interaction. The interviewer who can overcome the first factor and create, in the interviewee, a favorable image for the organization, is successfully promoting positive word-of-mouth advertising for future job applicants, as well as for products and services his company offers.

Participants

Different organizations use varying patterns of selection interviews, depending upon the nature of the job and the extent to which the interview is being relied upon for decision purposes. In a large number of interviews, of course, there will be two participants—interviewer and interviewee. The interviewer may be a company's personnel director, the owner of a small store, or perhaps the assistant manager of a large department store.

If the position being offered is an important one, then the *serial interview*, a series of successive interviews conducted by different individuals, may be used. At the same time, a *panel interview*, one interview conducted simultaneously by several individuals, might be employed. On rare occasions, when an extremely large number of applicants has applied for a relatively unimportant job, the panel interview may be reversed, with one interviewer questioning a number of job applicants at the same time. Thus, the actual number of people involved in an employment interview may vary from a dyad to a small group.

Structure

The nature of general interview structure will be discussed in detail in the following chapter. There the three major stages of opening, body, and closing, together with the subsidiary preplanning and follow-up steps, will be depicted. In this chapter, the concept of structure will be treated with reference to the specific interview type under examination.

Preplanning

Adequate preplanning of a selection interview is extremely critical. It usually involves three basic considerations. First is the element of *time.* Some practitioners claim, for example, that a successful employment interview can take place in the space of nine minutes.[8] Others maintain that at least an hour is required in order to satisfy the purposes of this aspect of the selection process.[9] Thirty minutes to an hour is probably the average minimum amount of time that the interviewer should allow for each applicant. The prospective employee should also be given an appointment, since his perception of the company will be more favorable and secure if he is not required to sit and wait for two or three hours.

The second basic consideration in preplanning is the written *application.* If there is one, then the interviewer should initially become familiar with the applicant on paper. This will save wasting time asking questions that are already answered on the application. Next, he should check off items that are clear and self-explanatory. Likewise, marking items that are unclear or incomplete will draw the interviewer's attention to them during questioning. Marking other items on the application that are of special interest to the company and the job requirements will aid the interviewer in probing important areas.

A third and final consideration in preplanning is the interviewer's overall *approach* to the interaction. Decisions regarding approach invariably entail process and style issues, as will become evident later. Basically, however, the interviewer is concerned with how much control he will maintain over the interaction and, consequently, how patterned the exchange of information will become. Research findings here indicate that something between a moderately directive and a highly directive style is desirable;[10] therefore, the interviewer may well use a combination of open and closed questions and hypothetical questions. Simultaneously, however, he will tend to avoid yes-no questions, which place the burden of interaction on the interviewer, and leading questions, such as "Our firm has a compulsory insurance program. Do you think you'd be willing to join?"

Adequate preplanning of the interview, then, in terms of *time,* the *application,* and the interviewer's *approach,* should enhance the interviewer's chances of acquiring information conducive to a reliable selection decision.

Opening

One of the most critical periods during the actual employment interview is the opening. Here a primary function of the interviewer is the establishment of rapport. An optimum level of *rapport* should create the best atmosphere for exchanging the most useful information.

Additionally, it is the interviewer's responsibility to outline his perception of the *purposes* of the interview. Though screening and good will might well remain implicit purposes, it is sometimes helpful to explicitly inform an applicant that one purpose of the interview is to allow him to ask questions and acquire information about the company. Furthermore, a general statement of what the interviewer expects to be accomplished during the interview (e.g. format, types of information he is seeking) will foster a mutual understanding of purposes.

Body

The body of this type of interview is where an exchange of information concerning the applicant and the company take place. Generally, it is the interviewer's responsibility to control the interview and, hence, the flow of information.[11] The moderately structured style he adopts naturally enhances his capacity for satisfying each of the purposes of the selection interview. Control, however, does not mean that the interviewer assumes the burden of conversation. Though his function is to control the interview, he must allow the respondent a chance to participate in the discussion of topics being explored.

In terms of specific suggestions for the body of the employment interview, an interviewer may wish to consider the following: 1) outline clearly the requirements for the position, as it is likely that not all applicants will be completely familiar with a job's specifications; 2) explain (without overselling) the benefits and promotional possibilities associated with the position; 3) encourage questions from the applicant; 4) avoid prying needlessly into the applicant's personal life; and 5) avoid registering approval or disapproval of answers to questions.

Closing

Unfortunately, many selection interviews close with an interviewer's apologizing for the procedure he has used—perhaps even building false hopes concerning the job—so as to maintain rapport and keep the applicant on friendly terms.

Actually, the interviewer should remain noncomittal. He should refrain from making any unnecessary statements about the possibility of an affirmative selection decision, yet carefully explain the company's next procedure, whether it be further interviewing, testing, or outright hiring of the applicant. Likewise, the applicant should leave the interview satisfied that he has secured enough information to make his own decision about the company.

Follow-up

An important consideration after completion of the actual interview is the immediate rating of the applicant, since as much as fifty percent of the information obtained may be forgotten if the interviewer delays.[12] Many companies use applicant rating forms for post-interview reactions; if one is not available, the interviewer should write his own summary of his reactions to the respondent.

Context

Perhaps the most important characteristic of the interview setting is that it should be private. The presence of other applicants in the interview room, for example, would certainly affect the flow of useful information. In short, anyone not directly concerned with the hiring of the applicant should not be part of the interview environment.

Exchange of Information

The exchange of information during an actual employment interview focuses generally on two points. First, information is provided to the applicant about the company, its goals, policies and procedures, and the position in which the applicant is interested. This is one of the basic purposes of the interview.

Second is the critical information that will help the interviewer make his selection—information about the applicant. This may be divided into five categories: 1) *personal history,* including domestic and educational background; 2) *work history,* focusing upon previous jobs held by the applicant; 3) *personality traits,* showing temperament, basic disposition, aggressiveness, dogmatism, etc. (hypothetical questions are often useful in probing this category); 4) *interests,* including outside activities, hobbies, and personal values (e.g., money versus job satisfaction); and 5) *physical attributes*, if such attributes are important factors in filling a particular position.

In summary, an employment interviewer has no easy task. This discussion has merely touched on the complicated and demanding responsibilities of rendering decisions about people—decisions that affect not only their futures, but also the continued success of an organization. The necessity of careful screening and selection of job applicants obligates the interviewer to devote his efforts to improving his interviewing skills.

THE PERFORMANCE APPRAISAL INTERVIEW

A second major type of interview commonly conducted in organizations is the performance appraisal. Unfortunately, there are few employees who will not readily admit that one of the most trying and frustrating work experiences is that time each year (or more frequently) when they must sit down with their immediate supervisor to be evaluated. Interestingly enough, it seems that supervisors find the performance review experience as unpleasant as do the employees being evaluated.[13] George A. Reider, in fact, has described some performance appraisal interviews as "unadulterated fault-finding sessions, featuring exaggerated statements about behavior and stale, yet previously uncommunicated, bad news about performance."[14] Douglas McGregor, finally, viewed the conventional approach to appraisal as a situation where the manager is placed in the distressing role of "playing God," rendering and communicating sometimes awesome judgments about individuals who work for him.[15]

Like the employment interview, performance review possesses a certain unhealthy aura; however, in most organizations appraisal is as critical a feature as the selection process. Hence, management's goal is not to simply rid itself of this distasteful process, but rather to work toward making appraisal a productive and positive experience.

Purposes

A common misperception of performance appraisal is that it has a single purpose—to let the employee know what management thinks of his performance. Consequently, numerous companies use a simple rating chart that includes such factors as appearance, promptness, and cooperativeness. The supervisor merely rates the appraisee on a scale, for example, from one to ten for each category, computes a total rating, shows it (sometimes) to the employee, and concludes the interview. Obviously, such an abrupt and superficial format can enhance the apprehension many experience at appraisal time.

Performance review is actually a multipurposed process. N. R. F. Maier, for example, lists eight goals of appraisal, each of which is appropriate in different situations. These goals are:

1. To let the subordinate know where he stands;
2. To recognize good work by the subordinate;
3. To point out how the subordinate can improve;
4. To develop the subordinate in his present job;
5. To develop or train the subordinate for a higher level job;
6. To let the subordinate know how to may progress in the organization;
7. To serve as a record, showing how the subordinate fits into the organization;
8. To issue a formal warning to the subordinate that he must improve.[16]

Because some of the goals (e.g., 2 and 8) are contradictory, and since too many goals may easily render the appraisal process an overly complex one, one does not attempt to incorporate all eight goals into a single interview. However, by selecting appropriate goals from those suggested here, the supervisor may make performance appraisal more meaningful.

Participants

Unlike the serial or panel forms of the selection interview, the performance review normally involves only two individuals, the supervisor and the employee being evaluated.

Structure

Preplanning

Initially, the supervisor decides upon the specific purpose(s) for a particular performance appraisal session. If, for example, he knows the employee has a solid performance and the potential to be promoted, then quite possibly the goals of this interview might be 1, 2, and 5 from the list. Conversely, should the worker's performance be less than expected, then the interviewer might select goals 1, 3, and possibly 8.

Once the purposes have been established, the supervisor has the option of allowing the subordinate to participate in the interview preplanning. A common practice in some organizations, for example, is to encourage employees to complete rating forms on themselves and submit the ratings to their supervisors before the actual interview. As part of his preplanning, the supervisor compares his ratings of the employee with those self-ratings. Any major discrepancies between the two sets of ratings then become part of the interview agenda.

The time allotted for a performance appraisal interview will vary according to the interviewer's estimate of the quantity and nature of the information to be exchanged. A supervisor who allows ten to fifteen minutes for each appraisal may rest assured that his subordinates will perceive its importance as corresponding to the minimal time involved. Fifteen minutes may well be sufficient time for some performance reviews, but others might easily take an hour or more.

Opening

As in the selection interview, the opening of a performance appraisal should serve to establish rapport and reveal the specific purposes of the interview. The interviewer also normally explains the format he will follow, including what he expects of the subordinate.

Body

Perhaps the most important characteristic of the body of an appraisal interview is its emphasis on subordinate involvement, in terms of both isolating performance problems and establishing objectives for future performance. This will make the interview at least moderately nondirective, with the interviewer posing open ended questions (rather than going through a rating chart) and allowing the subordinate ample opportunity to make whatever contributions are necessary.

Closing

The interviewer's first responsibility in concluding the performance review is to summarize what has taken place, focusing for the most part on what he and the subordinate agree to be points for improvement and methods for attaining that improvement.

Second, the interviewer should make plans for a follow-up, if it is necessary. If, for example, the subordinate has suggested certain performance standards for himself, then the supervisor might indicate how and when these standards will be applied.

Follow-Up

The follow-up to performance appraisal involves the interviewer's carrying out any plans agreed upon during the actual interview. Should both participants have agreed, for example, that the supervisor will observe the employee's performance for a specified period of time, then such observation becomes an aspect of the follow-up process.

Some organizations will also provide a written means of follow-up, where the subordinate is given a summary of the interview, together with a copy of his specific evaluation.

Context

To be an effective appraisal, the interview should be kept private. In organizations where performance review is a regularly scheduled occurrence, employees are prone to discuss upcoming interviews for days and sometimes weeks in advance. Given the significant but highly personal nature of the interview, then, it is important that the interaction be as confidential as possible.

Exchange of Information

One expert has claimed that performance appraisal is a problem in communication—the establishment of a constructive communication relationship between supervisor and subordinate.[17] Hence, the interviewer should concentrate not only on the information that is communicated, but also on how he does it.

In terms of these two facets of "what" and "how," research on appraisal offers several substantive suggestions: 1) involving the subordinate—both in talking during the interview and in self-evaluation; 2) separating the salary and promotional considerations from the actual appraisal; 3) conducting more "coaching" sessions with emphasis on short-run, specific performance objectives; and 4) using a futuristic approach with the employee participating in establishing his own work standards.[18]

A number of experts have sought useful guidelines for appraisal interviewers. Charles Redding, for example, suggests that the supervisor should focus not on personalities, but rather on situations and behavior; avoid quibbling about such items as rules, policies, and rating charts; avoid lengthy discussions of past failures; avoid kind responses that "sweep problems under the rug;" and focus on the "larger picture," rather than on minute and trivial details.[19]

Performance appraisal, then, is a multipurposed, moderately nondirective form of interview. It can prove to be a highly useful management tool, but only when the supervisor can make the process more than a ritual and can reduce the severe amount of ego threat involved in helping employees perceive their performance problems and establish ways of alleviating them.

THE CORRECTION INTERVIEW

One of the most difficult types of interviews supervisory personnel are required to conduct is the correction interview. The threat of dismissal, which too often permeates the climate of such an interview, may readily engender a sense of extreme wariness in both participants. For this reason, the interaction may be reduced to blatant accusation and indictment.

Yet, the skilled interviewer realizes that correction involves more than simply reprimanding or disciplining a subordinate. Satisfactory use of correction procedures can benefit not only the employee and the company, but also the supervisor-subordinate relationship.

Purposes

Generally, correction is associated with two purposes: 1) identifying undesirable behavior; and 2) substituting that behavior with proper activity. "Undesirable behavior" has a number of meanings and may range from a simple discourteous remark to stealing money from a cash register.

The supervisor's burden is to determine the gravity of the subordinate's violation and deal with it accordingly. If, for example, pilfering is not an "immediate termination" act, then the supervisor must decide exactly what tactics he will use in correcting the subordinate. Charles Redding has provided a very useful continuum of five situations involving problems of subordinates, each point representing an interview type that is, appropriately, "least" to "most" punishing. These situations are:

1. *Counseling:* to be used when the subordinate apparently lacks simple insights that could help him perform his job satisfactorily.

2. *Coaching:* to be used for more serious and long-term lack of insight, in a situation potentially dangerous to the subordinate's continued employment.

3. *Correction:* to be used when there is an actual *violation* of some premise, though the violation is apparently a result of ignorance or accident.

4. *Reprimand:* to be used when there is a violation of some premise, but said violation does *not* appear to be a function of ignorance or accident.

5. *Termination (dismissal, firing):* to be used when those with the proper authority decide that the subordinate is no longer a useful member of the organization.[20]

Thus, the purposes of a correction interview may vary within a specified range according to the supervisor's perception of the situation. In any case, however, the general goal is to instigate proper behavior.

Participants

Normally, only two individuals participate in a correction interview: the supervisor and the offending subordinate. As was indicated earlier, however, a shop steward may also be present if the company is unionized. Presumably, his function is to protect the subordinate through use of rules for correction stipulated in the union contract. Some supervisors, though, view such a situation as approximating a "two-on-one-free-for-all." Stories are widespread concerning abusive language, thrown cups of coffee, and worse. Those stories should only caution the supervisor to do a thorough job of preplanning for the interview.

Structure

Preplanning

Preplanning is an enormously critical stage of the correction interview. Unless proper groundwork is laid, the supervisor's attempts to correct an employee could not only fail miserably, but also result in permanent damage to the superior-subordinate relationship.

A number of requirements typify adequate preplanning. First, the supervisor must obtain all the facts pertinent to the subordinate's alleged infraction. Unless he possesses the specific details of most violations, outright denial by the interviewee can quickly lead nowhere.

Second, the supervisor should evaluate his own role as interviewer. Objectivity is the important criterion, for if the supervisor fails to understand his own motives for scheduling the interview or is unprepared to listen to the subordinate's version of the situation, then the interview should not occur in the first place.

Formulating potential solutions or corrective measures is the third element in successful preplanning. Though it is more beneficial for the subordinate to aid in determining appropriate corrective action, the supervisor should nevertheless be prepared in the event that the subordinate is unwilling or unable to contribute.

Fourth, the supervisor should schedule the correction interview as soon as possible after he becomes aware of the alleged violation. None of his subordinates cares to hear stale news about past errors, especially when those errors have since been repeated through ignorance.

Finally, the supervisor should consider the subordinate himself. Lopez, for example, describes nine kinds of employees who are likely to evolve as respondents in correction interviews: 1) the incompetent, who is not qualified to do his job; 2) the reluctant, the undisciplined individual who is chronically tardy or absent; 3) the disgruntled, whose unhappiness in life is attributed to his associates; 4) the disabled, the old and/or physically incapable; 5) the troubled, whose problems outside his job affect his performance; 6) the financially embarrassed, whose monetary problems affect his work; 7) the domestically "untranquil," whose home life is unbearable; 8) the alcoholic; and 9) the emotionally ill.[21] Not every correction interviewee can, of course, be categorized into one of these types; however, the supervisor should remain aware of their existence.

Opening

As in the selection and performance appraisal interviews, the opening of a correction interview should be devoted to establishing rapport and delineating the purposes of the interview. Rapport establishment here, however, should be brief or even nonexistent. Too much "atmosphere" can easily detract from the supposed gravity of the situation. The interviewer might instead move directly into an explanation of the interview purposes.

Body

A moderately nondirective style is well suited to the correction interview. The general structure involves outlining the alleged violation, hearing the subordinate's version of the situation, and working with the subordinate toward a solution. As such, the interviewee should be allotted ample time and some degree of control over these topics.

Closing

Closing a correction interview involves summarizing carefully what has taken place and planning the follow-up. One form of follow-up which should be discussed here is whether the violation should be entered into the subordinate's record. If the supervisor decides to record the infraction, then the employee should be so informed.

Follow-up

Ascertaining the effectiveness of the corrective measures is the central focus of follow-up. The supervisor must assure himself, through observation or discussion with the subordinates and his associates, that the plan of corrective action is being carried out.

Context

Privacy is a critical factor in the correction interview. An employee should not be corrected in the presence of his peers; the location should be one where the interview can be confidential.

Exchange of Information

A number of guidelines are appropriate to the communication behavior of the correction interview participants. First, the supervisor should focus on behaviors rather than personalities, concentrating upon correcting rather than blaming. He should treat the violation as a problem rather than as a crime. Second, the interviewee should be allowed ample time to communicate his perception of the incident. Often, rather compelling reasons exist for an employee's errors. Third, the subordinate should be encouraged to provide his own ideas about whatever corrective measures are being considered. Finally, the supervisor must reinforce the subordinate's value to the organization, thereby reemphasizing both the interviewee's responsibility and his importance to the company.

In general, then, a correction interview is not the most pleasant occasion. If improperly conducted, results obtained may well be useless, if not detrimental to the subordinate, the supervisor, and the firm. Yet, a knowledgeable, interested supervisor can use the correction interview to motivate his subordinates toward better performance while maintaining the good quality of his relationship with them.

THE GRIEVANCE INTERVIEW

Not many individuals will deny the importance our society places upon the "right to appeal." The grievance interview is an integral part of the appeal system in industry and government. It may take many forms, ranging from a simple "beef" between subordinate and supervisor to a formal series of confrontations preceeded by the employee's filing of a written complaint.

Purposes

Two general purposes characterize the use of a grievance interview. First, it is intended to serve as an arena for hearing *and* acting upon employee complaints. A second, much more implicit purpose, involves providing a usefully directed outlet for subordinates' frustrations. As such, the interview serves as a kind of cathartic mechanism, as well as a formal feedback device.

Participants

Normally, participants in the grievance interview are a supervisor and subordinate. In unionized companies, however, the shop steward often becomes a third participant. Like the correction interview, then, the grievance interview can take on emotional, hostile, and aggressive tones, depending on the people involved.

Structure

Preplanning

There is actually not much a supervisor can do to plan for a grievance interview. Often he has very little or no information concerning the nature of the subordinate's complaint. Consequently, preplanning involves mental preparation, the key to which is the assumption that the subordinate is convinced that he is *right* and that the supervisor or organization is *wrong*.[22] Frequently, employees will not register complaints immediately after an incident or supposed injustice. Instead, they will allow their feelings of hostility and injury to fester for a period of time before the grievance interview is requested. For this reason, when they finally enter the formal grievance action, their mental set is so rigidly fixed against management's version of the situation that they are almost incapable of examining the grievance objectively. Unfortunately, their hostile or aggressive manner is communicated to and perhaps adopted by the supervisor, and the interview progresses nowhere. Hence, the supervisor should develop an objective state of mind for a grievance interview and be prepared, on occasion, for an outburst of emotion from the subordinate.

Opening

As in the correction interview, too much time spent establishing rapport can be detrimental to the effectiveness of the interview. Rapport is, indeed, important, but a specified period of time devoted to it at the beginning of the interview may well appear to the subordinate to be a stratagem. Rather, the interviewer may make the effort *during* the interview to maintain an atmosphere of objectivity and openness.

The interviewer should provide a very brief statement of the purpose of the interview, thereby acknowledging his intention to listen carefully and provide as satisfactory solution as is possible.

In short, then, the opening of a grievance interview is brief. It serves as a springboard for moving into the important issue—the employee's actual complaint.

Body

The grievance interview is highly nondirective. Roles may, in fact, seem reversed at times, with the interviewee controlling the quality and quantity of the flow of information. What the supervisor must remember in this situation, is that his primary function is that of listener and helper, rather than teacher or moralist.

Closing

Closing a grievance interview involves three things. First, the interviewer summarizes what has taken place, making especially sure that there is complete agreement on the solution chosen for the complaint. Second, the supervisor, without overdoing it, apologizes for whatever inconvenience the subordinate has experienced.[23] Finally, he provides a definite and precise outline for carrying out the solution.

Follow-up

Immediate and decisive follow-up is a requisite of effective grievance. The total impact of a grievance program can be severely hampered if the supervisor fails to act immediately upon the solution he and the subordinate have chosen.

Context

Like the other interview types discussed so far, the grievance interview should occur in a location conducive to privacy. Especially because of the potentially explosive nature of some grievances, the interviewer should assure that confidentiality will not be endangered.

Exchange of Information

The flow of information in a grievance situation will be similar to that in a correction interview. Again, the interaction should concern the immediate problem, and both participants should be involved in selecting its solution. Scapegoating and discussions of personalities are generally avoided. The supervisor should listen carefully, admit the error if one does, indeed, exist, and make no unusual or impractical promises to alleviate the problem.

OTHER INTERVIEW TYPES

The selection, performance appraisal, correction, and grievance interviews constitute four major types of interviews that the manager has at his disposal. A number of other types exist, most of which are not used as frequently or are not directly relevant to the management function. For those reasons, they will be discussed briefly.

Exit Interview

An exit interview is designed to gain information about voluntary employee turnover. In effect, the objectives of the exit interview are: 1) to determine why an employee has decided to leave the organization; 2) to provide an opportunity to demonstrate appreciation for the employee's work; and 3) to foster a positive attitude of good will between employee and organization. Accomplishing any one—much less all three—of these objectives in an exit interview is extremely difficult.

The interview itself is normally conducted by a personnel specialist at some point prior to the employee's final day at work. His last day on the job is not the most opportune time for the interview, as he may well be preoccupied with simply getting through that day.

An unfortunate fact about exit interviewing is that it seldom discloses the employee's real reasons for quitting his job.[24] A number of organizations have adopted a procedure that includes a mailed questionnaire and a follow-up interview with the departed employee several months after his leaving and after he has acquired a new job. Given less fear of reprisal by the company (e.g., a poor letter of recommendation), the individual is more likely to reveal his true reasons for quitting the job.

Counseling Interview

Unlike the interviews discussed previously, the purpose of the counseling interview is less specific. It is normally concerned with matters of a personal nature. Though the counseling interview may not always be within the realm of responsibility of a line manager, one survey of companies revealed that eighty-seven percent of them engaged in counseling activities of some type with their employees.[25]

Counseling activities that involve actual supervisors are neither highly personal nor volatile. Many supervisors, in fact, serve as almost daily sounding boards with regard to normal family or job-related problems. In such situations, the interviewer adopts a highly nondirective style, serving as a listener rather than as an advisor. The interviewee, in fact, assumes a good degree of control in the interview, and the interviewer's major function is to help identify causes for problems and potentially useful solutions.

Induction Interview

Induction interviews are used to help new employees become oriented to their jobs and their particular work environment. Generally, the interview is moderately directive, with the interviewer providing information about the interviewee's place in the organization, opportunities for advancement, the specific job, special policies and procedures, and any other item that seems relevant and immediately important or in which the new employee expresses an interest.

The induction interview rapidly becomes an integral part of the overall interview program. Many employees form long-lasting opinions and attitudes about their job and the organization during their first few days at work. The induction interview can readily facilitate the formation of positive, favorable perceptions of the organization and its goals.

Sales Interview

A final type of interview, but one that is not directly relevant to all management personnel, is the sales interview. Much of a wholesale or retail organization's public relations work is accomplished through the sales interview, and the process consequently requires a high degree of skill.

Though many perceive the sales interview to have only one purpose— closing sales—associated with it, contemporary approaches to salesmanship usually recommend a dual purpose of closing sales and maintaining customer satisfaction. As a result, the stereotype of the high-pressure, fast-talking salesman is fast becoming an unpleasant memory throughout the selling profession.

Because the salesman concentrates on this dual purpose, the thrust of his presentation normally focuses on pointing to benefits and satisfying needs. The sales interview is often fairly directive, characterized by the salesman's asking pertinent questions about a prospect's interest in such factors as quality, price, guarantee, and so on. By adapting his presentation to the customer's frame of reference, the salesman hopes to make a sale, yet assist the buyer in selecting merchandise that is suited to his particular needs.

SUMMARY

This chapter has provided a basic introduction to various types of interviews a manager has at his disposal. In every interview type, the manager is concerned with such factors as purposes, participants, structure, context, and the critical exchange of information. Though a specific description of every aspect of each kind of interview has been well beyond the present scope, the information offered here has hopefully provided a basic foundation upon which the manager may build his knowledge about interviewing and his interviewing skills.

QUESTIONS FOR DISCUSSION

1. What are some advantages of having a personnel specialist conduct all the employment interviews for a company? Disadvantages?

2. Some managers maintain that effective selection of employees can be accomplished solely through the use of psychological tests (e.g., aptitude and personality tests). How do you feel about this position? Why?

3. Members of organizations quite often treat performance appraisal as an almost meaningless process where supervisor sits down with subordinate, rates him on an appraisal chart, makes a few general comments, and terminates the interview. Often, the interaction lasts no longer than ten or fifteen minutes. Why do you suppose this practice occurs? What specific steps would you as a manager take to preclude this practice?

4. Besides falsely accusing some subordinate of wrongdoing, what do you think is the worst mistake you as a manager could make in preplanning and conducting a correction interview? How would you avoid it?

5. What do you think is the most critical stage in the grievance interview? Why?

ENDNOTES

1. W. Bingham and B. Moore, *How to Interview* 4th edition. (New York: Harper and Row, 1959), p. 3.
2. J. Willing, "The Round-Table Interview—A Method of Selecting Trainees," *Personnel* 39 (2), 1962, pp. 26–32.
3. L. Ulrick and D. Trumbo, "The Selection Interview Since 1949," *Psychological Bulletin* 43 (1965), p. 100.
4. See, for example, E.C. Mayfield, "The Selection Interview—A Reevaluation of Published Research," *Personnel Psychology* 17 (1964), pp. 239–260; E.E. Ghiselli, "The Validity of a Personnel Interview," *Personnel Psychology* 19 (1964), pp. 389–394; E.C. Webster, *Decision-Making in the Employment Interview* Montreal: Industrial Relations Centre, McGill University, 1964; and R.E. Carlson, *et al.* "Improvements in the Selection Interview," *Personnel Journal* 50 (April, 1971), pp. 268–275, 317.
5. R.E. Carlson, D.P. Schwab, and H.G. Henneman III, "Agreement Among Selection Interview Styles," *Journal of Industrial Psychology* V (1970), pp. 8–17.

6. Carlson, *et al.* "Improvements in the Selection Interview," p. 270.
7. *Ibid.*
8. Bernice Jennings, "How to Interview Someone Fast!" *Business Management* XXII (September, 1962), pp. 57–60.
9. R.M. Robbins. "A Training Memo on Interviewing," *Canadian Personnel and Industrial Relations Journal* XVI (1969), pp. 63–64.
10. Eugene C. Mayfield, "The Selection Interview—A Reevaluation of Published Research." *Personnel Psychology* XVII (1964), pp. 239–260.
11. See, for example, Arthur Kellner, "Sharpen Up Your Interview Approach," *Supervisory Management* V (February, 1960), pp. 2–8; "Interview Pointers," *Personnel Journal* XLVII (1968), pp. 809–810.
12. Felix N. Lopez. *Personnel Interviewing* (New York: McGraw-Hill, 1966).
13. L.W. Gruenfeld and P. Weissenberg, "Supervisory Characteristics and Attitudes Toward Performance Appraisal," *Personnel Psychology* XIX (1966), pp. 165–172.
14. George A. Reider, "Performance Review—A Mixed Bag," *Harvard Business Review* July-August, 1973, Vol. 51, pp. 62.
15. Douglas McGregor, "An Uneasy Look at Performance Appraisal," *Harvard Business Review* May-June, 1957, p. 90.
16. N.R.F. Maier. "Three Types of Appraisal Interviews," *Personnel* (March-April, 1968), pp. 27–40.
17. K.E. Richards, "Some New Insights into Performance Appraisal," *Personnel* 37 (1960), p. 28.
18. H.N. Meyer, E. Kay, and J.R. French, "Split Roles in Performance Appraisal," *Harvard Business Review* January-February, 1965, p. 129.
19. W. Charles Redding, "Performance-Appraisal Interview," Purdue University, 1972, p. 1 (Mimeographed).
20. W. Charles Redding, "Suggestions on Communication Behavior: Reprimand (Correction) Interview." Purdue University, 1971, pp. 1–2 (Mimeographed).
21. Lopez, *op. cit.*, pp. 192–195.
22. W. Charles Redding, "Suggestions on Communication Behavior: Receiving a Complaint." Purdue University, 1970, p. 1 (Mimeographed).
23. *Ibid.*, p. 2.
24. Wayne L. McNaughton, "Attitudes of Ex-employees at Intervals after Quitting," *Personnel Journal* 35 (1956), pp. 61–63.
25. H. Eilbert, "A Study of Current Counselling Practices in Industry," *The Journal of Business* XXXI (1958), pp. 28–37.

11

Interviewing: Structure, Processes, and Style*

Common to all the interview types discussed in the previous chapter are the concepts of *structure, processes,* and *style.* Structure, as was indicated earlier, refers simply to the overall organizational pattern characteristic of an interview; *processes* denotes certain "events" whose occurrence is contingent upon skills possessed by the interviewer; and *style* means the degree or level of patterning associated with the interaction between interviewer and interviewee.

As will become evident, these three concepts are all interrelated; that is, the nature of one will almost invariably affect the essential character of another. Yet, despite the fact that these concepts are so inextricably interwoven, examination of them separately will help isolate both their unique attributes and the sources of their mutual influence.

INTERVIEW STRUCTURE

The concept of structure, as it pertains to the interview, is roughly analogous to the concept of organizational structure proposed by many organizational

---

*This chapter was prepared especially for this text by Robert L. Wells, Department of Management, University of Georgia.

theorists. Daniel Katz and Robert L. Kahn, for example, indicate that "a social system is a structuring of events or happenings rather than of physical parts and it therefore has no structure apart from its functioning."[1] The interview may be viewed in much the same manner, for it, too, consists of a "structuring of events." In this case, however, it is a social *event* and is composed of three rather distinct stages: the opening, the body, and the closing. Encompassed in each of these stages, furthermore, is still another series of events appropriate to that stage. Thus, the interrelationship between interview structure and process should already be apparent. One will invariably influence the other.

Interview Purposes

Before moving into an examination of the three steps of interview structure, it is useful to explore several general purposes for which interviews are conducted. As is obvious from the previous chapter, different types of interviews possess specific purposes unique to them. The employment interview seeks to screen applicants, provide information about a job, and create good will; the sales interview emphasizes acquiring both affirmative buying decisions and customer satisfaction. Yet there are broader purposes to interviewing, purposes that are just as significant as those specific ones discussed earlier. As John Keltner observes, it is certainly important to become familiar with those specific purposes; however, "we need always to examine it [the interview] in relation to the larger purpose for which it serves some function."[2]

Given this distinction, the broader purposes served by the interview include: 1) getting and/or giving information; 2) discovering new information; 3) problem solving and decision making; and 4) bringing about changes in attitudes and behavior.[3] Few interview situations, of course, would be designed to accomplish all four of these purposes, but most interviews would necessarily focus on one or more of them.

Getting and/or Giving Information

It should be remembered that the term "information" is used here in the general sense of including facts, opinions, attitudes, perceptions, observations, and feelings. Such information may be transferred either verbally or nonverbally. The interviewee who fidgets in his chair while explaining to the selection interviewer his reasons for holding three different jobs in the past six months may well be communicating information, so long as his activity is perceived and decoded in some manner by the interviewer.

This first broad purpose is plainly relevant to all types of interviews, as a central component of the earlier presented definition of interviewing was an "exchange of information." The correction interviewer seeks reasons for a subordinate's error, the induction interviewer intentionally or unintentionally communicates organizational values to a new employee, and the job applicant attempts to emphasize facts that he thinks will enhance his chances of being selected for a particular company position.

Discovering New Information

Closely related to the first general purpose of interviewing is the acquisition of new or previously uncategorized information. This second purpose differs from the simple getting or giving of information in that it serves a distinct segment of the interviewing profession. Among those to whom this purpose is important are criminal and credit investigators, social workers, market analysts, social scientists, writers, consultants, and opinion pollsters.

Quite often, because the focus of the interview is on discovering new information, such an interview is categorized as "research." Interviewing bank tellers to obtain information (attitudes and opinions) about a new service being offered to customers or interviewing shoppers concerning their preferences among brands of breakfast cereal are examples of interviews to discover new information.

Problem Solving and Decision Making

Interviews that facilitate problem solving and decision making constitute a large collection of interview types. The employment, performance appraisal, grievance, counseling, correction, and sales interviews may be classified according to this purpose. Holm describes the unique nature of this interview purpose:

> Problem solving is creative in the sense that the outcome develops from the interaction of the two participants in a way which neither had specifically forseen nor planned.[4]

Thus, the salesman adapts his presentation to the prospect's particular needs, the correction interviewer strives for a solution that alleviates the problem but is acceptable to both the company and the employee being disciplined, and the performance appraisal interviewer seeks to establish future work standards that the subordinate possesses the potential to meet.

Bringing about Changes in Attitude and Behavior

This fourth broad purpose of interviewing is perhaps the most difficult to achieve. One important reason for the challenge implicit in changing attitudes and behavior is that behavior is inherently goal-directed. Hence, the manager who wants to effect a successful and lasting change in the behavior of his subordinates must not only identify the appropriate goals, but also ensure that these goals are substituted for less suitable ones. The sales manager, for example, whose commissioned salesmen make unusual and impractical promises to customers simply because such behavior improves their chances of closing more sales, may often discover himself in a correction interview situation, where it is his obligation to point to the second purpose of a sales interview—guaranteeing customer satisfaction. Having identified this additional goal, the sales manager must then be assured that the two goals of closing sales and satisfying customers are substituted for the single goal of closing as many sales as possible.

The second difficulty associated with changing attitudes and behavior, however, is ascertaining if and when the proper change has occurred. The sales manager in the previous example may, of course, watch for a decrease in customer complaints about unkept promises. Yet, in many situations where the most subtle change may be a significant accomplishment, such a change may be extremely difficult to identify.

It should be obvious that changing attitudes and behavior are of critical importance in both the correction and the grievance interviews. In the latter, the responsibility for change may well be incumbent on the supervisor rather than the subordinate. Changes of attitudes and behaviors are relevant as well to performance appraisal and sales interviews. The difficulty in accomplishing such changes should implicitly demonstrate that only the most skilled interviewers should attempt them.

These four broad purposes of interviewing are not usually independent of one another. To some extent an "ordering of purposes" will provide some structure in the interview. Getting information as to *why* an employee constantly commits certain errors might well precede attempts to change the employee's error-prone behavior. Additionally, the purpose or purposes to be achieved in the interview may often influence the rapidity of transition from the opening to the body of an interview. Finally, purpose may also affect the total length of the interview, as well as the amount of time spent in the body and closing.

With these four purposes in mind, the actual structure of an interview will be discussed. It will be remembered that three distinct stages comprise the total interview: the *opening,* the *body,* and the *close.* Fourth and fifth "stages," moreover, are *preplanning* and *follow-up.* The following sections will examine each of these in detail.

Preplanning

Though not actually a part of the interview as it is normally conceived, preplanning is so critical to the successful interview that it cannot be overlooked. Though it is also obvious that the best made plans frequently go awry, consistently better results tend to be a by-product of effectively preplanning the interview.

The preplanning phase normally includes the following events:

1. Establishing the purpose or purposes to be achieved;
2. Collecting preliminary information on the subject and/or the interviewee;
3. Determining the amount of structure to impose;
4. Identifying, and perhaps recording, the strategic questions or responses that seem to possess potential for fulfilling the interview purpose;
5. Determining the time, place, and length of time for the interview;
6. Communicating the purpose, time, place, and length of time to the interviewee; and
7. Personal preparation (e.g., knowing where one stands on crucial issues, examining personal motives and attitudes, and predicting points of conflict and resistance.

Obviously, the extent of preplanning will be influenced by such factors as the purpose(s) to be achieved, the best climate for the interview, the gravity of the subject matter, and the nature and extent of previous relationships with the interviewee. Additionally, the amount of time spent with each of the steps listed may be partially determined by the type of interview to be conducted. While the employment interviewer normally has time to review an interviewee's written application before the interview, department store salesmen know very little about most of their prospects until the interview is well under way.

In a number of interview situations, moreover, substantial headway towards "communicative readiness" may be gained if the interviewee participates in establishing the time and place for the interview. In other situations, finally, the true purpose of the interview may not be made explicit prior to the interview. An interview between a superior and a subordinate for the supposed purpose of discussing promotional opportunities may be an attempt by the supervisor to help the subordinate identify his own shortcomings.

Adequate preplanning usually requires considerable time and effort. The additional structure it provides during the actual interview, however, will help attain the goal of the interview.

The Opening

The opening of the interview represents the initial face-to-face contact between interviewer and interviewee. If the interviewer provides a proper opening, then the interviewee can be induced both physically and psychologically to participate actively in the meeting.

Two general purposes are normally associated with the opening of an interview: 1) establishing rapport; and 2) explaining the interview purpose. Though the concept of rapport will be treated in detail in the discussion of interview process, it should be observed here that its primary function is to establish an atmosphere conducive to an interviewer-interviewee relationship. There should be an unconstrained dialogue. Social amenities are perhaps the most common type of communication occurring during rapport establishment; however, as will later become evident, prolonged unrelated conversation is sometimes unadvisable.

The second primary responsibility of the interviewer during the opening is to provide a statement of purpose. If the interviewer or the organization he represents is unfamiliar to the interviewee, several introductory comments may be required to fully explain the purpose of the interview. Charles Stewart and William Cash have identified a number of "attention getting" or "orientation" statements they call *starters*. These include:

1. Summarizing the problem;
2. Explaining how the problem was discovered;
3. Mentioning an incentive or reward for taking part in the interview;
4. Requesting advice or assistance;
5. Referring, if known, to the interviewee's position on an issue;
6. Referring to the person who suggested the interview;
7. Referring to the organization one represents; and
8. Requesting a specified period of time.[5]

In addition to merely stating the purpose, it is sometimes useful to involve the interviewee by asking for his understanding of the purpose. A participatory attitude may be encouraged by some type of personal involvement. Examples of such a strategy include "I feel you have some insight into the problem, and I thought you could help me"; "I knew you had an interest in this decision, and I didn't want to move on it without consulting you first"; and "Jack, you seem to be able to objectively evaluate new programs. . . .I wonder if you see any hitches in getting things started in Region 4?"

While often the shortest phase, the opening of the interview accomplishes a great deal. Relations are initiated and the overall climate for interaction is established. Purposes are identified and clarified. Failing to achieve what is required during this phase of the interview will greatly endanger the result of the interview.

Body

This second stage of the actual interview usually requires the majority of whatever time is allotted for the interview. It is not uncommon, for example, that in a fifteen-minute interview the opening and closing last approximately one minute each, with the body consuming the remaining time. Especially during this phase of the interview, the interviewer uses virtually every communication skill he possesses to both secure and impart relevant information. He asks questions, responds to questions, guides, supports, and provides feedback.

The experienced and effective interviewer pursues his pre-established plan by regulating the quantity and quality of the dialogue. He constantly reinforces and motivates the interviewee by listening carefully to what is said and uses this information to generate new or additional information. Since the interviewer normally controls the interview, he determines when the purpose has been achieved and is responsible for then terminating the interview.

A number of processes characterize the interviewer's behavior during the body of an interview. Several of them will be examined.

Closing

Interviews differ as to the ease of closing. Where there is a previously established time limit, closing may be a very simple matter. In situations where the incentive or reward for participating in the interview is perceived to be low or even nonexistent, the closing may be very perfunctory. In other situations, closing or terminating the interview may be one of the most difficult tasks. Commissioned salesmen often experience difficulty when closing sales interviews. Unfortunately, some of them are instructed to attempt to close every two or three minutes during the interview. On some occasions the interviewee may have just begun to participate fully; he may enjoy hearing himself talk; or he may enjoy the status he associates with talking with the boss for an extended period of time.

Whether simple or difficult, the closing usually includes a summary of the relevant points or decisions reached during the interview. Where decisions were made and subsequent activities are necessary, the interviewer may establish priorities and allocate these activities. Often, a follow-up interview will be scheduled if it is necessary to conduct unfinished business.

In almost all cases, whether or not the interview was productive, it is appropriate to express appreciation during the closing. Abruptness and impatience during a prolonged closing are generally avoided by the experienced interviewer.

In short, then, the closing provides opportunity for: 1) summary; 2) arrangement for follow-up, if necessary; and 3) expression of appreciation.

Follow-up

Like preplanning, the follow-up is not a part of the actual interview; however, a follow-up is occasionally important in order to ensure maximum benefit from the interview. It may be required for any of a number of reasons, and may take any one of several forms. The information that was exchanged during the interview may at times be important enough to preserve in written form. In this case, the follow-up may be a letter or a memorandum. In situations where critical decisions were reached, the actions required to carry out those decisions may be enumerated in written form. A telephone call is sometimes used to verify decisions and to engender impetus to subsequent actions that may have been initiated during the interview. It is standard practice among many salesmen, for example, to arrange for a follow-up visit with the customer to promote satisfaction and perhaps generate future sales.

Viewing the interview from preplanning to follow-up confirms the fact that it is not an isolated random event. Like its analogue, the social system, the interview as a social event consists of a specific structure. Within that structure, furthermore, are certain processes, each of which contributes directly to the structural composition of a particular interview. The interview should therefore be conceived as a major mode of communication that is not a static entity, but rather a dynamic structure of processes.

INTERVIEW PROCESSES

Interview *processes* were earlier described as certain "events" whose occurrence is contingent on the skills of the interviewer. Each of the processes to be discussed in this section is generic to every type of interview. Whether it serves a useful function, or even takes place within the interview structure depends, as will become evident, upon the skills of the interviewer. Such skills are not uniquely different from skills required in other communication situations, but they are all particularly critical to the effective interview.

Both participants in any interview obviously share the responsibility for employing their communicative skills as ably as possible. Unfortunately, the interviewee is not always as highly motivated to participate as is the interviewer. Consequently, the skill requirements for the interviewer are increased. Yet whether or not the interviewee is motivated, the interviewer possesses the burden of responsibility for ensuring that certain processes occur; and their occurrence depends extensively upon his skill.

The general effectiveness of any interview, therefore, will be a function in part of the following processes:

1. establishing rapport
2. asking questions
3. observing and listening
4. providing support
5. providing periodic internal summaries
6. responding to questions

A skilled interviewer will understand and successfully use these processes.

Establishing Rapport

As was indicated earlier, one of the functions of the interview opening is the establishment of rapport. To the untrained interviewer, rapport may connote the offering of a cigarette, the vigorous shake of a hand, a blissful smile, or some other technique to demonstrate interest and good will. To the trained, it is obviously a more complex and demanding process.

The function of rapport, it will be remembered, is to establish an atmosphere conducive to an interviewer-interviewee relationship that is characterized by an unconstrained dialogue. Rapport does not, according to Wilbert Beveridge, mean "chumminess," since the role relationship between interviewer and interviewee often demands the maintenance of a certain social distance.[6] Rather, rapport denotes:

> ...a confident and permissive relationship between interviewer and respondent (interviewee)...; the respondent is able to feel that the interviewer is genuinely interested in him as a person and will listen willingly to all he wants to tell him.[7]

Though the establishment of rapport is certainly essential, too much emphasis upon the atmosphere characterizing an interview is as perilous as too little:

> The interviewer may spend more effort on cultivating friendship than one eliciting information and may evaluate the interview in terms of the quality of the social relationship rather than the quality of the information obtained.[8]

Actually, the amount of time devoted to establishing rapport can be related directly to two factors: 1) the purpose of the interview; and 2) the relationship between interviewer and interviewee. It is quite possible, for example, that an overly friendly atmosphere in a correction interview may well affect the interviewee's perception of the gravity of the situation. Too little rapport in a counseling interview may render the interviewee uneasy and hence adversely affect how he receives the information. Then, too, time spent establishing rapport between two participants who are close friends can sometimes result in a stilted, awkward atmosphere, thereby hampering the flow of information. Obviously, there are no universal rules for rapport establishment. Rather, guidelines depend on the situation and participants.

The trained interviewer, draws from four sources when creating an atmosphere of rapport. The first of these is his own *personality*. A number of terms describe the interviewer who effectively establishes rapport. Among them are courtesy, interest, warmth, sincerity, and complete attention.[9] Negative qualities include pretentiousness, impersonality, punitiveness, and deference.[10] The interviewer's demeanor contributes to the level of rapport.

A second means of establishing rapport is *extraneous conversation*, or what Harold Zelko and Frank Dance have labeled "common-ground remarks."[11] The utilization of small talk about mutual interests can often benefit both interviewer and interviewee.

Simple courtesies constitute another way to bring about rapport. Such courtesies extend beyond the level of offering cigarettes or coffee and include such behaviors as thanking the interviewee for participating in the interview and ensuring that the interviewee is comfortable. Even explaining the need for such common place items as pencils, notebooks, or a tape recorder may enhance rapport.[12]

The fourth and final method involves *demonstration of respect and admiration.* A compliment or statement of agreement with or interest in one of the interviewee's beliefs, for example, may serve to create the proper atmosphere.

In general, therefore, rapport establishment is often, but not always, essential during the initial stages of the interview; the amount of time devoted to rapport will vary with the situation and participants; and the interviewer (as well as interviewee) can draw upon a number of sources to aid in developing an appropriate climate. Finally, it should be remembered that rapport *maintenance* is a continuous process, to be fostered throughout the course of the interview.

Asking Questions

Generally, the interviewer leads and controls the interview by asking a variety of questions. The skills involved in questioning may well be the most important ones required of the interviewer. The types of questions (e.g., open versus closed), as well as the manner in which they are asked, control both the quantity and quality of information provided by the interviewee. Questioning is normally the process by which one moves from the opening to the body of the interview, and the process usually predominates in the body of the interview. This section will focus on certain types of questions available to the interviewer. These include: 1) direct questions; 2) open questions; 3) probes; 4) mirror questions; 5) leading questions; 6) loaded questions; and 7) hypothetical questions.

Direct Questions

Direct, or closed questions constitute one of two major categories of questions. As will become apparent, some of the other question types described here (e.g., probes, leading questions) may occasionally take direct form.

Direct questions usually require a very brief and limited response. There exist three basic types of direct questions:

1. *Yes-No Type:* any question which can be answered yes or no. Examples: Do you have a college degree? Were you at work yesterday?

2. *Selection-Type* (also called Multiple Choice): any question in which the respondent is required to select one from two or more responses offered. Examples: Is your work a) highly satisfying, b) satisfying, c) dissatisfying, d) highly dissatisfying? Were you born in the a) North, b) South, c) East, d) West?

3. *Identification-Type:* any question requiring the interviewee to provide a specific, identifying response. Examples: Where were you born? Where did you last work?

Obviously, the direct question is best suited for acquiring factual information; however, use of the selection-type question may readily elicit limited information concerning attitudes, feelings, opinions, and perceptions.

Open Questions This type of question constitutes the second major category of questions. An open question is one that usually requires more than a few words for an adequate response. Such a question is generally very broad and allows the interviewee to decide upon the amount and kind of information he wants to provide.[13] The following are examples of open questions:

1. Would you describe the last job you had?
2. Tell me about your social life in college.
3. What type of company do you think you'd like to work for?

Probes Probes are normally used in conjunction with open questions to focus attention on particular information provided by the interviewee. They may be open or closed. For example, an interviewer probing responses to Question 2 in the preceeding list might employ one or all of the following:

1. How would you say you allocated your free time among sports, dating, and political activities?
2. What advantages do you think there were in belonging to a fraternity?
3. How many of your college friends do you still see on a regular basis?

A probe, then, is a question that is built upon an interviewee's response to a previous question. It's purpose is to elicit further information concerning that response.

Mirror Questions

The mirror question, much like the probe, is intended to acquire further information concerning an interviewee's response. It is used when the interviewer feels that the response was superficial or incomplete. It may also be employed merely to elicit further information about a specific response. The following examples illustrate the use of mirror questions:

INTERVIEWER	Where were you when the machine broke down?
INTERVIEWEE	Well, I was down on the floor, and Jack came up. . .
INTERVIEWER	Jack?
INTERVIEWEE	Yea, Jack Roberts. . .you know, out of quality control.

INTERVIEWER	I really can't understand why you've been out so much, Jim. You've always been pretty consistent about being at work.
INTERVIEWEE	Yes, but lately. . .well, the wife and I have been having some trouble, I guess, and. . .
INTERVIEWER	Trouble?

Quite often, the experienced interviewer will simply register an interviewee's response and pursue it later in the interview, especially if pursuing the issue immediately might result in substantial threat to the interviewee. In the second example above, the interviewer moved directly into the "trouble" between the interviewee and his wife. Often, however, the emotional nature of an issue dictates letting it pass for the moment and returning to it later.

Leading Questions

As their name implies, leading questions are structured so as to guide the interviewee to a specific response. A classic example is the courtroom lawyer who asks a witness, "Isn't it true, Mrs. Anderson, that on the night of the murder. . ." The clause "Isn't it true" implicitly provides the respondent with the appropriate answer.

Leading questions are perhaps most useful to interviewers in organizational settings who desire merely to validate factual information. Questions such as "You have a B. S. degree. Right?" and "You've talked to your supervisor about this, haven't you?" are entirely appropriate, so long as they don't present an opportunity for a biased response. Should the socially *desirable* response to the second question above be "yes," then the interviewer should not have structured the question in such a way as to render it a leading one.

Loaded Questions

The major characteristic of loaded questions is that they inherently produce some degree of ego threat. Although they are useful to highly skilled interviewers to create stress and explore emotional issues, the fledgling interviewer should avoid them. Because they focus on attitudes and feelings rather than on factual information, the level of interviewee resistance may increase dramatically if such questions are not well-handled.

Examples of loaded questions include: "What's your feeling about these asinine strikes the unions are causing?" and "What makes you think you have the ability to do your supervisor's job better than he can?" Yet even the most innocuous sounding question may, in fact, be unintentionally loaded, especially if the interviewee does not want to hear it. Consider the situation where an employment interviewer inadvertently asks an applicant with no college training, "How many accounting courses did you have in college?"

Hypothetical Questions

Questions of this final type are perhaps most useful to the employment interview. The "what if you were" or "let's assume" approach may well serve to relax the interviewee and enable him to fully consider all aspects of a given question. The interviewer might ask, for example, "If you were the project manager, what steps would you take now to get back on schedule?" Or he might say, "Let's assume the law passes and goes into effect on July 1. How would it affect your company?" "If you were to take the new position, what objectives would you establish initially?" is yet another example.

The hypothetical question, when not actually hypothetical at all, may have the same negative impact as a loaded question. Resentment and suspicion frequently result, and such a climate is likely to pervade the remainder of the interview.

Though they are representative of the most commonly employed questions, these seven types of questions do not exhaust the broad range of questions available to the interviewer. If an interviewee's response is incomplete, for example, the interviewer may simply request further information or restate the question in another way. Which type of questions an interviewer chooses to employ, as will be demonstrated later, has a significant impact on the quantity and quality of information exchanged during the interview.

Finally, regardless of the specific type of question posed, the interviewer must phrase it in words that are understandable to the interviewer. Such questions should also be germane to the purpose of the interview as it was communicated to the interviewee. They should be structured so that only one answer is required and should reflect clear thinking on the part of the interviewer.

Observing and Listening

The third critical process on which the skilled interviewer concentrates involves careful observation of the interviewee's physical behavior and attentive listening to what he says. What the interviewer should remember is that communication is *both* verbal and nonverbal.

In terms of the verbal mode, good listening requires more than simply perceiving and decoding the words employed by the interviewee. Such listening involves also making qualified judgments about the interviewee that will aid the interviewer in understanding his frame of reference. Alfred Benjamin, for example, lists eight factors the interviewer should attend to:

1. How the interviewee thinks and feels about himself; how he perceives himself.
2. What he thinks and feels about others in his world, especially significant others; what he thinks and feels about people in general.
3. How he perceives others relating to him; how in his eyes others think and feel about him, especially significant people in his life.
4. How he perceives the material that he, the interviewer, or both wish to discuss; what he thinks and how he feels about what is involved.
5. What his ambitions, aspirations, and goals are.
6. What defense mechanisms he employs.
7. What coping mechanisms he uses or may be able to use.
8. What values he holds; what his philosophy of life is.[14]

What the interviewer focuses upon, therefore, are not only the overt verbal responses of the respondent, but also information he can deduce from the covert aspects of an interviewee's answers to questions.

Such an approach will help the interviewer satisfy a basic requirement of good listening: *empathy.* Simply defined, empathy is the ability to "put yourself in someone else's shoes," to view the world from their perspective. Many communication problems arise during interviews, especially grievance and correction situations, simply because the interviewer is unable to comprehend *and* understand the interviewee's frame of reference. Empathy does not, of course, imply sympathizing with another's viewpoint. Yet, an objective view of the problems or issues from the interviewee's perspective will aid the interviewer in understanding reasons for the respondent's behavior or attitude.

The nonverbal mode of communication has been identified in recent years as an integral aspect of the total interpersonal communication process. Mark Knapp, for example, has described seven dimensions of nonverbal communication. These include: 1) kinetic behavior or body motion; 2) physical characteristics, such as height, weight, and general attractiveness; 3) touching behavior; 4) paralanguage, or vocal cues that accompany verbal utterance; 5) proxemics, or personal space; 6) artifacts, such as clothes, eye glasses, perfume, and make up; and 7) environmental factors, such as furniture, lighting, temperature, and room noises.[15]

Concerning these seven factors, the interviewer should be cognizant of two processes. First, he decodes nonverbal messages from the respondent unintentionally—almost unconsciously. Invariably, he makes judgments about the interviewee on the bases of his height, weight, clothes, the sound of his voice, and how near or far away he sits during the interview. At the very least, the interviewer is obligated to become aware of such nonverbal factors in his perception of the interviewee.

Second, the interviewer does conscious, intentional decoding of certain factors and assigns meanings. The example in the last chapter of the employment interviewer's use of personal space in making selection decisions is a crude but meaningful illustration of overreliance on nonverbal cues to form perceptions of others. Yet, this conscious decoding process is useful, for example, when the carefully observant interviewer detects extreme nervousness in the respondent's fidgeting.

Generally, then, the skilled interviewer listens to both the overt and the covert verbal responses of the interviewee. He is aware of nonverbal communication and his reactions to certain nonverbal factors. Finally, he realizes that nonverbal cues are useful in understanding an interviewee's responses but do not have universal meaning.

Providing Support

Closely tied to the process of establishing rapport is the necessity for providing support. Support is like rapport in that it connotes a certain atmosphere or climate that pervades the interview. It is unlike rapport in that, although rapport maintenance is important throughout the interview, it is emphasized especially in the interview opening. Support, conversely, is a process that is stressed throughout the entire structure of the interview.

A convenient perspective from which to view support is the classic dichotomy of defensiveness versus supportiveness provided by Jack Gibb. [16] According to Gibb, defensive behavior is "that behavior which occurs when an individual perceives threat or anticipates threat."[17] Among the behaviors that create a defensive climate and, hence, defensive behavior are:

1. *Evaluation:* when one is apparently evaluating or judging another.
2. *Control:* when one is apparently attempting to overtly influence another.
3. *Strategy:* when one is apparently employing strategems in trying to manipulate another.
4. *Neutrality:* when one is apparently uninterested in the personal welfare of another.

5. *Superiority:* when one is apparently communicating that he is superior to another with respect to such factors as intellect, wealth, position, and power.

6. *Certainty:* when one is apparently dogmatic or obstinate in his beliefs or attitudes.[18]

Gibb describes the impact of defense-creating behaviors upon an individual:

> Besides talking about the topic, he thinks about how he appears to others, how he may be seen more favorable, how he may win, dominate, impress, escape punishment, and/or how he may avoid or mitigate a perceived or an anticipated attach.[19]

Given a defensive situation in an interview, then, it is easy to understand how an interviewee might be inclined to distort or alter his communication to the interviewer.

A supportive climate, Gibb indicates, is characterized by behaviors that are the opposites of the six defense arousing behaviors cited above. These are:

1. *Description:* when one is apparently genuinely interested in acquiring information or employs communication with neutral loadings.

2. *Problem-Orientation:* when one is apparently interested in collaborating to define and solve a particular problem.

3. *Spontaneity:* when one is apparently communicating in a straightforward, nondescriptive manner.

4. *Empathy:* when one is apparently identifying himself with another's problems or viewpoint.

5. *Equality:* when one attaches little importance to such differences as status, power, intelligence, and position.

6. *Provisionalism:* when one is apparently taking a "wait-and-see," explorative, investigative attitude.[20]

Gibb outlines the outcomes of supportive behaviors:

> The more "supportive" or defense-reductive the climate the less the receiver reads into the communication distorted loadings which arise from projections of his own anxieties, motives, and concerns. As defenses are reduced, the receivers become better able to concentrate upon the structure, the content, and the cognitive meanings of the message.[21]

The process of providing support, then, may well be a complicated and demanding one. The benefits of such a climate, however, center on enhancing the quantity and the quality of information exchanged during the interview.

Providing Periodic Internal Summaries

Another process for which the interviewer is primarily responsible is the provision of summaries throughout the interview interaction. Such "internal summaries" occur normally during the body of the interview and are intended to capsulize and crystallize the problems or issues just discussed. They also provide convenient departure points for transitions into other important topics. A correction interviewer, for example, might move from the problem to solution stage of that interview by saying something like, "OK, Jack, from what's been said, it seems the problem is that you and Bill don't agree on the procedures for installing the pipe. What we need now are some concrete suggestions as to how we can correct this problem."

Notice first that by summarizing, the interviewer communicates his perception of the situation. If the interviewee disagrees with the accuracy of this perception, then he should be afforded the opportunity to submit his own ideas and rectify that perception before the interview continues. Second, notice that the interviewer was able to move smoothly from one segment of this particular interview to the next. In fact, his last statement provides an open-ended means for the interviewee to contribute to finding solutions.

Responding to Questions

A sixth and final process of which the skilled interviewer is aware is his own responding to questions posed by the interviewee. Especially in the employment interview, for example, the applicant should be given ample opportunity to ask questions about the company, the position for which he is applying, and any other issues he thinks are important.

Very simply, the interviewer should attempt to respond to those questions in the same manner he expects the interviewee to adopt when answering questions. Because he anticipates clear, specific, and honest answers from the interviewee, it becomes his obligation to reciprocate when the interviewee requests information from him.

This may appear to be a higly obvious and simplistic process, and it may well be; yet, how does the employment interviewer respond when the applicant asks about the potential for promotion or wage increases? How does the salesman respond when the prospect inquires into a television's guarantee? And what does the supervisor say when his subordinate complains that not everyone in the department is receiving equally fair treatment? The process is quite simple, indeed; the problem is not.

This discussion of but six crucial interview processes should establish first, that effective interviewing inherently requires the use of certain skills, many of which may be acquired only through extensive training and intensive practice. Second, it should be apparent that those processes, because they constitute, in part, the "events" comprising the interview structure, contribute directly to making the interview the dynamic social event that it is. Finally, interview processes, as will momentarily become evident, are also heavily interrelated to the third central concept—interview style.

INTERVIEW STYLE

As was indicated earlier, interview style means the degree or level of patterning of the interaction between interviewer and interviewee. More specifically, style is a function of the number and types of questions the interviewer employs. Stewart and Cash, for example, discuss nonscheduled, moderately scheduled, the highly scheduled, and highly scheduled standardized interviews.[22] "Schedule" refers to the list of questions an interviewer uses; therefore, the more scheduled an interview is, the greater the likelihood that all questions (including probes) are prepared beforehand.

The popular continuum of highly directive, moderately directive, and nondirective also represents stylistic differences among interviews. Like the Stewart and Cash schema depicted here, the primary criterion in classifying a particular interview involves the schedule. Furthermore, since there are both advantages and disadvantages associated with each of these three different styles, one necessarily foregoes the advantages and disadvantages of the others when he selects a particular style. Each of these styles will be considered below.

The Highly Directive Interview

This type of interview style is employed most frequently when: 1) the validity of the information to be obtained is a prerequisite; 2) the information acquired is to be used at a later date; 3) time for the actual interview is limited; and 4) unskilled interviewers are used.

The highly directive interview is well planned. Normally, the interviewer follows a prepared list of direct questions, and answers are usually recorded following each question. Probes may be used, but they, too, are generally planned. Open questions are typically avoided. The interviewer controls the interview and little time is devoted to developing interpersonal relationships.

This interview style is concerned primarily with factual information. Most appropriate to the selection situation, it lacks the flexibility and depth necessary to such types of interviews as grievance, correction, and counseling. The highly directive style is more commonly employed by market analysts, opinion pollsters, social science researchers, and census takers.

The Moderately Directive Interview

This style is similar to the highly directive one in that a schedule is also prepared in advance. The essential difference is that a combination of closed and open questions is used. Additionally, probes, both planned and spontaneous, are employed to acquire further information about specific responses.

The moderately directive interview provides more flexibility than its highly directive counterpart; yet, it imposes some degree of patterning of the interaction and permits the use of relatively unskilled interviewers. This style is certainly appropriate to the employment interview. It may also be used in performance appraisal, especially if the interviewer is prepared to adapt or alter his schedule according to the needs of a particular appraisal situation. Finally, although a number of critical questions may be planned for the correction or counseling interviews, for example, the moderately directive style would probably render such interviews inflexible and, consequently, rather unproductive.

The Nondirective Interview

This type of interview is characterized by heavy use of the open question. Interview preparation may involve forming a list of topics (rather than questions), but even this is not always the case. In the nondirective interview there normally exists a high degree of spontaneous interaction between participants, and the interviewer is quite often preoccupied with creating an atmosphere of permissiveness, acceptance, and participation. Interviews of this type, moreover, are generally problem-centered, in that the interviewer is attempting to help the interviewee discover his real problems. Similarly, one objective is to aid the interviewee in assuming the burden of responsibility for finding solutions to those problems.

Generally, the interviewee does most of the talking. The interviewer attempts to clarify, focus, and reflect the ideas provided by the interviewee. This style consequently engenders the maximum degree of flexibility with respect to topics and depth of discussion.

Associated with the nondirective style, however, are three major limitations. First, use of this style requires a high level of skill. Those who are not trained or improperly trained can easily defeat the purpose of the interview. Bias and lack of objectivity are not uncommon attributes of the unskilled interviewer who uses this style. Second, this style is sometimes prohibitive in that it is time consuming. Finally, the logistics involved in recording the responses of the interviewee make it extremely difficult to record accurately and later use the information obtained.

Essentially, then, interview style may be viewed in terms of directiveness. At the highly directive end is generally a schedule of planned, closed questions. The interviewer imposes a significant amount of control over both the quantity and quality of information exchanged. The extreme of this is the very nondirective style, consisting generally of a spontaneous, open question format and little obvious control by the interviewer over the information flow.

SUMMARY

Structure, processes, and style are three concepts central to the nature of the interview. Basically, the style chosen by the interviewer will affect the essential characteristics of the processes involved (e.g., a highly directive style demands posing direct questions; a nondirective style places unusual emphasis upon the observing and listening process). These processes, in turn, by serving as the inner workings of the interview structure, influence the nature of that structure. Hence, though they may, indeed, be viewed and discussed separately, structure, processes, and style are integral and integrated components of a dynamic social event—the interview.

QUESTIONS FOR DISCUSSION

1. Some suggestions were offered in this chapter for establishing rapport. What are some common behaviors that you think could occur during the opening of the interview that would inhibit rapport?

2. If you were forced to choose between the two, would you prefer to ask closed questions or open questions in an employment interview? Why? Which type of questions would you prefer to *be* asked? Why?

3. A common complaint of some supervisors in unionized companies is that the presence of the shop steward in all grievance and correction interviews creates a defensive communication climate. Why do you

suppose they feel this way? What could you as an interviewer/supervisor do to alleviate such a problem?

4. What kind of interview style do you think the typical automobile salesman employs? Why does he? What kind of style do you *think* he should employ? Why?

5. Suppose that you are conducting a correction interview involving a subordinate who has been stealing money from a cash register. Assume that you have just established whatever level of rapport you feel is necessary for this interview situation. Now write out, word for word, exactly how you would get into the problem at hand.

ENDNOTES

1. Daniel Katz and Robert L. Kahn, *The Social Psychology of Organizations.* (New York: John Wiley and Sons, 1966), p. 31.
2. John W. Keltner, *Interpersonal Speech-Communication.* (Belmont, California: Wadsworth Publishing Company, 1970), p. 264.
3. *Ibid.*, p. 265.
4. James N. Holm, *Productive Speaking for Business and Professions.* (Boston: Allyn and Bacon, 1967), p. 224.
5. Charles J. Stewart and William B. Cash, *Interviewing Principles and Practices.* (Dubuque, Iowa: William C. Brown Company, 1974), pp. 78–80.
6. Wilbert E. Beveridge, *Problem Solving Interviews.* (London: George Allen and Unwin Ltd., 1968), p. 47.
7. *Ibid.*
8. Stephen S. Richardson *et al., Interviewing: Its Forms and Functions.* (New York: Basic Books, 1965), p. 59.
9. Benjamin Balinsky, *The Selection Interview: Essentials for Management.* (New Rochelle, New York: Martin M. Bruce, 1962), pp. 13 and 34.
10. D. Keith Baker, "Correlates of the Effective Interview," *Personnel Journal,* XLVII (1969), p. 904.
11. Harold P. Zelko and Frank E. X. Dance, *Business and Professional Speech Communication,* (New York: Holt, Rinehart, and Winston, 1965), p. 148.
12. Samuel G. Trull, "Strategies of Effective Interviewing," *Harvard Business Review* XLII (January-February, 1964), p. 90.
13. Stewart and Cash, *op. cit.,* p. 47.
14. Alfred Benjamin, *The Helping Interview.* (Boston: Houghton Mifflin Company, 1969), pp. 48–49.

15. Mark L. Knapp, *Nonverbal Communication in Human Interaction.* (New York: Holt, Rinehart, and Winston, 1972), pp. 5–8.
16. Jack R. Gibb, "Defensive Communication," *Journal of Communication* XI (September, 1961), pp. 141–148.
17. *Ibid.,* p. 141.
18. *Ibid.,* pp. 142–148.
19. *Ibid.,* p. 141.
20. *Ibid.,* pp. 142–148.
21. *Ibid.,* p. 142.
22. Stewart and Cash, *op. cit.,* pp. 81–84.

12

The Public Presentation

In one of its advertisements, Gulf Oil inadvertently describes the predicament of big business in general when it states, "The trouble with being a big successful oil company is that nobody believes a word you say." This statement is accompanied by a drawing of a group of people of various ages and backgrounds. The faces reflect varying degrees of disbelief ranging from incredulousness to hostility.

"The public be damned" is a statement usually attributed to tycoon Cornelius Vanderbilt. While the historical accuracy of the quote is questionable, it is a sentiment that business is still suspected of not only harboring but nurturing. Until the decade of the sixties, such suspicions were rarely voiced publicly. Now, however, allegations about the motives of business and business people are found daily in the news media.

The group of nationally known figures who regularly denounce business is, for the most part, articulate and dynamic. Their comments usually receive more widespread publicity than do the rebuttals or representatives of business. While there are some exceptions, unfortunately, there is a general dearth of effective spokesmen for business.

PUBLIC SPEAKING IN BUSINESS

Various studies have been conducted on the role of public speaking in business and have revealed a growing awareness of its importance. This was indicated in 1966 when Knapp found many companies intended to offer training in public speaking to employees.[1] In 1969 Lahiff discovered that more than one-fourth of his national sample of undergraduates had been exposed to speeches by representatives of business organizations.[2] In 1970 Dees reported a growing interest of business in the establishment of speakers bureaus.[3] All three studies suggest recognition by business of the necessity of employing effective spokesmen, not solely to defend it against the onslaught of critics but it is one reason. Other reasons include the desire of the business organization for its employees to represent it effectively both in the immediate community and in its business transactions, sales and otherwise.

While it is indisputable—as those who deny the value of training in public speaking frequently remind us—that we spend much more time communicating in small groups than we do in giving public speeches, it is equally true that effective public speakers are in scarce supply both in the business world and out. Studies have shown that business wants its employees to be competent public speakers and views the ability to communicate as one of the prime requisites for those being considered for employment or promotion.

THE PARAD SEQUENCE

What are the characteristics of a good public speaker? Some of the most often-mentioned ones are self-confidence, knowledge, sincerity, and poise. How are these acquired? Some sources simply advise the novice speaker to practice, practice, practice; this in itself is unsound advice for it will result in misapplied efforts and compounded mistakes. What then is a better way? As with any problem, its solution is more likely if approached systematically. Just as a systematic approach to management problems is most likely to succeed so also will such an approach serve to develop you as a speaker. The ultimate goal of this chapter is to acquaint the speaker with a systematic program of communicative self-development and to illustrate the value of following it whenever faced with public speaking. Such a self-development program, here represented by the acronym PARAD, provides the structure for the rest of this chapter just as it should also provide the structure for the individual who learns that he is going to have to speak to a group of people.

The inexperienced speaker's initial response to the news that he must give a speech is often abject terror; however, this can be minimized, if not avoided, by adhering to PARAD. A comedian once described his perception of flying as "hours of boredom punctuated by moments of sheer terror."

Unfortunately this is how many view the public speaking situation with the boredom residing in the research and practice phases and the terror commencing upon arising to speak.

Phase One: Determing the Purpose

In this first phase in the PARAD sequence, the speaker determines what the purpose of his speech will be. What kind of behavior does he want the listeners to exhibit as a result of his speech?

If his purpose is to get the listeners to change one of their attitudes or beliefs, or if it is to get them to perform some specific action, his speech must be persuasive in nature. If he is trying to teach the listeners or explain something to them, the speech he gives is what is usually called informative. Sometimes his purpose may be neither to persuade nor to inform but to entertain the listeners. When George Jessel, often billed as "The Toastmaster General of the U.S.," gives an after-dinner speech his purpose is usually to entertain his listeners.

Categorizing speeches on the basis of purpose doesn't mean that these purposes are mutually exclusive. In fact, it is common for a speaker to have dual purposes. Ordinarily, however, one purpose will be predominant over the other. For example, when Senator George McGovern, Democratic nominee for President in 1972, broke precedent by urging the replacement of Senator Thomas Eagleton, his original choice for Vice President, with Sargent Shriver, his main purpose was informative. He sought to inform the public of his decision and of his reasons for it. His secondary purpose in this speech was to persuade the public that his decision was in the public interest and that his newly chosen candidate was well qualified for the office. While this is a dramatic example of a dual purpose speech the point is that few speeches are entirely persuasive or entirely informative but a combination of the two. Even the personality who appears on the television talk show and whose prime interest is to entertain and amuse the audience also usually presents some factual information in the course of his participation in the program.

One of the characteristics of an outstanding speaker is his urge for specificity. He seeks to satisfy this urge by being so specific that there is no question among his listeners as to what he is "getting at." In addition to determining his general purpose, to inform, persuade, or entertain, the effective speaker also remains aware of what his *specific* purpose is. The speaker who fails to decide on his own specific purpose before preparing his speech is the one who listeners criticize for being too vague.

Equally important as the need to recognize the difference between speeches in terms of broad purpose is the awareness of the differences in responses sought from the listeners. Understanding is the response most often sought from listeners by an informative speaker. Frequently, a beginning speaker is tempted to use his platform to try to impress the listeners with his extensive knowledge. Such a speaker has forgotten the primary purpose and is instead pursuing an ulterior one. The professor of statistics whose lecture on the characteristics of the normal distribution, in an introductory course in statistics, turns into a display of his knowledge of the principles of correlation and regression has most likely succumbed to such a temptation.

Speaking to Inform

The speech to inform is in itself a broad category of speeches and it can take many different shapes. Some of those shapes that are most recognizable to us are the lecture, the briefing, and the orientation. While their common purpose is to inform there are some not-so-subtle differences between them.

The most obvious characteristic of a lecture is that it is given by a person who is knowledgeable of a particular subject. The classroom is one of the most common settings of a lecture but far from the only one. One of the main functions of certain organizations such as the World Affairs Council is to provide a setting and format for authorities to transmit information on significant international problems to interested persons. No matter what the setting is or what type of organization is involved, however, the purpose of the informative speech remains the same—to build the listeners' understanding of special material.

The briefing is usually less formal than the lecture and, while its common purpose is to elicit understanding of the listeners, its uniqueness lies in its more specific purpose of bringing the listeners up to date on the subject. Usually the listeners have more than an academic interest in the subject. Very often a briefing is job-related—conducted for the occupational benefit of the listeners. The President's press secretary conducts briefings almost daily for news reporters who then transmit to the public the activities of the President for that day. A briefing is usually given to people who have a continuing interest in the subject and it is likely to be followed up by additional briefings as conditions change. The nature of the subject matter is such that there are not many other sources available to provide information on the subject.

Unlike the lecture, which is generally quite one-sided, and the briefing, a key characteristic of which is the immediacy of the subject matter, is the orientation. One of the characteristics of the orientation session is that the speaker and the listeners are usually all employees or associates in the same organization. There is often a clear status difference between the parties, with the speaker being in a position of authority. While the general purpose is like that of any informative speech, the speaker specifically tries to acquaint the listeners with something new or something that has recently been changed. Upon entering college, most students participate in some type of orientation program, the purpose of which is to familiarize the students with the policies and structure of the college and community. Several times each year, some large governmental agencies have programs for recently hired employees. While one purpose of such a program is to welcome new employees, the main purpose is to acquaint the people with their work environment. One feature of most orientation sessions is that opportunity is usually given for the listeners to ask questions. Such orientations are common in most business and governmental organizations.

When preparing to give any kind of an informative presentation the speaker must give special consideration to the level of knowledge that the listeners already possess on the subject. If he underestimates their knowledge, the listeners will feel that he is speaking down to them and may resent him. They will also, understandably, feel that there is no need for them to listen since they already understand the information that he is trying to transmit. Even though he may subsequently move on to material with which they are unfamiliar, it is likely that his original miscalculation will have caused some of them to lose interest completely.

Some speakers err in the opposite direction and overestimate the knowledge of the listeners on the subject. They assume that the listeners know more than they do and consequently fail to secure their understanding. After determining the listeners' level of knowledge, the speaker must decide how much information he will include in his presentation. The complexity of the material should also be taken into account. The informative speaker who is aware of these considerations is most likely to elicit understanding.

Speaking to Persuade

The second broad category of speeches is that which seeks to change the thinking and/or the behavior of the listeners—the persuasive speech. The sales presentation made by a salesman to a purchasing committee is an example. The congressional candidate speaking to groups throughout his district in pursuit of votes is another one.

An effective persuader is one who is aware of response. He knows the purpose of his speech and the kind of response he wants. All of the purposes for which a persuader may be speaking can be categorized into two very general ones: 1) to elicit a covert response; 2) to elicit an overt response.

A covert response is one that is not readily apparent to the speaker or to any observer. When the Director of Employee Benefits addresses a meeting of company employees to explain to them the ways in which the new group insurance program is superior to the previous one, he is seeking a covert response. Perhaps one or two employees may ask questions, but the majority will most likely not respond at all. The average speaker finds a covert response difficult to appraise since he can never be sure that he is relying on the appropriate cues to gauge his effect on his listeners.

When a speaker seeks an overt response, the appraisal process is simplified by the fact that the speaker will be able to observe the manner in which the listeners respond. The manager who seeks to persuade his staff to be on the lookout for errors will be able to measure his success by the degree to which errors are reduced. The Production Manager who urges increased output from his employees is similarly able to measure his success. In each of these examples, the speaker is seeking an overt response. The two examples differ only in the specific response being sought.

A prime reason for speakers failing to elicit the desired response, whether it is overt or covert, is that they lack the ability to be specific. Too many speakers assume that their listeners know what is expected of them. The necessity of pinpointing purposes for listeners is especially crucial when seeking a covert response, for it is usually more difficult for listeners to know in such a situation what the speaker is "getting at." This is not to say that the speaker does not also have such an obligation when he wants an overt response, for he does, but his effectiveness is much more readily observable then.

Another element to consider in the purpose of a persuasive speech is time. When is the response wanted, immediately or ultimately? The speaker seeking an immediate overt response is the easiest to evaluate since his success is readily apparent. The one striving for an immediate covert response is more difficult as is the speaker who is seeking an ultimate, rather than immediate, covert response. When a speaker seeks an overt response, evaluation becomes easier, unless complicated by the time element.

Speaking to Entertain

The third general type of speech is the speech to entertain. The general response sought from the listeners is their enjoyment. Many persons incorrectly equate entertainment and enjoyment with only humor. While it is true that humor is a common ingredient of entertainment, it is not the only one. You may have had a teacher at one time who didn't rely on humor but who entertained the class with his flair for drama, picturesque language, and boundless enthusiasm for his subject.

Phase Two: Analyzing the Audience

After he has established the type of speech to be made, the speaker should learn as much as he can about the group he will address. Thus we arrive at the second step of the PARAD sequence, the audience.

There are those who contend that American society is becoming obsessed with the analysis of audiences. They point with alarm to candidates who won't speak on issues until they have learned the results of the polls. They criticize the use of computers by the television networks to forecast the outcome of elections after only a minute sample of the vote has been counted. These critics contend that such emphasis on the various sophisticated techniques of audience analysis are converting the U.S. into a nation of "weather vanes," individuals fearful of speaking their mind without assurance that others agree with him. The greater the extent of homophily present between speaker and listeners, the easier it will be for the speaker to effectively appeal to them. *Homophily* means the degree to which individuals who interact are alike in regard to certain attributes. The opposite is called *heterophily*. This indicates the degree to which individuals who interact differ. The greater the extent of heterophily, the more complicated the task of the speaker.

Homophily and heterophily may be considered at two different levels: subjective and objective. At the subjective level, it refers to the degree to which speakers and listeners perceive one another as similar. At the objective level, it means the degree of similarity that is observable between the parties. It is the purpose of audience analysis to determine the h-h proportion present in the situation. More effective communication occurs when the source and the receivers are homophilous.[6] Having analyzed his audience, the speaker will be capable of pointing out the areas of homophily present in his situation.

In determining the present h-h proportion, the speaker must investigate a variety of aspects of the audience he will address. He will want to know the sex and age of the listeners. Numerous studies on the effect of sex differences on attitudes have confirmed what the married segment of the population has long known—that the sex of a person influences his frame of reference as well as his openness to persuasion and ideas. The effect of age upon attitudes and behavior is well known and has resulted in the widely publicized "generation gap."

The greater the similarities that exist among audience members, the fewer will be the uncertainties of the speaker. The greater the degree of group identification held by group members, the greater will be their homogeneity and their consequent predictability. When one addresses the average classroom group, the degree of identification will be low since the group is transient and there is little expectation or desire among group members for the group to continue outside the classroom.

Many people mistakenly regard the process of audience analysis as akin to extreme vacillation rather than what it is—a search for likenesses. The speaker who is able to point out similarities between himself and his listeners and who is able to appeal to their actual interests makes it easier for his listeners to identify with him. Such identification will help them accept the speaker's message.

Audience Adaptation

Another audience-centered activity that is intrinsic to effective public speaking is audience adaptation. Unlike analysis, which precedes the speech, adaptation occurs during it. A speaker may adapt to his listeners in many different ways. Sometimes, the speaker will recognize some condition existing in his audience, often unexpected, that requires the speaker to make some adaptation in order to increase the likelihood of effective communication. We have all, unfortunately, been exposed to the speaker who had memorized his speech so completely that, come what may, he could not vary his approach in the least. They suffer from the "future shock" as described by Alvin Toffler; they are unable to adapt to their changing environment.[7]

It is possible to adapt to such a degree, however, that the content of the message approaches meaninglessness and the credibility of the speaker becomes suspect. An example of this is the political candidate who was asked at a political rally, "What is your position on whisky?" Since he was unsure of the crowd's sympathies, and not wanting to alienate anyone, he replied: "If you refer to that evil brew that softens the brains, ruins the kidneys, distorts the judgment, wrecks marriages, obliterates moral values and turns man into an animal, I'm against it. But if, on the other hand, you refer to that magic potion that puts spring in the old man's step, stimulates conversation, enhances social contact, promotes the appetite and gives surcease of sorrow, then I am for it. That is my position on whisky, gentlemen, and whatever the consequences, I shall not compromise."[8]

Phase Three: Researching the Subject

Following the speaker's determination of his purpose and his analysis of his audience, he begins his research on the subject. The third step in the PARAD sequence is the research step.

For many the term "research" connotes boredom and drudgery and its locale ranges from antiseptic laboratories to musty libraries. While it is undeniable that research can be both difficult and time-consuming, it is also true that a knowledge of the methods of research is essential if one is to become an effective communicator. While the ideas presented by a speaker are certainly important, the discerning critic will recognize that the way in which the speaker presents his ideas is at least equally important. It is only through research that one is able to find support for his ideas—support that will appeal to his particular listeners.

Most of us perform considerable research each day as a prelude to taking action. The personnel administrator will review the employee's work record prior to discussing with that employee the transfer for which the worker has applied. The student will conduct "research" among his friends who have taken a particular course to determine which professor will be most to his liking. While these examples may appear to be of an informal nature, they still constitute research that Webster defines as "a systematic investigation" into a subject. We all routinely do research and are already familiar with the process. Now we are called upon to begin to refine our efforts.

Having selected a subject on which to speak, one must next decide how to research that subject. If he has had extensive experience in a given occupation, he might rely exclusively on that experience when planning to speak on the occupation. The insights acquired over a number of years in a given field will usually equip him to speak quite knowledgeably on it. When the speech is about a subject in which he has been immersed and on which his authority will be recognized, he will probably be his own prime source of material.

In most cases, however, research will not be quite that simple since a person will rarely be asked to speak solely on his occupation and even if such is the request, most people are not such authorities that their word alone will be accepted. Therefore, the speaker must look elsewhere for materials to support his ideas; often in fact he must look elsewhere for materials to clarify his own knowledge of the subject. At any rate, in most cases, he must go to outside sources for information.

Now he must decide where to seek out his information. If there are recognized authorities on his chosen subject located in his immediate vicinity, a most interesting means of research is to interview them. Provided that he makes an appointment in advance and prepares some questions, most such authorities are pleased with the recognition and willing, if not eager, to share their knowledge with others. Although the authority's views may be freely available in print, the interview can cover topics that have not been covered or that require clarification. If the speaker decides to use the interview for research, he has an obligation to familarize himself with the scope of his interviewee's expertise as well as with his background.

Use of the Library

Very often not only do we lack personal knowledge on the subject but also we have no authorities available. In that case, the local library is the most accessible source of information. Some students consider researching in the library such an unpleasant task that they will procrastinate doing it. The reason for such procrastination can usually be traced to personal ignorance about the library. Since a major characteristic of research is its orderly method, one would expect the library to be the epitome of organization, and rightfully so. Yet the comments of many students suggest that they view the library as a collection of books, randomly selected and arranged in as illogical manner as humanly possible. This misperception will continue unless they simply ask a librarian to explain the general scheme of the library.

If the speaker knows there are probably books about his subject, his first stop will be the card catalog. If he is not aware of any specific sources, he can check the books listed under that subject. If he does know some specific sources, he will check the card catalog under the title or author. When reading catalog cards many people don't use all of the information available on them. If one is looking for recent material, by noticing the date of publication one can avoid a needless climb to the fourth floor only to find that the source you are seeking was published in 1924. If time for research is limited, the awareness that a particular book is 900 pages in length will probably save a needless trip into the stacks and stimulate a search for materials that are more readily digested.

Current Sources of Information

Should the researcher want information of a more recent nature—perhaps the most recent—periodicals are most likely to yield the most relevant information. If seeking details about the current status of the problem of environmental pollution, *The Reader's Guide to Periodical Literature* is a likely starting point. This is an index of periodicals of general interest. It is published monthly and includes all of the articles from those periodicals arranged according to subject.

The Business Periodicals Index is another widely used source. It is similar in format to *The Reader's Guide* and includes all of the periodicals that specialize in information about business. While these are two of the better known indices, they are far from the only ones. For most esoteric topics, there is at least one index that will include subjects of interest to it.

In addition to the periodicals and journals that are published by private organizations, there are many pamphlets and brochures prepared under the auspices of the government. *The Monthly Catalog of U.S. Government Publications* is an index of such sources. Contrary to its title, the catalog is not restricted to materials about the government. A casual investigation of this catalog will impress the reader with the wide variety of subjects in it.

Newspapers are another prime source of information. Most libraries subscribe to several different newspapers, usually representing varying points of view and different geographical regions. While most smaller local papers are not indexed, some of the major newspapers are. *The New York Times* and *The Wall Street Journal* are two examples of the latter.

When doing library research, one must decide the quantity and nature of the material he is seeking. When making this decision, it is tempting to look only for information that will support his present point of view. A most important characteristic of a good researcher is his open-mindedess, however. If one loses his objectivity, he loses his credibility as a researcher. Without it, his ideas become impotent and the research process meaningless. It is human nature to have opinions on most subjects but it is mandatory that the researcher suspend his opinions and judgments until having thoroughly investigated all sides of the subject. Upon completing his research, there is a probability that he will be changed by the information obtained.

According to Oliver, Zelko, and Holtzman, listeners want to know: 1) How do you know? 2) Is this an accurate statement? 3) Does it agree with other sources? 4) What does it have to do with the subject? 5) What does it have to do with me?[9] Thorough research will equip one to respond to those and other questions.

Phase Four: Arranging Ideas

Having researched an issue, the speaker should have a fair grasp of all sides on the issue as well as the pros and cons concerning each side. It is now time to arrange the ideas, which he wishes to convey, in some orderly fashion. Both speaker and listeners will benefit from an organized presentation. The speaker will find it easier to recall his ideas if they have been arranged in a certain sequence. The listeners will appreciate this organization because the speaker's ideas will stand out and make them easier to follow. The value of a well organized speech has been confirmed through research also. Johnson found that the listeners recalled the central idea and main points better when the speech was well organized.[10] Weaver discovered that a well organized speech will be clearer to listeners and will help them also retain the information better.[11]

Central Idea

The speaker must now decide what his central idea will be. What does he want his listeners to retain if they should forget all else? If asked as to his central idea for a campaign speech the political candidate will most likely say that it is "Vote for me!" Another example of a central idea is "The U.S. must increase trade barriers against foreign textiles." Two characteristics of an appropriate central idea are its brevity and its clarity. It represents the minimum that the speaker wants his listeners to retain.

Supporting Ideas

Having determined his central idea, the speaker now seeks ideas with which to support it. The primary supports for the central idea are the main ideas. Since they are second in importance only to the central idea and since it is hoped that the listeners will also retain them they should be limited in number. It is generally suggested that the number of main ideas should be held to no more than five. It is the function of each main idea to support the central idea and the more clearly the relationship between central ideas and main ideas the greater the probability that the listeners will remember them.

The speaker's next step is to support the main ideas as best he can. It is important to remember that an argument that convinces one person won't necessarily convince all so the speaker must find supports that will impress each segment of his audience. It is possible that the speaker will recognize a need to explain the supporting ideas.

At this point the body, which is the main portion of the speech, is nearly complete. All that remains to be done is to ascertain that there is a continuity or flow from one idea to the next. A lack of continuity will result in a disjointed presentation, one in which the relationship between ideas is unclear. As long as he has taken pains to make sure that each of his main ideas supports his central idea, continuity can usually be insured by means of brief statements that function as "bridges" between the points of the speech.

Conclusion and Introduction

Following the completion of the body of the speech, the speaker should arrange the conclusion. The prime purpose of the conclusion is to restate for the listeners what he wants them to remember. Thus the speaker should repeat at least his central idea and his main ideas. If one or more of his ideas is highly controversial, he might also remind them of the supports he provided. Since the conclusion influences the final impression that the listeners will hold of the speaker, care should be taken in its construction.

The final task for the outliner is to arrange the introduction. The introduction is often rightfully described as springing from the listeners as much as from the speaker. Since he knows his listeners and main points, he must now determine how to integrate the two. Such factors as the listeners' level of knowledge and their apparent feelings on the subject must be considered. A main function of an introduction is to get the listeners' attention and interest and to make them receptive to the ideas presented. What must rank as one of the worst introductions and one which, therefore, should be religiously avoided begins with "My topic today is. . . ."

To place the subject of arrangement in its proper perspective, one must remember that a solid outline is not an end in itself but is a prerequisite for a good speech, the main points of which the listeners should be able to understand. Each of us has undoubtedly been subjected to speeches that have left us perplexed as to the speaker's intent or thinking. Few have described this genre of speech as vividly as William G. McAdoo who had this perception of Warren Harding's speeches: ". . . an army of pompous phrases moving over the landscape in search of an idea."[12] Any speaker can be spared similar embarrassing evaluations by first being sure that he has something to say and then arranging the material in a cogent, comprehensible manner.

Phase Five: Delivering the Speech

The final step in the PARAD sequence is delivery. While this should be the highest point in the sequence, the culmination of all of the speaker's efforts, it all too often doesn't reach its potential because of poor planning.

For some reason the person who is most thorough in covering the PARAD steps often completely neglects the last; there seem to be many members of the "Be Natural" school when it comes to delivery. They maintain that the best delivery is one that doesn't call attention to itself and for that reason the speaker should remain natural. There would be much merit to this suggestion if our body would cooperate and allow us to remain natural. Instead, it responds in a manner that is quite unusual. A novice speaker will show several signs of anxiety. He will perspire, his hands may tremble, his knees may knock, and he may feel a "knot" in his stomach. While these signs will subside somewhat as the speaker becomes acclimated, it is most unlikely that the advice "Be Natural" could be heeded.

These signs and feelings of nervousness are normal and to be expected. When we are excited, adrenalin is released into our system and our natural functions are accelerated. As a person accumulates more experience in public speaking, these signs of anxiety will be less visible, although they will probably never disappear completely. Stories are legion about famous personalities who, after years of public appearances, still remain extremely nervous when facing the public. It is also well to remember that those signs of nervousness are much more apparent to the speaker than to the observers.

Not only is it impossible to ever completely overcome such symptoms of nervousness when speaking—it is also undesirable. Such nervousness seems to give the speaker an edge that makes him more alert and responsive to his listeners. In fact, research has shown that speakers who were more anxious gave better speeches than did those who were less anxious.[13]

In direct opposition to the "Be Natural" advice is the idea that the speaker's delivery should be as rigidly programmed as possible. Proponents of this approach feel that the nonverbal aspects of the speaker should be as controlled as the verbal aspects. The late, late movies on television generally feature products of this school of thought. Their delivery is so rigidly programmed that the viewer can notice great uniformity among the actors in such factors as gestures. They will all gesture in the same manner to depict a certain emotion. No thought is given to individuality.

Obviously, the goal of effective delivery will not be reached along either of these extreme routes. Rather than striving for naturalness in what is, for most people, a decidedly unnatural situation, and rather than striving for the inflexibility inherent in the programmed approach, the speaker must consider the situation and determine the appropriate manner of delivery.

MAKING THE PRESENTATION APPROPRIATE

If the occasion appears likely to be informal, the speech is generally expected to be rather casual and impromptu in nature. An impromptu speech is one into which little effort has been expended. It is conversational.

At the other extreme, is the kind of situation that is considered highly formal and must trasmit much very specific information. In this type of speech, such as a State of the Nation address or a corporation President's annual report to the stockholders, the speaker will most likely prepare it completely in advance and read from a manuscript.

Midway between the impromptu and the manuscript speeches is the type most commonly given by businessmen, the extemporaneous speech. This is a speech for which research has been done but the material has neither been written in manuscript form nor memorized. It provides the speaker with flexibility in that he is not restricted to reading and can be conversational, but he usually does have brief notes to remind him of his main ideas and any quotes or specific figures that he wants to present accurately. There is no one "right" style of delivery. It must be determined by the situation.

The more complex the material to be presented, the more necessary it is for the speaker to prepare and use visual aids. Some of the most frequently used visual aids are charts, graphs, photographs, drawings on the blackboard, and slides in a slide projector. Regardless of the type used, its purpose remains the same—to help the listeners to understand and accept the speaker's central idea and main points. The most effective visual aids are those the speaker has carefully prepared in advance and with which he is thoroughly familiar. While a visual aid should never be expected to carry an otherwise poorly prepared presentation, it should clarify the message.

SUMMARY

A prerequisite for success in business or government is the ability to communicate. Most organizations today recognize the importance of effective spokesmen and for that reason many have initiated training programs in public speaking.

The purpose of the PARAD sequence is to provide the speaker with a structure within which to develop a speech. Such a systematic approach simplifies this task and reduces the uncertainty many experience when faced with having to give a public speech.

The first phase in the PARAD sequence is to determine one's purpose for speaking. The most common general purposes are: 1) to inform; 2) to persuade; and 3) to entertain.

The speaker must next analyze the audience in order to be able to appeal to the interests of the listeners and thereby help them accept him. Such an analysis should indicate the degree of homogeneity within the audience.

The research phase is third in the sequence. The nature of the research to be done will be determined by such factors as one's expertise in the subject and the amount of time available. Some of the more widely-used sources of current information are discussed in this chapter.

Having completed the research phase, the speaker is ready to arrange the ideas to be presented. If the research is thorough, he should have more material than can be presented in a single speech and the editing and arranging of ideas is crucial. After determining the central idea, he must find several main ideas to support it and subpoints with which to support the main ideas.

The final phase in the PARAD sequence is the delivery phase. If his preparation has been thorough throughout the first four phases, the speaker will be able to adapt the material to whatever the situation is. If any one of the first four phases was neglected, the most highly polished delivery will seldom compensate for it.

QUESTIONS FOR DISCUSSION

1. What do you consider the characteristics of an effective public speaker? Arrange these characteristics according to their importance.

2. Would you add to or modify any of the steps of the PARAD sequence?

3. Cite a general purpose for a speech and list ten specific purposes that would fall within the general purpose.

4. Imagine that you were assigned to give an informative speech to a group with which you were unfamiliar. What questions would you like to have answered about the group so that you might address its interests more effectively?

5. Name a national figure you consider to be an effective public speaker. How would you characterize that person's delivery?

ENDNOTES

1. Mark L. Knapp, "An Investigation and Analysis of Public Speaking in America's Largest Business and Industrial Organizations," (Ph.D. diss., Penn State Univerwity, 1966), p. 292.
2. James M. Lahiff, "Analysis of Sources of Information, Image Components and Attitudes of College Students Toward Six Large Corporations," (Ph.D. diss., Penn State University, 1969), p. 78.
3. Linda M. Dees, "The Speakers Bureau in Public Relations" (M.A. thesis, University of Georgia, 1970).
4. Knapp, p. 33.
5. Lahiff, p. 60.
6. Everett M. Rogers, Dilip K. Bhowmik, "Homophily-Heterophily," *The Public Opinion Quarterly*, XXXIV, Winter (1970–1971), pp. 523–538.
7. Alvin Toffler, *Future Shock* (New York: Random House 1970).
8. Edwin McDowell, "Give Three Cheers for Bucky O'Neill," *Wall Street Journal* October 20, 1972, p. 10.
9. Robert T. Oliver, Harold P. Zelko, Paul D. Holtzman, *Communicative Speaking and Listening* 4th ed. (New York: Holt, Rinehart & Winston. 1968), p. 104.
10. Arlee Wayne Johnson, "The Effect of Message Organization Upon Listener Comprehension," (Ph.D. diss., Purdue University, 1970).
11. James Franklin Weaver, "The Effects of Verbal Cueing and Initial Ethos

Upon Perceived Organization, Retention, Attitude Change, and Terminal Ethos," (Ph.D. diss., Michigan State University, 1969).

12. Eric F. Goldman, "A Sort of Rehabilitation of Warren G. Harding," *New York Times Magazine,* March 26, 1972, p. 43.
13. Daniel Kelleher, "A Study of the Relationship Between Stress and Performance During A Speaking Situation," (Ph.D. diss., University of Washington, 1960).

13

Written Communication

While he was Commissioner of the Federal Communication Commission, Nicholas Johnson chided his colleagues for issuing a forbidding technical ruling. He urged that they include "at least one small paragraph in each opinion providing a small clue as to the general subject at hand."[1] While he was probably being partly facetious, a personal survey of the quality of written communication in business or government would lead one to soon see some merit in Johnson's suggestion.

Written communication in business takes a variety of forms among which letters, memos, and reports are the most common. The term "paper explosion" was coined in the sixties to describe the flooding of correspondence in business organizations. Although the term is no longer in vogue, the problems inherent in the flow of written communication persist. The extent of such problems is suggested by the sheer amount of paper involved, one example being an estimate given by an official of the Celanese Corporation of America that the company sends 1500 letters a day.[2]

EXPENSE

In addition to often being aesthetically unpleasant, written communication is also expensive. Surveys estimate the average cost of a dictated letter ranges from $1.31 to $2.97 and that ten percent of all letters would not be necessary if the preceding correspondence had been understandable. One company believes it saves $25,000 a year by teaching its employees proper letter writing, and mails 10,000 fewer letters because those it does send are clearly written.[3]

Estimates of the amount of money spent in business, industry, and government on the improvement of communication vary widely; however, there is general agreement that the amount is staggering. A disproportionate share appears to be devoted to face-to-face communication and much of the balance seems misdirected because, all too often, no account is taken of the uniqueness of written communication. Until this is recognized and the training tailored to it, any improvement will be largely happenstance.

DIFFERENCES BETWEEN ORAL AND WRITTEN COMMUNICATION

One of the most significant differences between face-to-face and written communication is that the immediate feedback present in the former is absent in the latter. An effective oral communicator is cognizant of the feedback he receives and adapts his subsequent communicative efforts based on it. Since a writer is limited to feedback on a delayed basis, he is unable to do that immediately but must wait some time before being able to measure his effectiveness. Such a time lag can result in considerable distortion and misunderstanding that will remain undetected until the recipient of the message responds. In some cases, it will remain unapparent even after that, perhaps until the miscommunication is identified as the cause of a missent order or a broken policy.

Another important difference is that the written message has a permanency missing in oral communication. If the message is lengthy or highly technical, or if there are legal or contractual considerations involved, it is advisable to write it. Tape recorders and the more surreptitious recording devices have increased the permanency of the spoken word but have not bequeathed it with the credibility of writing. The fact that the sender and the receiver of written communication have a permanent record dictates that more care and planning go into it than into oral communication.

A major obstacle that is unique to written communication is that, with the exception of the message itself, there are few cues available. When interacting face to face with another, the participants have access to many sources of information besides the content of message. Such contextual factors as tone of voice, rate of speech, and facial expression provide the participants with additional cues as to the meaning of the message. The perimeters within which the writer must function, however, are both narrower and more rigidly defined.

Face-to-face communication is characterized by control, regardless if the format is the conversation, the interview, the conference, or the public speech. One or more participants exert varying degrees of control in order to reach the objectives. Such control is exerted not only over the participants but also over the environment in which the interaction occurs. The writer does not possess this kind of control and is not able to exert such influence over the situation in which his message is received. The effective writer remains aware of the constraints, recognizes their implications, and plans his strategy accordingly.

FAULTS IN GOVERNMENT WRITING

While there has long been considerable speculation on the most common shortcomings of business writing, there has been little empirical research. One exception to this is a study of the faults most commonly found in government reports. These faults, as reported in the Congressional Record, are:

1. Sentences are too long. The average sentence length in poor government writing exceeds 65 words per sentence. Average sentence length in good government writing is from 15 to 18 words per sentence.

2. There are too many modifications and conditional clauses and phrases. Such hedging causes suspension of judgment as to the outcome of the sentence, and therefore increases reading difficulty.

3. Writers overuse parts of the verb "to be" as well as too many weak verbs such as point out, indicate, or reveal.

4. Too many sentences begin the same way, especially with *The*.

5. An attempt to be impersonal results in too many passive and indirect phrases.

6. There is an overabundance of abstract nouns such as data, basis, and case, which cannot be visualized.

7. Samples of government writing show that many officials use at least one prepositional phrase to every 4 words. Samples from good writing contain only one prepositional phrase to every 11 words.

8. Expletives such as "It is" and "there are" are used too often.

9. Technical jargon is used too often when trying to reach a nontechnical audience.

10. There is a tendency to make ideas the heros of sentences despite the fact that people find it easier to think in terms of people and things.[4]

While few writers are guilty of all of these faults, few are completely faultless. Although the list is the result of a survey of government writing, it is equally applicable to written communication in business and industry.

STEPS TO BETTER WRITING

Having now been introduced to some of the features that make written communication unique and some of the most common faults in written communication, the moment of truth has arrived. It is time to begin to become a more effective writer. There is no magical formula that will transform the average writer into a superior one, despite what the various correspondence schools for writers proclaim. There is, however, a sequence of steps that, if followed, will increase the effectiveness of one's writing.

Determine the Objective

Before beginning to write, one should determine his objective, his reason for writing. While there is usually a passage of time between the recognition of the need to write and the actual commencement of the writing, few writers use that time purposefully. Instead, they simply procrastinate by busying themself with preliminaries. Stories abound of writers who delay their writing by devoting hours to menial chores such as sharpening pencils or rearranging the contents of their desk. Such activities are not to be confused with and do not take the place of determining one's objectives.

Robert Aurner and Morris Wolf discuss objectives on the basis of the function of the message. They divide messages into three categories:

1. Messages that help you seek information, assistance, services, or goals.
2. Messages that help you inform, explain, direct, or instruct.
3. Messages that help you gain or retain goodwill.[5]

Those categories are helpful in that they provide the various possible objectives; however, one must not consider the types exclusive of each other for one message may have more than one objective. While writing toward the objective may seem to be automatic that is often not the case. It is the writer's responsibility to indicate his objectives as specifically as possible. Had the Air Force pilot been more conscious of his objective when he noted on the "gripe sheet" in his plane, "Nose wheel almost needs changing," the mechanic who was unable to loosen the wheel would not have been able to avoid completing the chore by responding on the same sheet, "Nose wheel almost changed."

All written communication is intended to produce some change in the attitude, action, or the receiver's knowledge, or in any combination of these areas. While a clear statement of objective does not guarantee the intended change, the absence of such a statement greatly lessens its likelihood.

Identify Target Audience

Having determined his objectives, the writer should next identify the intended target of the message. The more that the writer knows about his reading audience, the easier it will be to adapt the message to them.

After the writer determines his target audience, he must gauge their knowledge of the subject. If the reader and the writer share the same occupation, jargon will most likely be understood. Jargon means the "shop talk" of a particular occupation. For example, oil drillers know that "suitcase sand" is rock too hard for drill bits; when they hit it they pack their suitcase and move on. There is nothing wrong with the use of such terminology when the message is intended for such a select group.

In recent years, occupational jargon has fallen into disfavor because many do not differentiate it from the inflated language so often associated with the government bureaucracy that the *Wall Street Journal* terms "Governmentese." When a government spokesman reveals where a new appointee will "office" that is governmentese. When "verbal information opportunity" is used in place of a briefing and "verbal posting" means a notice is read to newsmen when it goes up on a bulletin board, that also is governmentese. The difference between occupational jargon and governmentese is that the former is understandable to involved parties but the latter rarely is. Also, the writer should be aware of the depth of the reader's knowledge of the subject. If the reader is aware of necessary background information, the writer need not go into it, but if the reader doesn't know the background, the writer is obligated to provide enough details to promote understanding.

Another aspect that must be considered in the analysis of the intended receivers is the extent to which the receiver recognizes the competence of the writer. The reader should be given enough information to enable him to do so if the message is to be accepted.

As important as the receiver's knowledge, and more often ignored, is the receiver's attitudes toward the subject as well as toward the writer himself. If the office manager is known to be unfavorably disposed toward any altering of working hours, the writer must gear his message to that attitude and compensate for it in mapping his strategy.

If the writer is aware that his superior's negative attitude transcends the subject and is aimed at the writer, he must then compensate for this as best he can. This is usually attempted through extreme care in preparation and through thorough documentation of controversial points. Many business communicators stumble through the organizational morass needlessly simply because they fail to investigate the relevant factors.

Choose an Appropriate Format

Since the writer has a variety of formats available to him in which to present his ideas he must now determine which is best suited to his needs and to the nature of the material he wishes to present. The most commonly used formats are the memo, the letter, and the report. Sometimes the material will lend itself to graphic display in the form of a graph, chart, or illustration; however, this format is beyond the review of this chapter.

The Memo

When writing to another within one's business organization, the memo is most often used. Memos are briefer and more informal than letters and one's correspondence can be accelerated by using memos whenever possible.

Read the following two memoranda both of which deal with the same subject. Both were prepared as announcements for a company bulletin board.

> The purpose of this memorandum is to outline a procedure to assure that the oil in the crankcases of the Cushman motor scooters is changed at the properly designated intervals. The Cushman scooters are equipped with four-cycle gasoline engines having crankcases that contain oil in the amount of one quart. It is recommended by the manufacturer that the oil in these scooters be changed every 400 miles, but the scooters are not equipped with speedometer, and, therefore, it will be necessary to establish a time interval for oil change. Inasmuch as it is estimated that the maximum probable mileage is approximately 400 miles per month, it has been decided to have the oil changed at that interval.
>
> It will be the responsibility of the operator of each vehicle to see that such vehicle is driven or otherwise transported to the Auto Garage at 30-day intervals, for the purpose of obtaining a change of lubricant.

After rewriting, the memo read:

> To the operators of three-wheel scooters: Please bring your scooters to the Auto Garage every 30 days to have the oil changed.[6]

A memo should provide the necessary information on a particular subject. The first example was guilty of "overkill" in that it went well beyond what was necessary. Another point to be remembered when writing a memo is that each one should be limited to only one subject in order to facilitate its routing. Much of the purpose of the memo is defeated when it covers more than one subject. A copy must be sent to each party with an interest in any of the subjects, and each recipient will have to read the entire memo to extract that which pertains to him.

The Letter

When the message is to go outside of the organization or when it will be quite complex, the information is usually transmitted by letter. While the purpose of a letter will determine many of its characteristics, there are some features that remain independent of its purpose.

Since a letter must deal with a unique situation, it must be especially tailored to it. Thus both uniqueness and creativity are important. A letter is a personal format but this aspect should transcend its structure and be embodied in the content. In order to capitalize on the time and energy expended in preparing a letter, its message must be presented naturally rather than through the use of stilted language or jargon.

Free of the obligation to create a message understandable to many, the writer is able to appeal to the needs and interests of one person. This is as close as one comes, when writing, to personal conversation and the finished product should not resemble a form letter.

The Report

Unlike the writer of the memo and the letter, the writer of a report is clothed in considerable anonymity. The impersonal nature of the report leads many to feel that they can skirt responsibility for it. While the memo and letter are usually attributed to an individual, the report is the product of a committee or, even more impersonally, of a corporation.

While it is impossible to determine the number of reports written annually, various estimates have been given. "Today there are enough reports printed every day to fill seven sets of *Encyclopaedia Britannica;* over 190,000 man years each year are spent writing and reading these reports."[7] There are many organizations whose main, and sometimes sole, output is reports. Various service groups such as consulting firms and "think tanks" do little else.

The facelessness of the report writer belies its importance. Since reports provide many decision makers with the crucial information upon which major decisions are often based, another important characteristic of a report is its objectivity. The writer must not allow his personal biases to influence the content of the report and if he does include personal opinion it should be labeled as such.

Organize the Message

Now it is time to organize the message. If you follow the three previous steps, and have the necessary knowledge of the subject, all that will remain to be done prior to the actual writing is to arrange the material so as to achieve maximum understanding. If additional information is needed on the subject, the writer should refer to the third phase of the PARAD sequence in Chapter 12. Many writers pride themselves on their ability to organize their ideas mentally and thus reduce the time spent on it. Too often, however, such mental gymnastics culminate in a letter or report lacking in continuity, a finished product that fails to reflect the efforts invested in it.

While it is true that many students don't like the prospect of preparing an outline, it is the most effective method of organizing ideas. Their apprehension is unnecessary yet understandable, since the complexity of the outlining procedure, like operating a car with a standard transmission, has been greatly exaggerated.

One uncomplicated method of outlining is the "poker chip" outline. According to this method, the writer must first identify his ideas and their corresponding chip value. Thus, the main ideas are blue chips and the subordinate ideas, those that belong under each blue chip, are red chips. If there are any ideas that belong under the red chips, they become the white chips. After identifying and appraising the ideas, the writer must then arrange them in the appropriate sequence and arrive at an opening and closing.[8] Outlining need not be any more complex than as described here; however, one must not consider its simplicity as a measure of its value. It is the message whose organization has been assured through outlining that will be listened to and retained by the receiver. If each paragraph includes a topic sentence that states the thesis of that paragraph, it will also assist the reader.

Write and Rewrite

The four steps considered thus far—objective, target, format, and organization—all precede the actual writing. This is the fifth step. The person who has consciously followed these steps should discover that writing is less of a chore than he believed, but while it may be true that *The Rime of the Ancient Mariner* came to Coleridge in a dream such occurrences happen infrequently. If one wishes to be an effective writer he must write, revise, and rewrite.

Businessmen often protest that while they recognize the value of a systematic approach to writing, they simply do not have hours to devote to a memo or to a single letter. Such intensive efforts, however, are not expected in all instances. Like anyone else, the writer must establish priorities and appropriate his time accordingly.

One authority even admits that there may be a point in rewriting at which improvement ceases. "It may even be true that an article begins to deteriorate with too much rewriting, but it is easy to suspect that if this occurs it is during the thirty-seventh rewriting, or the fifty-fifth, and is thus not much of a threat to many writers."[9] While he is addressing himself primarily to professional writers, his point should be taken by all who ever touch pen to paper.

Just as the route signs which dot the nation's highways provide general guidance, so also do the five steps. Once off the highway, however, the driver depends upon street signs for specific direction to his destination. The writer's source of such specific directions is a collection of principles that, if heeded, will elevate the apprentice to a skilled craftsman.

COMPONENTS OF READABLE WRITING

Considerable research has been devoted to determining the components of readable writing and the findings, while not surprising, should be of interest to writers. Rudolf Flesch developed a readability formula that any writer can apply to his writing and thereby learn the level at which he is writing. It is based on sentence length and word load.[10] By word load he means the mix between easy and difficult words. Robert Gunning simplified the formula somewhat and called it the "Fog Index."[11] Some generally accepted principles for increasing readability follow.

Short Sentences

Keep sentences short. The fact that there are no popular magazines written at a level above grade twelve suggests short average sentence length. *The Reader's Digest* average is consistently between 14 and 17, and *Time* 16 or

17.[12] It is not coincidence that both magazines enjoy great popularity. Average sentence length in *Playboy* magazine is 8 to 10 words except for "The Playboy Philosophy" section which is 16 or more. Calkins astutely observes that "the magazine does not owe its large circulation to its printing of "The Playboy Philosophy.""[13] Argument could also be made that its success is not traceable to the short sentences in the remainder of the magazine either. The same argument would be less valid, however, in regard to *Reader's Digest* and *Time*. One occasionally encounters an idea that should be expressed in a single sentence and that requires the writer to violate the principle. As with most principles, there are exceptions to it and the writer should act accordingly.

Familiar Language

Simplify rather than complicate. Don't use a long word when there is a short synonym. Employee's account of accident: "When I pushed the file drawer closed, my right thumb got caught in the drawer." Supervisor's account of same accident: "Failure of employee to accurately estimate drawer closure speed for timely removal of digit."[14] Enough said.

Use words that are familiar to the target audience. The environmentalist who writes of ways to "advantageously impact" the auto pollution problems would be instantly understood if instead he wrote of ways to reduce or minimize the problem. Why do bureaucrats talk of "dedatifying" their records when all they mean is they no longer keep certain figures?

It sometimes happens that a writer or speaker seizes a familiar word and overuses it. Edwin Newman, an NBC newsman, described such an incident:

> At the Republican convention in Chicago in 1960 it fell to Mayor Daley, who though a Democrat was the host mayor, to make it clear at the outset that great would not be slighted and tradition would be upheld. Daley therefore referred to the great city, that being Chicago; the great year, that being 1960, the only year available to him at the time; the great convention city, again Chicago; our great country; the great convention, that being the one that nominated Abraham Lincoln a hundred years earlier; a great country, the United States; these great centers, the local urban communities; the great central cities of our nation, which include Chicago; our great beach, the beach of Lake Michigan; and a great people, this being the American people.
>
> This great speech by Chicago's great mayor lasted two minutes and drew great applause.[15]

Although Newman's example is from a speech, the principle is equally applicable to both speaking and writing. In order to increase the probability of being understood one should use familiar language; however, one must also employ variety and not be restricted to the same familiar words over and over and over and. . . .

Conciseness

Limit the number of words to only what is necessary. Verbiage results in loss of interest and incomprehension on the part of the reader. Just as consumers are urged to conserve fuel, so too should writers be urged to conserve words. While conservation of fuel is necessitated by a scarcity, however, conservation of words is necessitated by an overabundance. Businessmen are innundated with materials they must read. Their eyes and minds become overtaxed and yet the apparent attitude of most writers in business continues to be, "Damn the innundation; Full steam ahead." Consider these instructions taken from a state personnel board test:

> If you find a word in the narrative which could mean the same as the numbered word, then on the answer line on the answer sheet numbered the same as the number word, mark the answer which corresponds to the letter code of the line of the narrative containing the word you have chosen.

A reduction in the number of words would have probably been reflected in more applicants completing the test successfully.

As the writer separates that which is helpful from that which is excess, he should let this statement by William Strunk, Jr. be his guide:

> Vigorous writing is concise. A sentence should contain no unnecessary words, a paragraph no unnecessary sentences, for the same reason that a drawing should have no unnecessary lines and a machine no unnecessary parts. This requires not that the writer make all of his sentences short, or that he avoid all detail and treat his subjects only in outline, but that every word tell.[16]

Concreteness

Use words that are concrete rather than abstract. It is a simple matter to envision a blue, 1975, four-door Ford. It is more difficult to imagine an automobile and more difficult still to envision a vehicle. The writer who sacrifices the concrete for the abstract also risks sacrificing the reader's comprehension. The following statement from a state agency illustrates the problem:

> The objective of this pilot study is to process transactions documents generated from these departments in a more rapid and accurate manner.

The effort includes a substantial training process and major changes in the method by which documents flow. If this pilot effort is objective, there will be a major improvement in the speed with which transactions processing is completed.

A point closely related to using concrete words is suggesting meaningful examples. Examples are often used to illustrate ideas, but too many writers introduce examples with which the reader cannot identify.

Very often, an informative piece of the nature of the world's population will stagger the reader by the tremendous numbers so that he tunes out. One writer overcame that problem by reducing the numbers to a level that the reader could handle. He compressed the world's three billion people into a village of 1,000:

> In such a village there would be 90 North Americans, 60 of whom would be U. S. Citizens. There would be 50 South Americans, 210 Europeans, 85 Africans and 565 Asians.

> About 300 in the village would be white, about 700 non-white. About 300 would be Christians.

> The 60 U. S. Citizens would receive about half of the total income.[17]

When one writes on a complex subject for the layman, he is doomed to failure unless he constructs meaningful examples. By its very nature, raw economic data is boring to most noneconomists. One writer described the effects of inflation in Chile by writing from the standpoint of one individual and educated the reader in the process. He quoted an executive as saying "In April my salary covered our living expenses for 20 days. In May it covered only 15 days. In June we were out of money after 8 days. We have to live off our savings for as long as they last, but at this rate we won't get to the end of the year."[18]

Originality

Strive for originality in your writing style. According to Webster, a "cliche" is a "trite expression." While less thought is required of the writer who expresses himself with cliches, he has sacrificed clarity, for cliches rarely fit situations perfectly. Not only are they not precise, but they also are likely to cause sensory accomodation on the part of the reader. Sensory accomodation results when receivers are frequently confronted with the same stimulus and eventually cease to respond to it. Through overuse cliches have become useless.

Most scholarly and professional journals are lacking in readability and originality. The former deficiency precludes any but a select few from even attempting to expand their knowledge of topics. The latter deficiency causes many of those who are interested to feel such writing not worth the effort required to wade through it.

Superior writers will labor to record their thoughts in an original manner and all concerned will benefit. When this occurs in a subject not especially known for its concern for the reader, such as in scientific writing, the result may be memorable. Consider this paragraph from a paper dealing with circumcision in adults: "The patient is admonished to confine the function of the operated appendage to micturition only for two weeks after operation. After that period, if he is so disposed, he may without pain expand its field of usefulness."[19]

The above quotation features both originality and humor, two characteristics that are in short supply in most writing. While a few contend that humor is essential for good writing, its presence can add interest to the message while making it more memorable for the reader. As with all such devices, the most important criterion should be whether it contributes to clarity.

Tone

The tone of the message should be appropriate for the situation and for the intended receiver. Tone is one of the more nebulous concepts of written communication. Some define it as "the personality of writing" but many who write of it fail to define it. When one considers the "gut reaction" of the reader to the wording of the message one is talking about tone.

Shortly after his election, a first-term governor sent the following memo to his department heads, most of whom were veteran politicians in their respective offices for many years:

> Until further notice, no department shall employ personnel to fill budgeted positions which have been vacant for a period of one month prior to the date of this memorandum unless the filling of such positions is essential to the continued operations of the department and the prior approval of the State Budget Bureau has been given.

That memo precipitated an uproar from department heads who felt their authority was being usurped. The followup memo was more acceptable.

> The previous memo was not intended as a limitation on the authority of any department head, either appointed or elected. You were asked, how-

ever, not to fill any position unless that position is essential to the continued operation of your department. You are in the best position to determine essential needs.[20]

While the tone of the initial memo was authoritarian and brusque the second was the height of tactfulness. There was a significant yet subtle change in content in the second but the change in tone was even greater. Had the tone of the second one been incorporated into the initial memo the response to it would have probably been closer to what had originally been intended.

THE CHALLENGE OF WRITTEN COMMUNICATION

Some feel that the growth of modern technology signals a decline in the importance of written communication. There is little to lend credence to this feeling; however, there has been a significant national decline in the levels at which students read and write.

The Chronicle of Higher Education states that publishers now urge authors to write at a ninth grade level when writing college textbooks.[21] The *Wall Street Journal* reports that this decline is evident at even the most prestigious colleges and universities. More than one third of the applicants to the journalism school at one major university cannot meet the minimum requirements in spelling, grammar, word usage, and punctuation. At another university, the journalism school now requires all students to pass a high-school level spelling and usage test in order to graduate. Forty-seven percent of those taking the test for the first time failed it even though misspelling thirty percent of the words would still yield a passing grade.[22]

Both of the above examples involve students who aspire to careers as communicators; however, there is no reason to expect that the findings would be any different for students of business. It appears that while the demand for good business writers continues to grow, the shortage becomes more pronounced.

The ideas expressed in this chapter are intended primarily for persons who write as a part of their job. Because most businessmen are beset by the pressures of the clock and the calender, all of these principles will not always apply. One must attach priorities to tasks and devote time and attention appropriate to those priorities. In addition to the devotion of time and attention, a writer will benefit immeasurably if he has an associate who is a competent critic, providing that the writer is willing to accept criticism.

Discipline as well as purposefulness plays a part in effective written communication. It is hard work. Writers often express dismay at the problems inherent in getting started, forgetting that their project—like all projects—must begin as a small idea and that it is indeed the little things that count. When the English monk Roger Bacon wrote: "Take seven parts of saltpeter, five of charcoal, and five of sulpher" he had no forboding of the influence his recipe would have on the course of civilization. His small idea was the formula for gunpowder.

So, too, the advances made by the person trying to improve his writing seem small and tentative. As at first he warms up to the pursuit of his goal, his strides grow until he achieves it. He may then join the ranks of what many consider an endangered species—the competent writer.

SUMMARY

Despite the fact that there is a general recognition of the importance and expense of written communication in business, there has been little attempt to tailor its training to its unique features. Instead, a premise upon which most training is based is that writing is like speaking and the principles of effective speaking apply also to writing. The fact that written communication lacks immediate feedback, and that it is more permanent than speech is not considered. Neither is the scarcity of cues surrounding it nor the writer's relinquishment of control over the message.

There are five steps to follow that should improve any business writer. The first step is to determine one's objective as specifically as possible. Next the writer must identify the intended recipient(s) of the message. The more the writer knows about his intended reading audience the easier will be the task of reaching it. Such factors as the reader's level of knowledge of the subject as well as the reader's attitude toward the subject and toward the writer must be considered.

The third step for the writer is to choose the most appropriate format for the message. The most common of these are the memo, the letter, and the report.

The writer next organizes the message by arranging his ideas in the most appropriate sequence. The "poker chip" outline is a simple and practical method of organization.

The steps culminate in the actual writing of the message. The writer who uses short sentences, familiar language, conciseness, concreteness, originality, and appropriate tone will be read and understood.

There are very few to whom writing comes naturally. For most, it is hard work and will improve in proportion to the willingness to apply oneself.

QUESTIONS FOR DISCUSSION

1. Discuss the proposition that the growing sophistication of electronic communication devices will result in a decline in the importance of written communication.

2. State three situations in which each of the following formats would be appropriate: memo, letter, report.

3. In what ways does organizing a letter or report differ from organizing a speech?

4. An office manager feels that his employees spend too much time writing and that much of the necessary communication could be accomplished face to face or by phone. He wants to develop a policy that would govern whether communication in a specific instance should be oral or written and, if written, the format to be used. What factors must be considered in creating such a policy?

5. The list of faults in government writing presented in this chapter is far from exhaustive. Describe at least two other faults you feel are significant that you find in written communication.

6. Which of the components of readable writing would you consider as applicable to a writer of novels as to a business writer? Why?

7. Describe a situation in which the steps to better writing might be more appropriate if arranged in a different sequence?

ENDNOTES

1. "Minor Memos," *Wall Street Journal,* October 12, 1973, p. 1.
2. Smith, Terry C., *How To Write Better and Faster* (New York: Thomas Y. Crowell Company, 1965), p. 67.
3. Smith, T. C., p. 67.
4. William Dow Boutwell's Study of Government Reports, *Congressional Record,* Vol. 88, Part IX, p. A1468.
5. Aurner, Robert R., Morris Philip Wolf, *Effective Communication in Business* (Dallas: South-Western Publ., 1967).
6. Robert Gunning, *How To Take The Fog Out Of Writing* (Chicago: The Dartnell Press, 1960), p. 21.
7. Smith, Terry C., p. 93.

8. John O. Morris, *Make Yourself Clear* (New York: McGraw-Hill, 1972), p. 16.
9. Rivers, William L., *Free Lancer and Staff Writer* (Belmont, California: Wadsworth Publishing Co., 1972), p. 101.
10. Rudolph Flesh, *The Art of Plain Talk* (New York: Collier Books, 1962).
11. Robert Gunning, *The Technique of Clear Writing* (New York: McGraw-Hill, 1960).
12. Gunning, 34.
13. Ken-Calkins, "Cognate the Averation Fraught," *ABCA Bulletin*, Vol. 36, #4 (December, 1973).
14. *Atlanta Journal*, February 2, 1973, p. 1.
15. Edwin Newman, *Strictly Speaking* (New York: Bobbs-Merrill, 1974), p. 91.
16. William Strunk, Jr., E. B. White, *The Elements of Style* (New York: Macmillan Company, 1962), ix.
17. Atlanta Journal & Constitution, July 4, 1973, Section A. p. 28.
18. Everett, G. Martin, "The Crucial Year for Chile's Allende," *Wall Street Journal*, July 6, 1973, p. 6.
19. A. K. Swersie, "Suggestions on Adult Circumcision," *New York State Journal of Medicine*, Vol. 50, 1950, p. 1108 as quoted in Alexander Kohn, "The Journal in Which Scientists Laugh at Science," *Impact of Science on Society*, Vol. XIX, No. 3 (July-September, 1969), p. 266.
20. *Atlanta Journal & Constitution*, Jan. 31, 1971.
21. *Chronicle of Higher Education*, October 15, 1974, p. 11.
22. *Wall Street Journal*, December 4, 1974, p. 26.

Name Index

Subject Index